Thoughts for Food

Thoughts for Food

"Strange to see how a good dinner
and feasting reconciles everybody."
Samuel Pepys

 Houghton Mifflin Company Boston

ISBN: 0-395-07824-5

c 20 19 18 17 16

Foreword

THIS BOOK, consisting of one hundred twenty-five menus, with recipes, is intended for the woman who is both home-maker and hostess. The menus, which range from intimate family dinners to meals for more elaborate occasions, have been carefully planned. They provide delightful surprises for the members of the household as well as a variety of unusual and delicious suggestions for guests.

To the woman who is interested in serving meals with that "something different" touch, *Thoughts for Food* is offered, in the hope that it may help her achieve her purpose.

Table of Contents

Brunch

```
Filled Grapefruit Shell
Chicken Livers en Brochette
Apple Rings
Toasted English Muffins
Soufflé au Rum
Coffee
```

Filled Grapefruit Shells

Remove core and pulp from halved grapefruits. Sugar, and fill center with sliced fresh fruits of the season. Sprinkle with chopped crystallized ginger.

Chicken Livers en Brochette

Soak the livers in milk for one-half hour, drain and dry. Cut livers into halves. Sprinkle with salt and pepper. Alternate pieces of liver and pieces of thinly sliced bacon on skewers, allowing four pieces of liver and five pieces of bacon for each skewer. Balance skewers in an upright position on a rack in a dripping-pan. Bake in a hot oven (400° F.) until the bacon is crisp. Serve with one teaspoon of melted butter poured over each.

Fried Apple Rings

Core eight medium-sized Jonathan or Spitzenberg apples. Slice crosswise into half-inch slices. Melt one-third cup butter in a large iron skillet. Place the apples in it and sprinkle them with two-thirds cup sugar mixed with a half teaspoon cinnamon. Cover and cook slowly for a half hour or until the apples are tender. Baste, but do not turn the apples.

Soufflé au Rum

4 egg yolks	6 tablespoons rum
1 teaspoon salt	8 egg whites
½ cup confectioner's sugar	Guava jelly

Powdered sugar

Beat the egg yolks, salt, sugar, and two tablespoons of rum until light; fold in the stiffly beaten egg whites. Cook slowly in a hot buttered omelet pan until puffed and delicately browned on the under side. Place in the oven to finish cooking the top. Spread with jelly. Fold one half over the other; turn on a hot serving platter and sprinkle with powdered sugar. Pour the remaining rum around it and send to the table lighted.

Melon Balls
Shirred Eggs in Tomato
Mixed Grill
Toast   Strawberry Preserves
Assorted Kipfel
Coffee

Melon Balls

Cook to a thin syrup orange juice, lemon juice, sugar to taste, and a few sprigs of mint. Cool and pour over assorted melon balls. Serve in chilled cocktail glasses.

Shirred Eggs in Tomato

Cut a thin slice from the stem end of each tomato. Scoop out the pulp, slip in an egg sprinkled with salt and pepper. Cover with buttered crumbs and bake until the tomato is tender and the egg set.

Mixed Grill

Serve shirred eggs in tomatoes on a large platter. Surround with broiled lamb chops with a sautéed mushroom placed on each. Bacon and small fried pork sausages may also be added.

Fried Pork Sausages

Prick sausages with a fork; place in a skillet; add enough boiling water to cover the bottom of the pan. Cook until the water evaporates and the sausages are brown.

Kipfel

½ pound butter ½ pound cream cheese
½ pound flour   ¼ teaspoon salt

Cut butter into small pieces. Mix with the flour until the butter is absorbed. Add the cheese and salt. Place on ice until firm. Roll and cut into three-inch squares. Fill the centers with a teaspoon of thick apricot marmalade or red raspberry jam. Bring corners up to center and press together. Bake in a hot oven. Sprinkle with 'vanilla sugar.'

Note: Keep a jar of 'vanilla sugar' on your supply shelf to sprinkle over cakes, cookies, desserts, such as soufflés, etc. It is prepared by placing a split vanilla bean in a jar of powdered sugar.

Other Fillings for Kipfel

Puréed prunes mixed with lemon juice, cinnamon, chopped walnut-meats, and sugar.

One-half pound dry cottage cheese mixed with three egg yolks, lemon juice and rind, half cup sugar, two tablespoons butter, and two tablespoons sour cream.

Mix one-fourth pound grated nuts with one tablespoon bread crumbs, the juice of one-quarter lemon, sugar and cinnamon to taste, and enough cream to form a thin paste. Cook until thick, stirring constantly. Cool before using.

> *Broiled Grapefruit*
> *Smelts à la Meunière*
> *Lyonnaise Potatoes*
> *Nut Muffins   Jelly or Marmalade*
> *French Toast — Hot Maple Syrup*
> *Coffee*

Broiled Grapefruit

Cut grapefruit in half, core, remove pits and white skin. Cover with orange marmalade and place under broiler ten minutes.

Smelts à la Meunière

Clean smelts, leaving heads and tails on. Season with salt, pepper, and lemon juice. Cover and let stand for ten minutes. Roll in cream, dip in flour, and sauté in butter. Arrange on a platter. Add to butter in the pan finely chopped parsley, lemon juice, and anchovy paste to taste; mix and pour over smelts.

Lyonnaise Potatoes

8 cold, boiled potatoes	Salt, pepper
1 onion, chopped	½ cup bacon drippings or butter
2 tablespoons parsley, chopped	

Peel and cut the potatoes into small cubes, add the onion, salt and pepper to taste. Heat the fat in a frying-pan, turn in the potatoes. Mix well, and cook until well heated. Pack solid and allow the potatoes to brown. Fold one half over the other, remove to a platter and sprinkle with parsley.

Nut Muffins

2 eggs	$\frac{1}{4}$ cup sugar
2 cups flour	3 tablespoons butter, melted
4 teaspoons baking powder	1 cup milk
1 teaspoon salt	$\frac{3}{4}$ cup chopped pecan meats

Beat the eggs until light. Add the sifted dry ingredients alternately with the butter and milk. Beat thoroughly. Fold in the nuts. Pour into well-greased muffin pans and bake in a hot oven (400° F.), twenty to twenty-five minutes.

French Toast

4 eggs	$\frac{1}{2}$ teaspoon salt
1 pint cream	2 tablespoons sugar

Bread, not too fresh

Beat the egg lightly, add cream, salt, and sugar. Cut bread two inches thick. Cut each slice in half; remove crusts. Soak in the egg mixture until soft. Fry in deep hot fat until golden brown. Sprinkle with confectioner's sugar. Serve with maple syrup.

> *Strawberries in Orange Juice*
> *Boiled Salt Mackerel*
> *Scrambled Eggs and Tomatoes*
> *Sautéed Potatoes*
> *Toasted Rolls   Jam*
> *Wheat Cakes*
> *Maple Syrup*
> *Coffee*

Strawberries in Orange Juice

Mix strawberries with sweetened orange juice. Serve very cold in fruit cocktail glasses.

Boiled Salt Mackerel

Soak the mackerel with skin side up, in cold water overnight. Drain. Place in a shallow pan, cover with cold water, and boil ten to fifteen minutes, or until the flesh separates from the bone. Remove to a platter. Pour melted butter mixed with minced parsley and lemon juice over mackerel. Garnish with lemon slices.

Scrambled Eggs and Tomatoes

Drain the juice from a can of tomatoes. Heat the tomato pulp with salt and pepper. Pour off excess juice and keep tomatoes as whole as possible. Scramble eggs in butter, and, when almost done, fold in the tomatoes.

Sautéed Potatoes

Cut cold boiled potatoes into one-fourth-inch slices. Season with salt and pepper. Put into a hot, well-buttered frying-pan; brown one side, turn and brown the other side.

Wheat Cakes

2 cups sour milk	$\frac{1}{4}$ teaspoon salt
2 eggs	1 teaspoon soda
2 cups flour	2 teaspoons baking powder

2 teaspoons melted butter

Mix the milk and well-beaten eggs. Sift flour, salt, and soda. Gradually add to the eggs and milk. Beat until smooth. Add baking powder and butter. Drop by spoonfuls on a buttered hot griddle. When puffed around the edges, turn and cook the other side.

Grapefruit Cocktail
Shirred Eggs and Sausages
Hashed-Brown Potatoes   *Rye Toast*
French Pancakes
Coffee

Grapefruit Cocktail

Sugar to taste skinned segments of grapefruit. Flavor with maraschino liqueur and garnish with chopped maraschino cherries.

Shirred Eggs and Sausages

1 pound link country sausages   ½ cup chili sauce
6 to 8 eggs   Salt, pepper

Brown the sausages; place around edge of a buttered shallow casserole. Cover with chili sauce and break the eggs into the center. Bake in a moderate oven (350°) fifteen to twenty minutes, or until the eggs are set.

Hashed-Brown Potatoes

Chop raw potatoes very fine; season with salt and pepper. Place enough beef or bacon fat in an iron skillet to be about one-eighth inch deep. Heat and drop in the potatoes. Sauté over a medium flame, shaking pan occasionally so potatoes won't stick to bottom of pan, and add more fat as needed. When potatoes are cooked and bottom is brown, turn out upside down on serving platter.

French Pancakes

6 eggs, beaten   6 tablespoons melted butter, not hot
2 tablespoons sugar   1 quart milk
2 scant level cups sifted flour

Stir sugar into beaten eggs. Add butter, milk, and flour. Have frying-pan hot and use a teaspoon of butter for each pancake as you fry them.

Pour a small amount of batter in the pan and tilt it back and forth so the batter will spread and cover the whole frying-pan. When brown, turn and brown on the other side.

Sprinkle shaved maple sugar and pieces of butter over each pancake and stack on top of each other. Keep in a warm oven while other pancakes are being made.

Cut in pie-shaped wedges, but leave intact. Serve with hot maple syrup or blueberry sauce. (If blueberry sauce is used, spread only with butter.)

Blueberry Sauce

Pick over and wash one quart of blueberries; drain. Add one cup of thinly sliced peaches, half cup sugar, the juice of half a lemon, and a half teaspoon cinnamon. Cook slowly until tender. Add one teaspoon cornstarch diluted in a little cold water. Cook three minutes longer. Chill.

> *Red Orange Juice*
> *Mushrooms Stuffed with Hamburger*
> *French Fried Potato Balls*
> *Baked Bananas*
> *Waffles*
> *Coffee*

Red Orange Juice

Mix equal quantities of cranberry and orange juice. Sweeten to taste and serve cold.

Mushrooms Stuffed with Hamburger

Large mushrooms	$\frac{1}{4}$ cup cold water
Salt, pepper	$\frac{1}{2}$ teaspoon lemon juice
1 pound ground round steak	1 teaspoon A-1 Sauce
1 tablespoon bread crumbs, grated	1 onion, grated
1 egg	Bacon slices

Remove the stems from mushrooms. Wash, drain, sprinkle with salt and pepper. Mix the meat with the bread crumbs, egg, cold water, lemon juice, A-1 Sauce, onion, and ground mushroom stems. Fill the mushrooms heaping full. Place on a buttered pan with a slice of bacon over each. Bake for fifteen minutes, basting with strong soup stock or a bouillon cube dissolved in half cup water.

French Fried Potato Balls

Pare large potatoes and soak in cold water for a half hour. Dry. With a French vegetable-cutter scoop into balls. Fry in deep hot fat until tender and golden brown. Sprinkle with salt and serve promptly.

Baked Bananas

Remove the skins from six bananas. Cut into halves lengthwise. Place in a shallow pan. Mix two tablespoons melted butter with one-third cup brown sugar and two tablespoons lemon juice. Cover the bananas with half the mixture and baste with the remainder. Bake twenty minutes in a slow oven (325° F.).

Sour Cream Waffles

3 eggs, separated	1 tablespoon sugar
1 cup and 2 tablespoons flour	1 pint rich sour cream
$\frac{1}{4}$ teaspoon salt	1 teaspoon soda
2 teaspoons baking powder	1 tablespoon hot water

Beat egg yolks until thick and lemon-colored. Sift the flour, salt, baking powder, and sugar together; add to beaten yolks alternately with the cream. Fold in the stiffly beaten egg whites. Add the soda dissolved in the water. Bake on a hot waffle iron.

Note: If the cream is not rich, add one-fourth cup melted butter.

OR

Crisp Waffles

2 cups cake flour	1 cup milk
4 teaspoons baking powder	$\frac{1}{2}$ cup cream
$\frac{1}{2}$ teaspoon salt	2 eggs, separated
1 tablespoon sugar	$\frac{2}{3}$ cup melted butter

Sift flour, measure. Add baking powder, salt, and sugar. Sift together twice. Add milk and cream slowly, beating mixture until smooth. Add beaten yolks, then stir in melted butter. Fold in stiffly beaten whites.

Figs with Cream
Calves' Liver and Bacon
Potato Cakes   Smothered Onions and Peppers
German Pancake
Apple Sauce
Coffee

Calves' Liver and Bacon

Soak sliced calves' liver in milk for thirty minutes. Drain, dry, and remove the thin outside skin. Sprinkle with flour mixed with salt and pepper and sauté in hot bacon fat until brown on both sides.

Place slices of bacon in a cold frying-pan. Heat slowly and when the bacon begins to curl, turn it often until it is crisp and light brown. Drain on unglazed paper.

Potato Cakes

Shape cold mashed and seasoned potatoes into small cakes; roll in flour. Place in a hot buttered frying-pan. Brown on both sides, adding butter as needed to prevent burning.

Smothered Onions and Peppers

2 tablespoons butter	2 green peppers, sliced
6 onions, sliced	Salt

Melt the butter in an iron skillet. Add the onions and peppers. Cover and simmer until the vegetables are tender but not brown. Season.

German Pancake

6 eggs	$\frac{1}{2}$ teaspoon salt
1 cup flour	1 cup milk
6 tablespoons butter	

Beat the eggs until very light. Add the sifted flour and salt alternately with the milk, beating continually. Spread the bottom and sides of a ten-inch frying-pan with butter. Pour in the batter and bake in a hot oven (400° F.) twenty to twenty-five minutes. Serve with powdered sugar and lemon, or with apple sauce.

Persian Melon
Chicken Livers with Madeira Sauce
OR
Veal Kidneys with Madeira Sauce
Bacon
Corn Ring   Baked Candied Tomatoes
Orange Marmalade Toast
Thin Apple Cake OR   Busy-Day Coffee Cake
Coffee

Chicken Livers with Madeira Sauce

Clean one pound of chicken livers. Soak them for a half hour in milk. Drain and dry. Sprinkle with salt and pepper; dredge with flour and sauté in butter.

To prepare Madeira Sauce, brown two tablespoons butter in two tablespoons flour. Gradually add one cup soup stock (or one cup water with a bouillon cube dissolved in it), three tablespoons Madeira wine, one-half tablespoon minced parsley, salt and pepper to taste. Reheat the livers in the sauce. Serve in a corn ring surrounded with bacon.

Veal Kidneys

Trim the kidneys and parboil until tender. Drain, cut into small pieces and reheat in Madeira Sauce.

Corn Ring

2 cups corn kernels	1 teaspoon salt
4 eggs, separated	Pepper
2 teaspoons sugar	1 cup cream

To the corn add the well-beaten egg yolks, sugar, salt and pepper to taste. Add cream and fold in the stiffly beaten egg whites. Pour into a buttered and floured ring mold. Place in a pan of hot water and bake in a moderate oven (325° F.) one-half hour or until firm.

Baked Candied Tomatoes (see page 58)

Orange Marmalade Toast

Remove the crusts from thin slices of white bread; spread with creamed butter and orange marmalade; put two slices together. Fry slowly on both sides. Cut into halves before serving.

Thin Apple Cake

Line the bottom of a spring form with Kipfel dough (see page 6). Cover with thinly sliced apples. Sprinkle with sugar mixed with a few grains of cinnamon and a few drops of lemon juice. Bake in a moderate oven (350° F.) until the apples puff. Spread melted apple jelly over the top. Cool.

Busy-Day Coffee Cake

$\frac{1}{3}$ cup butter	$2\frac{1}{2}$ teaspoons baking powder
1 cup sugar	$\frac{1}{4}$ teaspoon salt
1 egg	1 cup milk
$1\frac{3}{4}$ cups pastry flour	1 teaspoon vanilla

Cream the butter and sugar; add the egg and beat until light. Add sifted dry ingredients alternately with the milk and beat for several minutes. Add vanilla and pour into a shallow pan. Spread with topping and bake in a moderate oven (350° F.) twenty-five to thirty minutes.

Topping

2 egg whites   1 cup brown sugar
Nut meats

Beat egg whites stiff. Fold in the sugar. Spread on batter and sprinkle with chopped nut meats.

> *Jellied Melon Slices*
> *Scrambled Eggs on Anchovy Toast*
> *Icebox Rolls*
> *Filled Coffee Cake*
> *Coffee*

Jellied Melon Slices

1 honeydew melon	Raspberries or pitted cherries
Seedless grapes	1 package Raspberry Jello
Diced pears	1½ cups boiling water

Cut the melon in half, scoop balls from pulp and reserve the shells. Fill shells with melon balls combined with other fruits. Dissolve Jello in hot water. Cool, pour over fruit in melon shells. Place in refrigerator to set. Cut into slices and serve on green leaves.

Scrambled Eggs on Anchovy Toast

Spread anchovy paste on buttered toast. Cover with scrambled eggs, Garnish with rolled anchovies. Serve with slices of broiled tomatoes. topped with crisp chopped bacon.

Icebox Rolls

½ cup sugar	2 eggs, beaten
2½ teaspoons salt	2 tablespoons lard
2 cups hot water	1 cake yeast
6 cups flour	

Place sugar, salt, and lard in a large mixing bowl. Add one cup of the hot water to melt the lard; then add the other cup of water, lukewarm. Add yeast, eggs, and flour.

Keep in icebox overnight before making rolls. After shaping rolls, let stand and rise three hours before baking. Bake in hot (500° F.) oven for about five minutes, and then at 350°.

Filled Coffee Cake

¼ cup butter
1 cup sugar
2 eggs, separated
1½ cups flour

2 teaspoons baking powder
1 teaspoon salt
½ cup milk
1 teaspoon vanilla

Filling

½ cup brown sugar
1 tablespoon flour

1 teaspoon cinnamon
1 tablespoon butter, melted

¼ to ½ cup nut meats, broken

Cream butter, add sugar, and beat in yolks. Add sifted dry ingredients alternately with liquids; fold in beaten whites.

Combine filling ingredients. Pour two-thirds of batter in a buttered pan (7 by 11 inches); spread on filling and pour over the rest of the batter. Bake in a moderate oven (350° F.), about forty minutes. Cool, sprinkle with powdered sugar, and cut in squares.

Summer Luncheon

Fruit Shrub

Into one quart of chilled orange juice mash one pint of raspberry ice.
Serve in chilled glasses with a sprig of mint.

Soft-Shell Crabs

Remove sandbags, raise aprons, and cut from crabs with the spongy
substance around them. Wash and dry. Sprinkle with salt and pepper.
Dip in crumbs, egg, and crumbs again. Fry in deep fat three to five
minutes, turning once during cooking. Drain on unglazed paper.
Serve with Sauce Tartare or Hot Sauce Tartare.

Hot Sauce Tartare

1 tablespoon butter	1 teaspoon vinegar
1 tablespoon flour	½ tablespoon chopped
½ cup milk	pickles
⅓ cup mayonnaise	½ tablespoon chopped
1 chopped shallot	olives
½ tablespoon chopped	½ tablespoon chopped
capers	parsley

Cayenne

Make a white sauce of butter, flour and milk. Add the remaining ingredients. Stir constantly until the mixture is thoroughly heated.
Add a dash of cayenne.

23

Lattice Potatoes

Wash and pare potatoes. Slice with a vegetable-slicer. Stand in cold water for two hours. Drain and dry. Fry in deep fat. Drain on unglazed paper and sprinkle with salt.

Broccoli Vinaigrette

Select fresh stalks of broccoli, tie in bunches. Cook in boiling salted water until tender. Drain, chill, and serve with Vinaigrette Sauce (see page 111.)

Poppy-Seed Twists

Make Refrigerator Dough (see page 18). Divide small uniform pieces of dough into three parts. Lightly roll into even strands and braid. Brush with butter, cover and let rise until light. Bake in a hot oven (400° F.). When nearly done, brush with butter and bake five minutes longer. Again spread with butter and sprinkle with poppy seeds. Return to the oven for a few minutes.

Apricot and Pineapple Icebox Cake

1 cup apricot pulp (made from soaked dried apricots)	2 eggs, well beaten
	$\frac{1}{2}$ cup sweet butter
	1 cup powdered sugar
$\frac{1}{3}$ cup shredded pineapple	1 cup whipped cream
1$\frac{1}{2}$ dozen ladyfingers	

Place apricot pulp and shredded pineapple in a double boiler. Add eggs and cook until thick, stirring constantly. Chill thoroughly. Cream butter, gradually adding powdered sugar, and beat until creamy. Add cold apricot mixture. Mix well and fold in the whipped cream. Line the bottom and sides of a spring form with ladyfingers. Pour in half of mixture; cover with ladyfingers, then pour in rest of mixture and cover with ladyfingers. Put in icebox for several hours. Take out of mold and garnish with additional whipped cream before serving. Make double recipe for large spring form.

Chicken Salad
Biscuits   *Plum Conserve*
Iced Russian Chocolate
Pecan Macaroons

Chicken Salad

4 cups chicken, cubed	Whipped cream or sour cream
2 cups celery, diced	French Dressing
1 cup hard cooked eggs, diced	Capers
Mayonnaise	Asparagus tips, tomato or cucumber slices

Cook chicken the day before it is to be used. Chill and cut into half-inch cubes. Marinate with French Dressing (but omitting onion and garlic). Wash, scrape, and dice celery. Chill in ice water, then drain and dry. Mix together two parts of mayonnaise and one part cream. Just before serving, add dressing to chicken and celery, then lightly fold in the diced egg. Mound on a salad dish, garnish with capers, and surround with lettuce-leaf cups filled with marinated asparagus tips, tomato or cucumber slices.

Baking-Powder Biscuits

2 cups flour	2 tablespoons lard
4 teaspoons baking powder	2 tablespoons butter
1 teaspoon salt	$\frac{2}{3}$ cup milk

Mix dry ingredients; sift twice. Cut in the shortening; add the milk gradually, mixing to a soft dough with a knife. Toss on a floured board. Roll lightly to half-inch thickness. Shape with biscuit-cutter. Place on a buttered pan and brush the top with melted butter or heavy cream. Bake in a quick oven (450° F.) for twelve to fifteen minutes.

Plum Conserve

6 pounds blue plums	2 lemons
3 oranges	5 pounds sugar
1 pound English walnuts or pecans	

Stone plums and cover with juice of oranges and lemons. Let stand for two hours. Cut peel of oranges and lemons into strips. Boil all together until mixture is thick. Remove from fire and add nuts. Place in sterilized jars and seal.

Iced Russian Chocolate

Hershey Chocolate Syrup	Hot strong coffee
Ice cubes	Ice cream
Whipped cream	

Put two to three tablespoons of chocolate syrup and an ice cube into each tall glass. Fill with hot coffee and a ball of chocolate ice cream; top with a teaspoon of whipped cream.

Pecan Macaroons

1 pound yellow sugar	2 egg whites
1 pound pecans	$\frac{1}{8}$ teaspoon salt
Candied cherries	

Mix the sugar and nuts; put through a nut grinder. Add the unbeaten egg whites and salt. Form into small balls. Press a piece of candied cherry into each. Bake on a buttered tin for ten minutes in a moderate oven (350° F.).

> *Fish Tartare*
> *Bran Muffins   Red Raspberry and Currant Jelly*
> *Pineapple Havana*
> *Chocolate Fudge Squares   Chocolate Icing*
> *Coffee*

Fish Tartare

Clean a five- or six-pound pike or trout, leaving head and tail on. Boil in water with a few slices of onion, carrot, couple of celery stalks, and seasoning. Skin and cut into pieces for serving. Arrange on platter as a whole fish and serve with following sauce:

Sauce

½ large Bermuda onion
1 green pepper
2 hard-cooked eggs
2 garlic dill pickles
1 pint mayonnaise
¼ bottle prepared horseradish
¼ cup Chili sauce

1 tablespoon capers
½ clove garlic, grated
Dash of cayenne
Salt, pepper
½ cup whipping cream
   or thick sour cream
Caviar

Put the onion, green peppers, egg yolks, and pickles through a food-chopper. Add these to the mayonnaise, horseradish, chili sauce, capers, seasoning, and cream. Mask fish with sauce. Place caviar down the center of the fish with the riced egg whites on either side. Garnish platter with cold cooked and marinated vegetables in lettuce cups.

Bran Muffins

2 eggs
2 tablespoons molasses
1 cup flour
1 cup bran flour

1 teaspoon soda
½ teaspoon salt
⅞ cup milk
2 tablespoons melted shortening

Beat the eggs until light. Add the molasses. Sift the dry ingredients together and add to the eggs alternately with the milk. Then add the shortening. Beat thoroughly. Pour into buttered muffin pans. Bake in hot oven (400° F.) twenty minutes.

Red Raspberry and Currant Jelly

2 parts red raspberries   1 part currants
Sugar

Pick over raspberries and currants, but do not remove stems. Wash and drain. Cook slowly until the currants look white. Strain through a coarse strainer. Then allow juice to drip through a double layer of cheesecloth or a jelly bag. Measure, bring to a boil and boil for five minutes. Add an equal measure of heated sugar and boil gently for three minutes or until a drop jells on a cold plate. Remove all scum. Fill sterilized glasses. Let stand for twenty-four hours. Cover with paraffin and adjust lids.

Pineapple Havana

Peel pineapple and slice crosswise in slices about a half-inch thick. Sugar to taste and let stand about an hour. Arrange rings of pineapple on a platter with a bowl of coconut sauce in the center. Coconut sauce comes ready for use in cans or, if not available, can be made by cooking grated fresh coconut in sugar syrup.

Chocolate Fudge Squares

2 ounces bitter chocolate	2 eggs, well beaten
2 tablespoons water	1 cup and two tablespoons flour
1 tablespoon sugar	3 teaspoons baking powder
$\frac{1}{8}$ pound sweet butter	$\frac{1}{8}$ teaspoon salt
$\frac{7}{8}$ cup sugar	$\frac{1}{2}$ cup water
2 teaspoons vanilla	

Cook the chocolate, two tablespoons water, and one tablespoon sugar until the chocolate is dissolved and the mixture is thick. Cream the butter and sugar. Add the eggs and the chocolate mixture. Add the sifted dry ingredients gradually to this, with the water and vanilla. Bake in a shallow pan in a hot oven (400° F.) for fifteen to twenty minutes. Frost while warm. When cold cut into squares.

Chocolate Icing

1 tablespoon butter	1 ounce bitter chocolate
1 cup confectioner's sugar	½ teaspoon vanilla

2 to 3 tablespoons boiling strong coffee

Cream the butter. Add a little sugar, then the melted chocolate and vanilla. Continue adding the remainder of the sugar with just enough coffee to make it the right consistency for spreading.

Sea Food Plate

Nut Bread   Yellow Tomato Preserves
Strawberry Bavarian Cream
Ladyfinger Sandwiches

Sea Food Plate

½ pound crab meat	Shredded lettuce
¾ pound shrimps, cooked	2 large tomatoes
½ pound lobster meat	16 asparagus tips
2 hard-cooked eggs	Celery Solari
Tuna fish	Sauce Louis

On each plate place crisp shredded lettuce; arrange in the center a thick slice of peeled tomato, on which place one-half egg stuffed with tuna fish. Around this place four asparagus tips like the spokes of a wheel. In one section place a tablespoon of Crab Meat Ravigote; in the next a like quantity of shrimps with mayonnaise; in the next the lobster with Sauce Louis or Ravigote Sauce (page 360), and in the last space Celery Solari. Dust all with riced egg yolk mixed with minced parsley and watercress.

Sauce Louis

1 hard-cooked egg, riced	½ tablespoon tarragon vinegar
1 egg yolk	½ cup chili sauce
½ teaspoon mustard	½ tablespoon chopped chow-chow
Salt, pepper	¼ tablespoon minced shallots
Clove of garlic	¼ tablespoon minced parsley
½ cup olive oil	¼ tablespoon minced watercress
¼ tablespoon minced chives	

Blend the egg, egg yolk, mustard, salt and pepper. Place in a bowl rubbed with garlic; add oil, a drop at a time, beating with a rotary beater. As mixture thickens, dilute with vinegar. When it reaches the consistency of mayonnaise, add chili sauce, chow-chow, and remaining ingredients. Mix thoroughly and keep in refrigerator.

Celery Solari

6 stalks celery
Chicken stock
Anchovy fillets
⅓ cup tarragon vinegar

⅔ cup salad oil
4 tablespoons minced shallot and
watercress
Black pepper, freshly ground
Salt, paprika

Trim celery, place in an enameled pan, cover with chicken stock, cook until tender (about twenty minutes), and let cool in the broth. Before serving, drain well, cut lengthwise, decorate with anchovies and moisten with dressing made of the combined remaining ingredients.

Nut Bread

2½ cups flour
4 teaspoons baking powder
½ cup sugar

½ teaspoon salt
½ cup walnuts, broken
1 egg

1 cup milk

Mix dry ingredients; add egg to milk and combine the two mixtures. Place in greased bread tin, let stand twenty minutes, then bake in a moderate oven about a half-hour or until thoroughly baked. (This keeps for days and is even better toasted than it is fresh.)

Yellow Tomato Preserves

4 quarts small yellow tomatoes
1 lemon, sliced thin

Sugar
4 pieces whole ginger, crushed

Scald tomatoes, immerse in cold water, skin, and then weigh. Add an equal weight of sugar, then the lemon and ginger. Cook in a preserving kettle slowly until sugar is melted; continue cooking until tomatoes are transparent (one to one and one-half hours), being careful not to crush them. Place in sterilized glasses and seal.

Strawberry Bavarian Cream

1 quart strawberries
1 cup sugar
1 tablespoon gelatin

¼ cup cold water
½ cup boiling water
1 pint whipping cream

Sugar berries and let stand about an hour, and crush. Dissolve gelatin in cold water, add the boiling water, stir over hot water until thoroughly

dissolved; add to crushed fruit. When cool, fold in the whipped cream.
Pour in mold and let stand several hours. Serve very cold, garnished
with whole berries and fluted whipped cream.

(One pint of peach pulp may be substituted for berries.)

Ladyfinger Sandwiches

Split ladyfingers and fill with jelly, sandwich fashion.

Melon with Berries
Lobster Farci   *Potato Curls*
Tomato Filled with Cucumber
Sour Cream Dressing
Parker House Rolls
Angel Food Mocha Torte
Coffee

Filled Melons

Select ripe cantaloupes. Cut them into halves, remove seeds and stringy portions, and point the tops of the melons. Fill with red raspberries and blueberries mixed with a half tablespoon sloe gin, half teaspoon lemon juice, and one teaspoon powdered sugar for each portion of berries. Serve cold.

Lobster Farci

4 two-pound lobsters	$\frac{1}{2}$ teaspoon paprika
Boiling water	$\frac{1}{4}$ cup vinegar
1 teaspoon salt	2 bay leaves
$\frac{1}{3}$ teaspoon peppercorns	

Drop lobsters into the above, being sure that they are entirely covered. Cook twenty minutes. Cool, cut lobsters in halves lengthwise and take out intestinal vein. Remove meat and cut into cubes.
    Prepare the following:

4 tablespoons butter	4 tablespoons flour
$\frac{1}{2}$ onion, grated	1 pint cream
1 teaspoon parsley	1 teaspoon lemon juice
$\frac{1}{2}$ green pepper, chopped	Sherry wine
Buttered crumbs	

Melt butter, add onion, parsley, and green pepper; simmer for five minutes. Blend in the flour, gradually adding cream. Cook until thick.

Remove from the fire, add the lobster meat, lemon and sherry to taste. Refill lobster shells. Cover with buttered crumbs and bake until the crumbs are brown.

Potato Curls

Wash and pare large, long potatoes. Shape with potato-curler, then soak one hour in cold water. Drain and dry. Fry a few at a time in deep fat. Drain on unglazed paper and sprinkle with salt.

Tomato Filled with Cucumber

Peel medium-sized tomatoes. Remove a thin slice from the stem end of each, and with a round cutter remove the seeds and pulp. Invert and let stand a half hour. Fill tomatoes with cucumbers which have been soaked in salted ice water for an hour, then drained, pressed dry, and mixed with sour cream dressing (see page 41).

Parker House Rolls

Prepare Refrigerator Dough (see page 18). Toss on a floured board and roll one-third inch thick. Cut into rounds two and one-half inches in diameter. Brush well with melted butter. Fold one half of each roll over the other and place close together in rows in buttered pans. Let stand until they double their size. Bake in a hot oven (450° F.) for twelve minutes. Brush with an egg yolk mixed with one tablespoon of heavy cream. Return to oven for three more minutes.

Angel Food Mocha Torte

Angel Food Cake	8 egg yolks
1 tablespoon gelatin	1 pint whipping cream
$\frac{1}{4}$ cup cold water	1 teaspoon vanilla
1 cup powdered sugar	$\frac{1}{2}$ cup roasted, blanched almonds
2 tablespoons Mocha essence or	or
2 tablespoons strong coffee	$\frac{1}{2}$ pound pecan brittle, crushed

Soak gelatin in cold water. Put over boiling water to dissolve, then add sugar and Mocha essence. Cool. Beat egg yolks until light. Add gelatin mixture. And fold in the whipped cream. Chill until it begins to stiffen. Cut Angel Food Cake in two, just a little above the center (which prevents top layer from slipping). Spread cream mixture between layers and over the top and sides. Sprinkle thickly with almonds or brittle. Place in refrigerator for several hours before serving.

Angel Food Cake

10 to 12 egg whites	1 cup and 2 tablespoons pastry flour
1 teaspoon cream of tartar	$\frac{1}{8}$ teaspoon salt
1½ cups sugar	1 teaspoon vanilla

Beat the egg whites until frothy, add cream of tartar and continue beating until the eggs are light. Sift the sugar four times. Sift the flour mixed with salt four times. Add the sugar to the egg whites, two tablespoons at a time, then gradually fold in the flour and add the vanilla. Pour into ungreased tube cake pan. Bake for one-half hour in slow oven (275° F.), then increase the heat to 325° and bake thirty to forty minutes longer.

Cottage Cheese Ring

Scones   Apricot-Ginger Conserve

Coffee Freeze

Dream Cakes

Cottage Cheese Ring

2 tablespoons gelatin   1 quart cottage cheese
¼ cup cold water   ½ pint whipped cream
1 cup milk   Salt

Soak gelatin in cold water, dissolve in hot milk. Cool and fold in cheese and whipped cream. Pour into an oiled ring mold and chill until firm. Serve surrounded by an assortment of melon balls and fresh berries, pineapple slices, and halved peaches or pears. In center of ring place a bowl of cream salad dressing (see page 93).

Scones

2 cups flour   ½ teaspoon salt
4 teaspoons baking powder 4 tablespoons butter
2 teaspoons sugar   ⅓ cup cream
              2 eggs, well beaten

Sift the dry ingredients together. Chop in the butter, add cream and eggs (reserving a small amount of unbeaten whites). Toss on a floured board. Roll into three-fourths inch thickness. Cut into small squares. Brush over with reserved egg, sprinkle with sugar and bake in a hot oven for fifteen minutes.

Apricot-Ginger Conserve

1 pound dried apricots   1 tablespoon grated orange rind
2 quarts water   ½ cup lemon juice
1 cup candied ginger (sliced)   5½ cups sugar
              1 cup sliced almonds

Soak apricots and boil in the two quarts of water for forty-five minutes (until soft). Press through a sieve and to the pulp add the ginger, orange rind, lemon juice, and sugar. Cook twenty minutes, stirring often and lowering heat as mixture begins to thicken. Add almonds five minutes before cooking is completed. Pour into scalded jelly glasses and seal.

Coffee Freeze

3 tablespoons cornstarch	$\frac{1}{4}$ cup cream
1 cup sugar	3 egg yolks, well beaten
$\frac{1}{8}$ teaspoon salt	$1\frac{1}{2}$ cups strong coffee

1 pint whipping cream

Mix the cornstarch, sugar, and salt; stir in gradually one-fourth cup of cream; add the egg yolks and then the coffee. Cook slowly in double boiler until thick, stirring constantly. Cool; fold in the whipped cream. Freeze in ice-cream freezer.

Dream Cakes

1 cup sweet butter	2 cups flour
$\frac{1}{2}$ cup brown sugar	$\frac{1}{8}$ teaspoon salt

Cream the butter and sugar. Add the flour and salt. Press into a shallow baking pan; bake fifteen minutes in a moderate oven (325° F.). Do not brown.

Top with

2 eggs	1 cup walnuts, grated
1 cup brown sugar	$\frac{1}{2}$ cup cocoanut

Beat the eggs and sugar until light. Fold in nuts. Spread on cake. Sprinkle coconut over the top. Bake for another fifteen minutes. While warm, cut into small bars. These may be iced with an orange frosting (see page 296).

Jellied Tomato Juice
Singapore Salad
Orange Muffins   *Blueberry Pudding*
Coffee

Jellied Tomato Juice

Dissolve one package of Royal Gelatin Aspic in one cup of hot, well-seasoned tomato juice. Add two cups more of tomato juice and season with lemon juice, Worcestershire Sauce, and salt if necessary. Fill bouillon cups and chill until firm. Serve with one tablespoon of sour cream in each cup and garnish with thin slices of unpeeled radish.

Singapore Salad

1 small head cabbage	1 red pepper
1 green pepper	3 cups chicken, cut in strips

1 cup beef tongue, cut in strips

Shred vegetables and add meats. Just before serving add dressing. Mix carefully, using forks so as not to break the meat.

Dressing

½ cup mayonnaise	1 tablespoon chives, chopped
½ cup cream	1 teaspoon salt
3 tablespoons chili sauce	Paprika, cayenne
Juice of ½ lemon	1 tablespoon Worcestershire Sauce

Mix until well blended.

Orange Muffins

2 tablespoons shortening	⅔ cup orange juice
½ cup sugar	1 cup flour
1 egg	½ teaspoon salt
1 cup corn flakes	2½ teaspoons baking powder

2 tablespoons grated orange rind

Blend shortening and sugar thoroughly. Add eggs and beat well. Stir in corn flakes and orange juice. Sift flour with salt and baking powder and add to first mixture. Add grated orange rind. Stir only until flour disappears. Fill greased muffin pans two-thirds full and bake in a moderately hot oven (400°) about thirty minutes.

Blueberry Pudding

1 quart blueberries	1 cup flour
1 tablespoon lemon juice	1 cup sugar
$\frac{1}{8}$ teaspoon cinnamon	$\frac{1}{2}$ cup butter

Whipped cream

Wash the berries. Put them into a baking dish. Add lemon juice and cinnamon. Sift flour and sugar and blend in butter with a pastry mixer. Spread this mixture over the berries and perforate top. Bake for forty-five minutes at 400° F. Serve with whipped cream.

Bouillon with Cracker Balls
Fillet of Trout Almondine
Parsley Potatoes
Tomato Aspic Surprise
Cucumbers in Sour Cream
Corn Meal Sticks
Watermelon Basket　　*Shell Cookies*

Bouillon (see page 77)

Cracker Balls

2 tablespoons butter
1 egg
½ teaspoon salt
1 teaspoon chopped parsley

½ teaspoon grated onion
Dash of ginger
6 tablespoons cracker meal
Soup stock

Cream butter, add egg, seasonings, cracker meal, and enough soup stock to form a drop mixture. Place in refrigerator for an hour. Form into small balls. Drop into boiling soup and cook ten minutes. (If mixture is too thick, add more broth or balls will be heavy.)

Note: Onion, parsley, and ginger may be omitted and one-half teaspoon lemon juice and a dash of mace added instead.

Fillet of Trout Almondine

Clean and bone fish. Cut into pieces the desired size and dry. Sprinkle with salt and pepper. Dip into corn meal or flour and cook in frying-pan with enough butter to prevent it from sticking to the pan. Brown on one side, turn and brown on the other. Remove to a platter and pour sautéed almonds over fillets. Garnish with lemon.

Sautéed Almonds

Blanch almonds. Split or cut in slivers and brown in butter.

Parsley Potatoes

Scrape small new potatoes and put into cold water for a half-hour. Cook in boiling salted water until tender. Drain. Add butter and chopped parsley. Shake well over the fire.

Tomato Aspic Surprise

1 large can tomatoes	2 tablespoons gelatin
6 cloves	$\frac{1}{2}$ cup cold water
2 onions	2 tablespoons vinegar
2 bay leaves	1 tablespoon lemon juice
1 teaspoon salt	1 teaspoon sugar
6 whole peppers	Cottage cheese

Chives, finely cut

Boil the first six ingredients until the tomatoes are soft, press through a sieve. There should be two cups. Soften gelatin in the cold water, then dissolve in the hot tomato mixture. Add vinegar, lemon juice, and sugar. Pour into oiled ring mold and chill.

When aspic is partially set, drop six to eight tablespoons cottage cheese, seasoned with salt and chives, into the mold at equal distances apart. Fill center with cucumbers.

Cucumbers in Sour Cream

Cucumbers	1 teaspoon salt
1 cup sour cream	Paprika
2 tablespoons vinegar	Chopped chives

Peel cucumbers with French paring-knife. Cut paper-thin cross-sections. Let stand for one hour in salted ice water. Drain and press dry. Mix remaining ingredients together, chill, and add cucumbers.

Corn-Meal Sticks

1 cup corn meal	$\frac{1}{4}$ cup sugar
$\frac{1}{2}$ teaspoon salt	2 tablespoons melted butter
2 eggs	1 cup milk
1 cup white flour	4 teaspoons baking powder

Mix and sift the dry ingredients. Add the milk, the well-beaten eggs, and the melted butter. Fill well-greased corn-stick pans half full of the batter and bake twenty to twenty-five minutes in a moderately hot oven (400° F.).

Watermelon Basket

Make an oval basket of a small, well-shaped watermelon. Cut a thin slice off the long side to make a flat base; from the opposite side cut off about one-third of the melon; scoop out balls and scrape remaining pulp down to the white rind; cut a saw-tooth edge around basket. To the melon balls add fresh pineapple cubes, cantaloupe or honeydew balls, cherries, grapes, and berries. Flavor with two tablespoons brandy and one-fourth cup kirsch. Chill fruits and arrange in the basket. Top with balls of Raspberry Ice. Decorate the platter with leaves.

Shell Cookies

1 cup butter	1 egg yolk
¾ cup powdered sugar	2½ cups flour
Almond extract	

Cream butter and sugar. Add egg yolk, almond flavoring, and flour. Work dough well, with hands until well blended. Fill buttered shell forms (Madeleine molds), place them on a large cooky sheet and bake several at a time. Sprinkle with powdered sugar before serving.

> *Jellied Bouillon*
> *Puffed Crackers*
> *Frogs' Legs Provençale*
> *Potato Balls*   *Green Salad*
> *Orange Biscuit*
> *Peach and Raspberry Mélange*
> *Rum Balls*
> *Coffee*

Jellied Bouillon

1 large can tomatoes	1 egg white and shell
¾ cup water	2 tablespoons and 1 teaspoon gelatin
1 onion	2 cans Campbell's Consommé
2 bay leaves	1 tablespoon Worcestershire Sauce
4 cloves	½ teaspoon sugar
1 carrot	½ teaspoon lemon juice
	Salt

Simmer the tomatoes, half cup water, onion, bay leaves, cloves, and carrot for twenty minutes. Strain. Add the gelatin, soaked in one-fourth cup water. Stir until thoroughly dissolved. Clarify. There should be two and one-half cups. Mix with consommé and seasonings. Fill bouillon cups. Set in refrigerator until firm. Serve with a slice of lemon.

To clarify soup (all kinds): Allow white and shell of one egg to each quart of stock. Beat egg slightly, break eggshell into small pieces and add these to the stock; place over a low fire and stir constantly until the boiling point is reached; boil two minutes. Add one tablespoon of ice water; set aside for ten minutes, strain through a double thickness of cheesecloth placed over a fine strainer.

Puffed Crackers

Soak soda crackers in cold water for ten or fifteen minutes and lift carefully from water with a pancake-turner that has holes in it, so the water can drain off. Place in a pan, far enough apart to allow them to expand. Put a teaspoonful of melted butter on each cracker and bake in a hot oven about thirty to forty minutes until light brown and crisp.

Frogs' Legs Provençale

Dip frogs' legs in milk, roll in seasoned flour and sauté in hot cooking oil until golden brown. Drain on unglazed paper. Brown butter with a grated clove of garlic, add a few drops of lemon juice and pour over frogs' legs. Sprinkle with minced parsley and garnish with lemon slices.
Note: Allow four to six legs to a serving, depending on size.

Potato Balls

Cut potatoes into balls with a round cutter. Cook in boiling water until done. Mix with butter and minced parsley.

Green Salad

Mix lettuce, endive, chicory, romaine, celery, watercress, and French artichokes in a salad bowl. Toss thoroughly with Jar French Dressing.

Jar French Dressing

5 tablespoons honey	1 teaspoon paprika
2 teaspoons salt	2 tablespoons tarragon vinegar
1 tablespoon dry mustard	$\frac{1}{2}$ cup vinegar
1 tablespoon Worcestershire	1 can Campbell's Tomato Soup
Sauce	$1\frac{1}{2}$ cups olive oil
1 shake Tabasco	1 clove garlic

Mix all the ingredients. Put into a quart jar. Keep in the refrigerator. Shake well before using.

Orange Biscuit

2 cups flour	$\frac{3}{4}$ cup milk
4 teaspoons baking powder	4 tablespoons butter
$\frac{1}{2}$ teaspoon salt	3 tablespoons orange juice
3 tablespoons butter	Grated rind of one orange

4 tablespoons sugar

Sift flour, baking powder, and salt together. Cut in the three tablespoons of butter and gradually add milk. Mix with a knife to a soft dough. Roll to one-fourth inch thickness. Cook the remaining ingredients until thick; cool and spread over the dough. Roll like a jelly roll. Cut into half-inch slices. Brush with cream and sprinkle with sugar. Bake in buttered muffin tins in a hot oven (400° F.) ten to fifteen minutes.

Peach and Raspberry Mélange

Wash and drain two pints of red raspberries. Mash one pint and press through a coarse strainer. Sweeten to taste. Add the juice of one-half lemon. Fold in the remaining berries. Place in a serving bowl. Add peeled halves of small ripe peaches and garnish with blanched almonds. Chill thoroughly. Serve with whipped cream, passed in a separate bowl.

Rum Balls *or* Kentucky Colonels

$\frac{1}{2}$ pound vanilla wafers	$\frac{1}{2}$ cup light corn syrup
2 tablespoons cocoa	$\frac{1}{4}$ cup rum or bourbon
1 cup pecans, finely chopped	Powdered sugar

Grind vanilla wafers very fine. Add nuts, cocoa, syrup, and rum and stir until mixture is blended. Coat hands with powdered sugar and roll mixture into balls the size of a walnut. Let stand for about an hour to dry out partially and then roll in powdered sugar to coat them.

Dairy Salad

Popovers   *Orange Marmalade*

Apricot Torte

Coffee

Dairy Salad

Tomatoes	Cottage cheese
Cream cheese	Sour cream
Anchovy paste	Caviar
Hard-cooked egg	Lettuce

Select uniform tomatoes, peel, and cut off a thick slice. Spread tomato with a thick layer of cream cheese mixed with anchovy paste, replace top and cover with sliced egg.

Place each tomato on lettuce and surround the base of the tomato with cottage cheese. Pour sour cream, to which a generous amount of caviar has been added, over all.

Popovers

1 cup flour	1 cup milk
¼ teaspoon salt	2 eggs, beaten until light
1 teaspoon melted butter	

Sift flour and salt. Add milk and butter to eggs; then stir gradually into the flour to make a smooth batter and beat until well blended. Butter glass custard cups and pre-heat in a hot oven for ten minutes. Fill one-third full, and bake twenty minutes in a hot oven (450° F.) then reduce the heat to 350° and bake for fifteen to twenty minutes longer.

Apricot Torte

2½ cups flour (sifted)	1 yeast cake
1 cup butter	3 tablespoons sugar
3 tablespoons cream	3 egg yolks
Vanilla	

Work butter and flour as for piecrust. Soak yeast in the cream. Beat egg yolks; add sugar and cream and yeast. Blend in with butter and flour.

Line a spring form with a thin layer of dough. Sprinkle bottom lightly with cornflakes. Place halved canned apricots (in heavy syrup) in rows; fill centers with almonds. Sprinkle heavily all over with sugar and dots of butter. Bake about a half-hour in moderate oven (350° F.).

Cook juice from apricot can with some sugar and butter, to a syrup. Baste cake with this three times in last ten minutes of baking.

Luncheons

```
Chicken Rolls          Mushroom Sauce
          Deviled Tomatoes
          Devonshire Toast
           Vienna Torte
              Coffee
```

Chicken Rolls

2 cups cold finely diced chicken
2 tablespoons butter
2 tablespoons flour
1 cup hot milk and cream or
   chicken broth
2 egg yolks

1 tablespoon minced parsley
1 tablespoon grated onion
Few grains ginger
$\frac{1}{2}$ teaspoon lemon juice
Salt, pepper
Pie dough

Melt butter, add flour, and then add the liquid. Cook until thick, then blend with egg yolks. Add to the chicken, with seasonings. Cook over hot water for ten minutes. Cool. Roll rich pie paste one-eighth inch thick, cut into five-inch squares; spread with chicken mixture and roll. Pinch ends together and place in a greased pan. Brush with additional egg yolk diluted with two tablespoons cream, and bake for thirty minutes in hot oven (400° F.). Serve with Mushroom Sauce (see page 71).

Rich Pie Paste

$1\frac{1}{2}$ cups flour
$\frac{3}{4}$ teaspoon salt

$\frac{2}{3}$ cup shortening
Ice water

Add salt to the flour and cut in shortening. Moisten to a dough with water, handling as little as possible. This dough can be used at once or covered and kept in the refrigerator.

Deviled Tomatoes

3 large, firm tomatoes	1 teaspoon mustard
Salt, pepper	1 hard-cooked egg yolk
Flour	1 egg, slightly beaten
Butter	2 tablespoons vinegar
4 tablespoons butter	$\frac{1}{4}$ teaspoon salt

Dash of cayenne

Wipe tomatoes and cut them into thick slices. Sprinkle with salt and pepper. Dredge with flour and sauté in butter. Cream the four tablespoons of butter and add the mustard, riced egg yolk, egg, vinegar, and seasonings. Cook over hot water, stirring constantly until it thickens. Place sautéed tomatoes on a serving dish and pour sauce over them.

Vienna Torte

7 eggs, separated	$\frac{1}{8}$ teaspoon salt
1 cup sugar	$\frac{1}{4}$ pound marshmallows
1 tablespoon pulverized coffee	$\frac{2}{3}$ cup strong coffee
$\frac{1}{2}$ pound pecans, grated	1 pint whipping cream

Add the sugar to the egg yolks, beat until thick and lemon-colored. Mix dry coffee and nuts, fold into the egg yolks alternately with the stiffly beaten egg whites. Bake in two layer-cake pans (with removable bottoms) in a moderate oven (350° F.) for twenty minutes. Cook the marshmallows and coffee in a double boiler until blended. Chill thoroughly. Fold into whipped cream. Spread between layers and over the top of the cake.

Eggs Robin Hood
Italian Salad
Baked Peaches
Coffee

Eggs Robin Hood

Split and toast English muffins. Sauté circular pieces of boiled ham and place them on the halves of muffins with slices of broiled tomato. Arrange on each a poached egg and cover with Cheese Sauce.

Cheese Sauce

2 tablespoons butter	$\frac{1}{2}$ teaspoon salt
$1\frac{1}{2}$ tablespoon flour	1 cup hot milk
$\frac{1}{8}$ teaspoon paprika	1 cup grated cheese

Melt the butter, then add the flour and seasonings. Gradually pour on the milk, stirring constantly. Add the cheese and cook until smooth and creamy.

Italian Salad

1 cucumber	$\frac{1}{4}$ pound Roquefort cheese
4 tomatoes	1 small tin anchovies
6 shallots	$\frac{1}{3}$ tube anchovy paste
1 bunch water cress	1 small can caviar
1 head lettuce	French Dressing
1 clove garlic	

Peel the cucumber. Cut all the vegetables and greens into small chunks. Cream the cheese, add the anchovies cut into halves, the paste, and the caviar. Combine ingredients and add French Dressing. Marinate and serve from a salad bowl, rubbed with garlic.

Baked Peaches

6 large ripe whole peaches $\frac{1}{2}$ cup water
1 tablespoon butter   1 cup sugar
$\frac{1}{2}$ teaspoon mace   1 lemon, juice and rind
     $\frac{1}{4}$ cup white wine or brandy

Peel peaches and put them in a covered glass baking dish. Add butter, mace, water, sugar, lemon juice, wine or brandy. Grate the rind of lemon over the top and bake in hot oven (400° F.) until peaches are tender, which will be about thirty minutes. Serve either hot or cold.

Crab Ring, Saint Anthony
Brioche   *Orange Marmalade*
Pears with Sabayon Sauce
Brown Wafers
Coffee

Crab Ring, Saint Anthony

2 tablespoons gelatin
¼ cup cold water
1 can Campbell's Tomato Soup
3 cakes cream cheese
1 cucumber

1 teaspoon grated onion
1 large stalk celery
4 cups crab meat
1 teaspoon salt
Few grains cayenne

1 cup mayonnaise

Soak gelatin in the cold water. Bring the soup to a boil, dissolve the gelatin in it, then mix with the riced cheese. Put the vegetables through a meat-grinder. Combine all together with crab meat, add seasonings and pour into an oiled mold. Chill until firm and then remove to a salad platter. Garnish with stuffed eggs, marinated asparagus tips, artichoke hearts, and cucumbers placed in lettuce cups. Serve with Thousand Island Dressing.

Mayonnaise Dressing

1 teaspoon mustard
1 teaspoon salt
1 teaspoon powdered sugar
Few grains cayenne

2 egg yolks
2 tablespoons vinegar
1½ cups olive oil
2 tablespoons lemon juice

Mix dry ingredients, add egg yolks, and, when well mixed, add one-half teaspoon vinegar. Add oil gradually, at first drop by drop, and beat constantly. As mixture thickens, dilute with vinegar and lemon juice.

Thousand Island Dressing

To one cup of mayonnaise, add one-third cup chili sauce, one tablespoon chopped chives, two tablespoons chopped green pepper, and one tablespoon chopped pimiento. Fold in one-half cup of whipped cream or sour cream.

Stuffed Eggs

4 hard-cooked eggs
2 tablespoons grated cheese or,
2 tablespoons deviled ham
Melted butter

1 teaspoon vinegar
¼ teaspoon mustard
Salt and cayenne

Cut eggs in halves, remove yolks and mash. Add remaining ingredients with enough melted butter to make the right consistency to shape. Form into balls and refill whites.

Brioche

1 cake yeast
⅓ cup sugar
½ cup lukewarm water
½ cup milk, scalded

5 cups sifted flour
1 cup butter
3 eggs and 4 yolks
1 tablespoon salt

Dissolve yeast and sugar in water. Add milk when lukewarm. Add two and one-half cups of flour to make a sponge. Beat ten minutes, cover and let rise in a warm place for one hour. Add creamed butter with unbeaten eggs and yolks, beating mixture thoroughly after the addition of each egg. Add remaining flour and salt. Knead five minutes and set aside to rise (five to six hours). Shape dough into balls, placing one in each well-greased muffin pan. On top of each ball place another ball, the size of a hickory nut. Cover this and let rise until double in bulk. Bake in hot oven (400° F.) for fifteen to twenty minutes.

Pears with Sabayon Sauce

Heat a can of whole pears; drain off syrup. Place pears in serving dish. Pour over one-half cup brandy and bring to the table flaming. Serve with Sabayon Sauce.

Sabayon Sauce

8 egg yolks
⅛ teaspoon salt
1 cup sugar

Juice of ½ lemon
1 cup sherry wine
2 teaspoons brandy

1 cup cream, whipped

Beat egg yolks, salt, sugar, and lemon juice until light. Cook in a double boiler, stirring constantly until thick and gradually adding the wine and brandy. Cool, then fold in the whipped cream.

Brown Wafers

½ pound butter
1 pound brown sugar
3 eggs, well beaten

2 teaspoons vanilla
2 cups flour
⅛ teaspoon salt

1 cup pecan meats

Cream the butter and sugar. Add the eggs and vanilla. Sift flour and salt and add with pecan meats gradually to the butter mixture. Drop from a teaspoon on a buttered cooky pan. Bake in a moderate oven (350° F.) until the edges are brown.

Eggs Tip-Top
Baked Candied Tomatoes
Maryland Biscuit
Almond Torte
Coffee

Eggs Tip-Top

8 croustades	Pepper
1 pound crab meat	8 poached eggs,
Thin cream sauce	Hollandaise Sauce
Salt	Chopped truffles

Add crab meat to cream sauce; season with salt and pepper. Fill croustades half full. Place a poached egg on top. Cover with Hollandaise Sauce. Garnish with truffles.

Croustades

Cut stale bread in two-inch slices, and cut in rounds, three inches in diameter. Remove centers, leaving shells. Brown in deep fat or brush with melted butter and brown in the oven.

Hollandaise Sauce

$\frac{1}{2}$ cup butter	$\frac{1}{4}$ teaspoon salt
2 tablespoons water	Pinch of pepper
4 egg yolks	Juice of $\frac{1}{2}$ lemon

Cream butter, add yolks, and beat well. Add lemon juice, salt, and pepper. When ready to serve, add water and cook in double boiler until sauce thickens, beating constantly.

NEVER ALLOW THE WATER IN THE LOWER PART OF THE DOUBLE BOILER TO GET TO THE BOILING POINT.

Baked Candied Tomatoes

12 tomatoes	White pepper
1 tablespoon salt	2 cups sugar
12 teaspoons butter	

Place tomatoes in baking-pan, stem side down. Sprinkle with salt, pepper, and sugar. On each put one teaspoon butter. Bake until tomatoes are tender. Then cook on top of the stove, basting frequently until only one-half cup of juice is left in the pan. Time required — one hour.

Maryland Biscuits

2 cups flour ~ ~ ~ ~ $\frac{1}{3}$ cup lard
$\frac{1}{2}$ teaspoon salt ~ ~ Milk and water in equal quantities

Sift dry ingredients, cut in lard, and add enough liquid to make a stiff dough. Beat with rolling pin or flatiron, continually folding over the dough until it blisters. Roll one-half inch thick. Shape with a small cutter. Prick with fork, place on a buttered tin and bake twenty minutes in a hot oven (400° F.).

Almond Torte

6 eggs, separated ~ ~ ~ ~ ~ ~ 1 teaspoon vanilla
1 cup sugar ~ ~ ~ ~ ~ ~ ~ ~ ~ $\frac{1}{2}$ teaspoon lemon juice
$\frac{2}{3}$ pound almonds, grated ~ ~ 1 tablespoon Sherry wine
1 teaspoon baking powder ~ Raspberry jelly
$\frac{1}{8}$ teaspoon salt ~ ~ ~ ~ ~ ~ Whipped cream

Beat egg yolks with sugar until thick and lemon-colored. Mix nuts and baking powder. Fold into the egg yolks alternately with the stiffly beaten egg whites and salt. Add flavorings. Bake in two layers in a moderate oven for twenty minutes. Put raspberry jelly between layers and ice with whipped cream.

Asparagus Mold with Stuffed Avocado
French Dressing
Date Nut Bread and Butter Sandwich
Chocolate Waffles
Coffee

Asparagus Mold

1 large can asparagus	2 tablespoons flour
2 tablespoons gelatin	4 eggs, well beaten
2 tablespoons butter	$\frac{1}{2}$ pint whipping cream

Salt, cayenne

Drain the water off the asparagus and add enough water to it to make one cup. Soak the gelatin in one-fourth cup of the mixture. Melt the butter and add flour. Gradually add the remaining liquid and eggs. Cook until thick. Add the gelatin and stir until dissolved. When cool, add seasonings and fold in the whipped cream. Cut tips from asparagus and line oiled mold with them, tip-end down. Cut remaining stalks into one-inch pieces, add to the gelatin mixture, and pour into mold. Chill until firm. Serve on a bed of shredded lettuce. Surround with stuffed Avocado pears, and serve with French Dressing, to which one bunch chopped watercress, one-fourth cup pearl onions, and one tablespoon caviar have been added.

Stuffed Avocado Pear

Select five small ripe pears. Peel and cut into halves. Fill with a stuffing made from six riced hard cooked eggs, one small can caviar, one tin of anchovies, chopped, and enough mayonnaise to hold all together.

Date Nut Bread

1½ cups dates	1 egg
1½ cups boiling water	2¾ cups pastry flour
2 tablespoons shortening	1 teaspoon soda
1½ cups sugar	1 teaspoon cream of tartar
1 teaspoon salt	1 cup chopped walnut meats

½ teaspoon vanilla

Wash and remove stones from dates, cut in quarters and pour water over them. Add shortening, sugar, and salt and set aside. When cool, add egg, flour sifted with soda and cream of tartar, nut meats and vanilla. Beat well, turn into a buttered and floured bread pan and bake in a moderate oven (350° F.) for one hour and fifteen minutes.

Chocolate Waffles

½ cup butter	1½ cups pastry flour
1 cup sugar	2 teaspoons baking powder
2 eggs, separated	⅛ teaspoon salt
½ cup milk	2 squares bitter chocolate

1 teaspoon vanilla

Cream butter and sugar; add the egg yolks well beaten, milk, sifted dry ingredients, melted chocolate and vanilla. Beat thoroughly. Fold in the stiffly beaten egg whites. Bake in a heated waffle iron. Serve with whipped cream or Chocolate Sauce.

Chocolate Sauce

2 squares bitter chocolate	1 tablespoon butter
⅓ cup hot water	¾ cup cream
1½ cups sugar	⅛ teaspoon salt

1 teaspoon vanilla

Melt the chocolate in the water. Add sugar, butter, cream, and salt. Cook in double boiler for ten minutes. Add vanilla. Serve hot or cold.

Egg Croquettes in Tomato Sauce
Glacéed Lemon Carrots
Oriental Salad
Potato Flour Muffins   Orange Marmalade
Gingerbread Ring   Caramel Sauce
Coffee

Egg Croquettes

9 hard-boiled eggs	½ cup hot milk
2 tablespoons butter	1 tablespoon chopped parsley
1 tablespoon flour	Pepper, salt

Rice the eggs. Make a white sauce of the butter, flour, and milk. When thick, add the eggs and seasonings. Place in refrigerator until stiff. Form into croquettes. Roll in fresh bread crumbs, using no crusts. Dip in egg and again roll in crumbs. Fry in deep, hot fat and drain on unglazed paper.

Tomato Sauce

2 cans Campbell's Tomato Soup	Salt, pepper
Milk	Chopped parsley

Heat tomato soup. Rinse out can with a little milk and add to soup. Add seasonings and chopped parsley. Pour sauce on a hot platter and arrange croquettes in it.

Glacéed Lemon Carrots

Wash, scrape, and cut carrots into shreds lengthwise or into balls with a French vegetable-cutter. Simmer in enough salted water to cover, until tender. Drain. For one pint carrots, add one teaspoon minced parsley, one tablespoon sugar, one-half teaspoon paprika, four tablespoons butter, and the juice of half a lemon. Sauté for ten minutes, shaking the pan so that each piece of carrot will be coated with the sauce.

Oriental Salad

4 ounces Camembert cheese	Salt
4 ounces cream cheese	½ cup Bengal chutney
4 tablespoons olive oil	Romaine
2 tablespoons tarragon vinegar	

Blend cheese and place a tablespoon of it on a few leaves of romaine. Make a dressing of the oil, vinegar, chutney, and salt and pour over the cheese.

Potato Flour Muffins

4 eggs, separated	½ cup white potato flour
⅛ teaspoon salt	1 teaspoon baking powder
1 tablespoon sugar	2 tablespoons ice water

Beat whites of eggs until dry and stiff. Add salt and sugar to the beaten yolks and fold into whites. Sift flour and baking powder twice and fold into egg mixture. Add ice water last. Bake in moderate oven (350° F.) fifteen to twenty minutes.

Orange Marmalade

5 large navel oranges	12 cups sugar
9 cups of water	Juice of 4 lemons (¾ cup)

Cut oranges in thin slices, then cut each slice into eight segments. Add water. Allow to stand twenty-four hours. Cook for twenty minutes. Add sugar, mix thoroughly and simmer for forty-five minutes. Add lemon juice and cook for ten minutes more. Place in sterilized jars and seal.

Gingerbread Ring

1 cup molasses	2 eggs, beaten separately
2 teaspoons baking soda	½ cup sugar
1 teaspoon cinnamon	½ cup melted butter
1 teaspoon ginger	2 cups flour (scant)
1 cup boiling water	

Mix molasses, soda, and spices. Add sugar, butter, flour, and water; beat well. Add egg yolks and fold in whites. Pour in a greased ring mold and bake in a moderate oven.

Note: This is a very thin batter.

Caramel Sauce

2 egg yolks	1 tablespoon butter
1 cup cream	1 teaspoon vanilla
1 pound light brown sugar	$\frac{1}{8}$ teaspoon salt

Add egg yolks and cream to sugar. Cook until creamy in a double boiler. Add butter. When cool, add vanilla and salt.

> *Meatball Pancakes*
> *Stuffed Onions*
> *Tropical Fruit Salad*
> *Delmonico Bavaroise*
> *Coffee*

Meatball Pancakes

¾ pound round steak, ground fine
6 eggs, separated
½ teaspoon baking powder
Salt, pepper
½ teaspoon lemon juice
1 teaspoon minced parsley
Grated onion

Add meat and other ingredients to the well-beaten egg yolks; fold in the stiffly beaten egg whites. Drop by spoonfuls on a hot buttered frying-pan; when puffed and brown around the edges, turn and brown the other side.

Stuffed Onions

Remove skins from eight Bermuda onions and parboil ten minutes in boiling salted water. Drain and remove a part of the centers. Pour one cup soup stock over the shells and bake in the oven until tender, basting frequently. Boil six potatoes, mash, season with salt, pepper, butter and hot milk. Beat until fluffy. Fill centers of onions with potatoes, sprinkle with buttered crumbs and bake until brown.

Tropical Fruit Salad

Mix equal parts of diced fresh pineapple, sliced bananas and sections of tangerines. Marinate with French Dressing. Serve on a bed of lettuce leaves and sprinkle generously with paprika.

Delmonico Bavaroise

1 tablespoon gelatin $\frac{1}{16}$ teaspoon salt
$\frac{1}{2}$ cup milk $\frac{1}{2}$ pint whipping cream
1 egg $\frac{1}{2}$ cup chopped glacéed fruits
$\frac{1}{2}$ cup sugar $\frac{1}{2}$ cup broken pecans

Sherry

Dissolve gelatin in the milk. Beat egg, sugar, and salt until light; add to the milk. Cook in a double boiler until creamy. Chill and, when it begins to stiffen, fold in whipped cream, fruits, and nuts and flavor with sherry. Pour into a mold, chill until firm. Serve with Raspberry Sauce.

Raspberry Sauce

Melt one glass of raspberry jelly in a double boiler. Add one teaspoon lemon juice and two tablespoons water. Chill.

> *Clam Juice*
> *Egg Timbales with Anchovy Sauce*
> *Ham Cornucopias   Asparagus Tips*
> *Salad Glacé with Pineapple Ice*
> *Swedish Wafers*
> *Coffee*

Egg Timbales with Anchovy Sauce

Butter individual timbale molds and sprinkle with chopped parsley. Drop one egg into each mold, place in hot water and cook until the white is set (three to five minutes). Mix two tablespoons anchovy paste with Hollandaise Sauce (see page 58). Pour sauce on a hot platter and arrange timbales in it.

Ham Cornucopias

Steam thin slices of ham until thoroughly heated. Roll into cornucopias. Fill with heated asparagus tips. Use as a border around platter of eggs.

Salad Glacé

$\frac{1}{2}$ teaspoon gelatin   2 packages cream cheese
1 tablespoon cold water   Chopped nuts
2 cups hot water   1 quart fresh strawberries, lightly
1 package Raspberry Jello   sugared
                1 quart pineapple ice

Soak gelatin in the cold water and dissolve in the hot water with the Jello. Make twelve cheese balls and roll them in chopped nuts. Place in an oiled ring mold. Cover with strawberries. Over this pour the Jello mixture. Place in the refrigerator until firm. Serve on lettuce. Fill center of ring with pineapple ice. Serve with French Dressing.

Pineapple Ice

1 cup sugar	2 cups grated pineapple
2 cups water	Juice of three lemons

2 egg whites, stiffly beaten

Boil the sugar and water for ten minutes. Cool. Add the pineapple and lemon juice. Freeze until slightly thickened, then add egg whites. Mix well, and continue freezing.

Tamale Ring with Meat Balls
Bohemian Salad
Rye Toast
Jelly Roll
Coffee

Tamale Ring

1 No. 2 can tomatoes	1 clove garlic, grated
2 eggs, separated	1 pint pitted ripe olives
1 can corn kernels	1 cup corn meal
1 green pepper, chopped	$1\frac{1}{2}$ tablespoons chili powder
Salt	

Press the tomatoes through a sieve. Add to the well-beaten egg yolks and the remaining ingredients. Fold in the stiffly beaten egg whites. Pour into a buttered and floured ring mold. Place in a pan of hot water and bake one hour in a moderate oven (350° F.).

Fill center of ring with small meat balls (see page 307). Pour tomato soup heated and seasoned to taste over the meat balls and sprinkle with minced parsley.

Bohemian Salad

Cut celery cabbage crosswise in half inch slices. Put in a salad bowl lined with watercress. Arrange over the top alternate slices of hard-cooked egg and boiled beets. Sprinkle with minced chives, cover with French Dressing. Toss, and serve.

Jelly Roll

3 eggs, separated	1 teaspoon baking powder
1 cup sugar	$\frac{1}{4}$ teaspoon salt
6 tablespoons hot water	Grated rind of one lemon
1 cup flour	Jelly

Beat egg yolks and sugar until thick and lemon-colored. Add the water and sifted dry ingredients, fold in the stiffly beaten egg whites. Add lemon rind. Pour into a ten-by-sixteen-inch baking-pan which has been greased, lined with paper, and again greased. Bake in a hot oven (375° F.) for fifteen minutes. Quickly cut off crisp edges of cake. Turn from pan at once on cloth covered with powdered sugar. Remove paper. Beat jelly with a fork until soft and spread quickly over cake. Roll while warm. Wrap in cloth and set aside to cool.

Lemon filling may be used instead of jelly.

Lemon Filling

½ pound granulated sugar	2 tablespoons butter
Juice and grated rind of 2 lemons	2 whole eggs

Put in double boiler and stir until thick.

Egg Soufflé with Mushroom Sauce
Persimmon Royal
Toasted Fingers
Hazelnut Roll
Coffee

Egg Soufflé

2 tablespoons butter	½ tablespoon grated onion
2 tablespoons flour	1 tablespoon chopped parsley
½ pint cream	Salt
5 hard-cooked eggs	Paprika
4 eggs, separated	

Melt butter, add flour and cook, stirring constantly until light brown. Gradually add the cream. Cook until thick. Rice eggs and add to the sauce. Cool and season. Add the egg yolks beaten light and fold in the stiffly beaten egg whites. Pour into a greased and floured ring mold. Place in a pan of boiling water, and bake in a moderate oven (350° F.) until firm (thirty minutes).

Mushroom Sauce

Peel and slice one pound of fresh mushrooms. Sauté in butter. Add one cup cream and one-half cup milk mixed with two tablespoons flour. Cook until smooth and creamy. Season with salt, paprika and sherry wine. Serve in the center of the egg ring.

Persimmon Royal

Select eight ripe persimmons. Remove stems. Cut each into six sections, leaving them connected at stem end. Arrange on serving platter, on crisp lettuce. Between persimmons put sections of grapefruit, orange, and avocado pear; separating the grapefruit and oranges with very thin slices of unpeeled apple. Serve with Lorenzo Dressing (see page 78).

Toasted Fingers

Cut bread into one-inch slices. Remove crusts. Cut into one-inch fingers. Brush all sides with melted butter. Toast in a slow oven.

Hazelnut Roll

4 eggs, separated	$\frac{1}{2}$ teaspoon rum
5 ounces sugar	$\frac{1}{8}$ teaspoon salt
3 tablespoons stale bread crumbs	5 ounces shelled hazelnuts

1 pint cream, whipped

Stir yolks with sugar until light and lemon-colored. Add bread crumbs, rum, and salt. Alternately fold in the stiffly beaten egg whites and the nuts. Pour into a shallow, well-greased, and floured baking-sheet. Bake in a moderate oven fifteen to twenty minutes. Remove from pan at once onto a cloth covered with powdered sugar. Cut off crisp edges of cake and roll while hot. When cold, unroll, and spread with sweetened whipped cream flavored with vanilla and roll again. Ice with a caramel frosting (see page 319).

Baked Noodles Antin
Grapefruit and Malaga Grape Salad
Orange Bread
Coffee Torte
Coffee

Baked Noodles Antin

1 package fine noodles (5 ounces) 1 onion, finely chopped
1 cup cottage cheese 1 tablespoon Worcestershire Sauce
1 cup sour cream Dash of Tabasco sauce
½ clove garlic, minced Salt

Cook the noodles in boiling salted water for ten minutes. Drain. Mix
other ingredients and add to the noodles. Put in a buttered casserole,
and bake forty-five minutes in a moderate oven (350° F.) or until brown
and crusty on top. Serve piping hot, with sour cream and Parmesan
cheese.

Grapefruit and Malaga Grape Salad

Carefully remove the pulp from grapefruit, leaving sections whole.
Use half the amount of Malaga grapes cut into halves, peeled with seeds
removed. Place grapefruit on a bed of lettuce in a salad bowl, with
grapes in the center. Cover with Lorenzo Dressing, and serve very cold.

Orange Bread

1 cup orange peel 1 egg, beaten
Water 2 cups milk
1¾ cups sugar 4 cups flour
1 tablespoon butter 4 teaspoons baking powder
⅛ teaspoon salt

Cut orange peel into small pieces. Cover with water and cook until
peel is tender. Add one cup sugar and boil to a syrup. Cream butter
and remaining sugar, add egg, milk and sifted dry ingredients. Beat

well and fold in the orange peel. Pour into two buttered bread pans. Let stand twenty minutes. Brush top of loaves generously with melted butter. Bake forty to fifty minutes in a slow oven (325° F.).

Coffee Torte

6 eggs, separated
$\frac{1}{2}$ pound confectioner's sugar
$\frac{1}{8}$ teaspoon salt

$\frac{1}{2}$ pound almonds, grated
2 ounces pulverized coffee
1 teaspoon vanilla

Beat egg yolks, sugar, and salt until thick and lemon-colored. Add the almonds, coffee, and vanilla. Fold in the egg whites, beaten very stiff. Bake in two layers in a moderate oven (350° F.) for twenty minutes. Put chocolate filling between layers and ice with coffee icing.

Chocolate Filling

$\frac{1}{3}$ pound Maillard's chocolate
2 tablespoons sugar
$\frac{1}{8}$ teaspoon salt

3 tablespoons cream
1 tablespoon butter
2 egg yolks

Grate chocolate, mix with sugar, salt, and cream. Cook in a double boiler until thick. Add the butter, stir until melted, then beat in egg yolks. Cool before putting between layers.

Coffee Icing

1 tablespoon sweet butter   2 cups confectioner's sugar
Strong coffee

Cream butter; add sugar and enough coffee to make the proper consistency for spreading. Ice cake, and decorate with part of the chocolate filling forced through a pastry tube.

Tomato Soufflé Ring with Creamed Chicken
Broiled Mushrooms with French Peas
Bread Loaf   Gherkins
Lemon Fluff Icebox Cake
Coffee

Tomato Soufflé Ring

1 large can tomatoes	1 large onion
1 bay leaf	1 teaspoon sugar
2 cloves	2 tablespoons butter
1 teaspoon salt	4 tablespoons flour
Pepper	3 eggs, separated

Simmer the tomatoes and seasonings for twenty minutes; strain. Melt butter, add flour and pour one cup of the tomato mixture in slowly. Cook until thick. Cool and add to the well-beaten egg yolks. Beat the egg whites very stiff and fold into the tomato sauce. Pour into a well-buttered and floured ring mold. Place in a pan of boiling water. Cover with a lid and bake in a moderate oven twenty to thirty minutes.

Creamed Chicken

Melt four tablespoons butter, add four tablespoons flour, and gradually pour on two cups hot milk and one-half cup cream. Cook until smooth and thick. Add three cups diced chicken, one tablespoon minced parsley, salt, paprika, and one minced pimiento.

Broiled Mushrooms

Select large white mushrooms. Wash, remove stems, and dry. Place on a buttered broiler and broil for five minutes, turning them once. Sprinkle with salt, pepper, and a little melted butter. Fill with French peas and serve around Tomato Soufflé.

French Peas

To two pounds of fresh cooked peas, add three tablespoons of butter and six shallots, finely chopped. Season with salt and pepper and let simmer for a few minutes.

Bread Loaf

Remove all the crust from a loaf of bread. Cut into one-inch slices three-fourths of the way through the loaf. Brush the sides and the cut sections of the loaf with melted butter. Toast on all four sides; serve hot.

Lemon Fluff Icebox Cake

$\frac{3}{4}$ pound vanilla wafers or graham
    crackers
$\frac{1}{3}$ cup melted butter
2 tablespoons gelatin

$\frac{1}{3}$ cup cold water
7 eggs, separated
2 cups sugar
3 lemons, juice and rind

$\frac{1}{4}$ teaspoon salt

Crush wafers or crackers; add butter. Line the sides and bottom of a spring form with this mixture, reserving one-half cup. Soak the gelatin in the cold water. Beat the yolks of the eggs with one cup of sugar until light. Add lemon juice, rind, and gelatin. Cook in a double boiler until thick. Cool. Add the salt to the egg whites; beat stiff. Fold in other cup sugar and the cooled lemon mixture. Pour into spring form. Sprinkle the remaining crushed crumbs on top and place in refrigerator.

> *Bouillon*
> *Stuffed Celery*
> *Sweetbread and Mushroom Crêpes*
> *Lorenzo Salad   Lorenzo Dressing*
> *Toast Melba*
> *Chocolate Pot au Crème*
> *Vanilla Butter Wafers*
> *Coffee*

Bouillon

5 pounds lean beef	2 cloves
4 ounces beef liver	1 tablespoon salt
2 tablespoons lean raw ham	3 carrots
Cold water	2 stalks celery
2 marrow bones	2 large onions with skins
1 No. 2 can tomatoes	1 turnip
1 teaspoon peppercorns	6 sprigs parsley
2 bay leaves	Dash of paprika

Wipe and cut meat into small cubes; put two-thirds of meat into soup kettle and soak in water thirty minutes. Brown the remainder in hot frying-pan with marrow from the marrow bones. Put browned meat and bones into the kettle. Heat to the boiling point, skim thoroughly, and cook at temperature below boiling for two hours. Add remaining ingredients and cook three hours; strain and cool. Skim fat from the top and clarify (see page 43). Add a dash of maggi, reheat, and serve with a slice of lemon and minced parsley, or slices of avocado.

Stuffed Celery

Celery stalks	Salt
½ pound Roquefort cheese	Pepper
½ cup sherry	Paprika
1 teaspoon Worcestershire Sauce	Melted butter
Pecans	

Mash cheese, add seasonings with enough melted butter to make a paste. Fill celery stalks and garnish with coarsely chopped pecans.

Sweetbread and Mushroom Crêpes

2 pounds sweetbreads   1 pound mushrooms

Soak sweetbreads in cold water for fifteen minutes. Cook twenty minutes in a quart of boiling salted water, to which one tablespoon vinegar or lemon juice has been added. Plunge in cold water; chill in refrigerator.

Remove all membrane; cut or break into small pieces.

Sauté mushrooms in butter. Combine sweetbreads and mushrooms with Sauce Suprème, reserving some sauce to pour over the finished crêpes.

Sauce Suprème

3 tablespoons butter   ½ cup cream
3 tablespoons flour   Salt
1 cup hot chicken stock   Paprika
           Sherry wine

Melt butter and add flour. Gradually add the chicken stock and the cream. Bring to a boil, stirring constantly. Add the seasonings and the sherry.

Make crêpes (see Pancakes, page 11, using half of recipe). Spread each pancake with sweetbread and mushroom mixture and roll. Cover with the remaining Sauce Suprème.

Lorenzo Salad

Select firm ripe pears. Peel, core, and cut into slices. Cut lettuce into chunks. Place in a salad bowl lined with watercress, add Lorenzo Dressing and toss until well mixed.

Lorenzo Dressing

⅔ cup olive oil   Paprika
⅓ cup vinegar   1 cup chili sauce
1 teaspoon salt   1 cup chopped watercress

Stir all together until thoroughly mixed; serve cold.

Toast Melba

Cut paper thin slices of bread and remove crusts. Place in a slow oven until golden brown.

Chocolate Pot au Crème

1 pint milk	1 pound Maillard's
6 egg yolks	sweet chocolate

Scald the milk, add the chocolate, and cook, stirring constantly, until it is melted and boiling point is reached. Pour this over beaten egg yolks and stir well. Strain through cheesecloth or a fine sieve. Pour into small custard cups (ramekins) and chill. Serve very cold.

Vanilla Butter Wafers

1 cup sweet butter	2 cups flour
1 cup sugar	2 teaspoons vanilla
2 eggs, well beaten	Candied cherries or pecans

Cream butter and sugar; add eggs, then gradually add flour and vanilla. Drop mixture from tip of teaspoon on to a buttered pan. Top with a small cherry or a pecan, and bake in a hot oven (400° F.) until the edges are brown.

American Cheese Ring
Lorenzo Dressing
French Lamb Cutlets with Cuban Sauce
Sautéed Corn with Green Pepper
Graham Gems　　　　Spiced Pears
Macaroon Pudding
Coffee

American Cheese Ring

1 can pineapple, medium size	1 cup Processed American cheese,
Juice of 2 lemons	finely diced
2 tablespoons gelatin	1 cup white grapes
1 cup sugar	Shredded lettuce
$\frac{1}{2}$ pint whipping cream	Persimmons
	Avocado pears

Drain pineapple. To pineapple juice add the lemon juice and enough water to make two cups. Soften gelatin in one-half cup of the liquid; to remaining liquid add sugar and bring to a boil. Remove from fire and add gelatin, stirring until dissolved. Set aside until it begins to stiffen. Fold in the whipped cream, cheese, grapes, and pineapple cut into small pieces. Put into an oiled ring mold. When firm, turn out on a platter covered with shredded lettuce. Garnish with sections of persimmons and avocado pears. Serve with Lorenzo Dressing.

French Lamb Cutlets

8 rib lamb chops, cut thin	$\frac{1}{2}$ teaspoon salt
1 tablespoon butter	$\frac{1}{8}$ teaspoon pepper
4 tablespoons flour	1 cup cream
	$\frac{1}{2}$ cup chopped ham

Make a white sauce of the butter, flour, salt, pepper, and cream. When thoroughly cooked, add the finely chopped ham. Mix well and set aside to cool. Broil the chops and season with salt and pepper. Spread both sides with the sauce. Allow them to stand on a buttered plate until firm, then dip in crumbs, egg, and crumbs again. Fry in deep fat until brown.

Cuban Sauce

2 tablespoons chopped ham   Paprika
$\frac{1}{4}$ cup butter $\frac{1}{2}$ teaspoon salt
$\frac{1}{4}$ cup flour $1\frac{1}{2}$ cups soup stock
1 cup tomato catsup

Sauté ham and butter until the butter is well browned. Add the flour, paprika, salt, stock, and catsup slowly. Cook slowly for ten minutes and serve with chops.

Sautéed Corn with Green Pepper

3 tablespoons butter   2 tablespoons chopped green pepper
3 cups corn   Salt, paprika
                                          $\frac{1}{4}$ cup cream

Melt the butter in a frying-pan. Add corn, pepper, seasonings, and cream. Cover and cook slowly until all the liquid is absorbed.

Graham Gems

$\frac{1}{2}$ cup flour   4 teaspoons baking powder
1 cup graham flour   1 egg, well beaten
$\frac{1}{4}$ teaspoon salt $\frac{3}{4}$ cup milk

Sift the flour. Sift again with salt and baking powder. Add egg and enough milk to make a heavy batter. Bake in buttered muffin pans for twenty minutes in a hot oven (400° F.).

Spiced Pears

$\frac{1}{2}$ peck pears   1 pint vinegar
2 pounds sugar   1 ounce stick cinnamon
                              Cloves

Carefully pare fruit. Boil sugar, vinegar, and cinnamon for twenty minutes. Put fruit into syrup. Cook until tender when pierced with a straw. Cook one-half the fruit at a time. Put into sterilized jars, adding to each some cloves and a stick of cinnamon; fill to overflowing with the syrup and adjust lids.

Macaroon Pudding

18 macaroons	1½ pints milk
½ cup sherry	2 tablespoons gelatin
5 eggs, separated	2 tablespoons water
1 cup sugar	1 teaspoon vanilla
⅛ teaspoon salt	Whipped cream

Line a pudding mold with macaroons and pour wine over them. Beat egg yolks and sugar until light. Add the salt and milk and cook over hot water until creamy. Soften the gelatin in the water, and then dissolve in the hot custard. Fold in the stiffly beaten egg whites and add the vanilla. Pour over macaroons in mold and place in refrigerator until firm. Serve with whipped cream.

> ### Bouillon Rosa
> ### Celery   Olives
> ### Chicken Casino
> ### Soufflé Potatoes
> ### Toasted English Muffins
> ### Apricot and Pineapple Jam
> ### Green Salad
> ### Almond Sponge — Wine Sauce
> ### Coffee

Bouillon Rosa

Mix equal quantities of chicken broth and tomato juice. Season to taste.

Chicken Casino

6 whole tomatoes	1½ cups Bengal chutney
Salt, pepper	3 cups finely diced chicken
1 teaspoon sugar	1½ cups thin cream sauce
Sliced ham	2 eggs, beaten
½ cup butter	Chopped parsley

Peel tomatoes, season with salt, pepper, and sugar. Steam until soft. Sauté ham in butter and chutney. Mix chicken with white sauce, add eggs. Cook until thoroughly heated and thick, stirring constantly. Place ham on platter, pour chutney over it. Cover with chicken and place a tomato on each portion. Garnish with chopped parsley.

Soufflé Potatoes

Use white baking potatoes and slice them lengthwise, about a sixteenth inch thick. Soak in ice water, and when ready to use, drain and dry.

Have two kettles of fat heating, one at 225° and the other at 425° F. Drop a few at a time in the first kettle (225°). Fry for four or five minutes or until they rise to the surface of the fat. Transfer the partly fried potatoes to the other kettle (425°), where they should puff immediately. Drain on unglazed paper and sprinkle with salt.

Green Salad

Combine an assortment of salad greens (lettuce, watercress, escarole, endive) with French Dressing and toss lightly. To have a crisp salad, do not add dressing until ready to serve.

French Dressing

½ teaspoon salt	1½ tablespoons vinegar
1 teaspoon paprika	1½ tablespoons lemon juice
¼ teaspoon white pepper	¾ cup olive oil

Mix the ingredients and beat until well blended.

Apricot and Pineapple Jam

1 large pineapple	6 dozen apricots
Sugar	

Pare, core, and cut pineapple into small pieces. Cut apricots into halves and remove stones. Allow three cups sugar to four cups fruit. Bring slowly to boiling point. Cook until thick and clear. Pour into glasses. When cold, cover with paraffin.

Almond Sponge

2½ ounces butter	9 ounces almonds, blanched and grated
2½ ounces sugar	⅛ teaspoon salt
6 eggs, separated	1 teaspoon vanilla

Beat butter until creamy with sugar and yolks. Add almonds, stiffly beaten whites, salt, and vanilla. Pour into a buttered pudding form sprinkled with sugar. Cover tightly and steam for one hour.

Wine Sauce

$\frac{1}{4}$ cup sugar
$\frac{1}{16}$ teaspoon salt
2 teaspoons cornstarch
$\frac{1}{2}$ lemon sliced

$\frac{3}{4}$ cup white wine
$\frac{1}{2}$ cup water
1 stick cinnamon bark
2 egg yolks

Mix sugar, salt, and cornstarch. Add wine, one-fourth cup water, cinnamon, and lemon. Cook in a double boiler for five minutes, stirring constantly. Strain. Blend yolks with remaining water. Gradually add strained hot liquid, return to boiler and cook until it coats a spoon. Serve hot or cold.

Scallops Madeleine
Macédoine Salad
Muffins   *Cherry Preserves*
Crème Brulé
Green Gages
Coffee

Scallops Madeleine

1 quart scallops	1½ cups soup stock
Boiling salted water	2 tablespoons flour
2 pounds fresh mushrooms	1 cup cream
Celery salt	2 egg yolks, beaten slightly
Pepper, paprika, salt	1 tablespoon butter

Simmer scallops until tender in boiling water. Sauté mushrooms, seasoned with celery salt, pepper, paprika, and salt. Blend flour and soup stock and add to mushrooms. Add most of the cream, and cook, stirring constantly, until thick and smooth. Combine mushroom mixture and scallops, add butter and egg yolks to which remaining cream has been added. Heat thoroughly. Serve with toast points and garnish with chopped parsley.

Macédoine Salad

Marinate separately cold cooked beans, asparagus, cauliflower, and tomatoes. Place cauliflower in center of the dish and arrange vegetables around it. Garnish the beans with pearl onions. Serve with Lorenzo Dressing.

Muffins

¼ cup butter	2 cups flour
¼ cup sugar	4 teaspoons baking powder
1 egg, well beaten	¼ teaspoon salt
	¾ cup milk

Cream butter; add sugar and egg. Sift flour, baking powder, and salt, and add to the first mixture alternately with the milk. Bake in hot oven (400° F.) in buttered muffin pans for twenty-five minutes.

Crème Brulé

1 quart cream	2 teaspoons vanilla
2 tablespoons sugar	8 egg yolks
Brown sugar	

Scald cream, remove from heat and add sugar and vanilla. Pour slowly over well beaten egg yolks, beating constantly. Pour into greased shallow baking dish. Bake one hour or until set, at 300°. Chill and then cover with a layer of brown sugar. Place under broiler to caramelize sugar. Chill thoroughly before serving.

Dill Tomato Juice
Saltines
Chicken Doris with Corn Fritters
Green Salad
Blueberry Muffins
Café Soufflé
Coffee

Dill Tomato Juice

Make a cheesecloth bag and fill it with six to eight heads of dill, broken in pieces. Cut into quarters, a half bushel of tomatoes. Cook over low flame until soft, with the dill bag in it, watching to see that the bag stays down in the tomatoes. Strain and bring to a boil. Pour into sterilized jars, putting one teaspoon of salt in each quart jar.

Chicken Doris

Boiled chicken breasts	White pepper
3 cups cream	Dash cayenne
1 tablespoon paprika	1 tablespoon cornstarch
Salt	1 tablespoon cream

Cut chicken into one-inch cubes. Put into a double boiler with three cups of cream and seasonings. Cook slowly for twenty minutes. Thicken sauce with cornstarch, blended with remaining cream. Serve on a corn fritter covered with a thin slice of sautéed ham, and top with a broiled mushroom.

Corn Fritters

3 egg yolks	$\frac{1}{2}$ teaspoon salt
1$\frac{1}{2}$ cups corn	$\frac{1}{4}$ teaspoon pepper
$\frac{1}{4}$ cup flour	3 egg whites

Beat egg yolks well. Add corn, flour, salt, and pepper. Beat egg whites until stiff and fold into the corn mixture. Drop by spoonfuls onto lightly greased griddle.

Green Salad (see page 84)

Blueberry Muffins

1 cup blueberries	1 egg, well beaten
2½ cups flour	½ teaspoon salt
¼ cup butter	4 teaspoons baking powder
¼ cup sugar	1 cup milk

Dredge berries with one-fourth cup flour. Cream the butter and sugar, add egg, then the sifted dry ingredients alternately with the milk. Fold in the berries. Bake twenty-five minutes in a hot oven (400° F.) in buttered muffin pans.

Café Soufflé

3 ounces butter	¾ cup strong coffee
2¼ ounces flour	5 ounces sugar
$\frac{1}{16}$ teaspoon salt	1 teaspoon vanilla
1 cup milk	6 eggs, separated

Melt butter, add flour, salt, milk, and coffee. Cook until thick, stirring constantly. Cool and add to the well-beaten egg yolks and sugar. Fold in the stiffly beaten egg whites. Add vanilla. Pour into a buttered pudding dish, set in pan of boiling water. Bake forty-five minutes in moderate oven (375° F.). Serve with Café Cream.

Café Cream

½ cup cream	3 tablespoons strong coffee
3 egg yolks	½ teaspoon vanilla
Sugar	$\frac{1}{16}$ teaspoon salt
½ pint whipping cream	

Mix all the ingredients but the whipping cream; cook in a double boiler until thick. Cool, then fold into the whipped cream.

Bouillon — Almond Balls
Sea Food Pancake Pie
Celery Vinaigrette
Rye Toast Melba
Orange in Syrup with Coconut
Pinwheel Cookies
Coffee

Almond Balls

⅛ pound almonds, grated   ⅛ teaspoon salt
1 egg, separated   Grated lemon rind

Add egg yolk, salt, and a little lemon rind to almonds. Fold in beaten egg white. Drop from the end of a teaspoon into hot fat. Drain on unglazed paper. Put into boiling bouillon just before serving.

Sea Food Pancake Pie

½ pound cream cheese   Caviar
1 tube of anchovy paste   Sea Food Newburg Sauce
Pancakes (see page 11)

Blend cream cheese, anchovy, and a little cream to soft paste. Place a pancake on the serving platter; spread with the cheese mixture; top with a pancake spread with caviar, and continue alternating until all the pancakes are used. There should be about ten or twelve. Slice in pie-like wedges, but keep intact. Cover with Sea Food Newburg Sauce (see page 105).

Celery Vinaigrette

Wash, scrape, and cut celery stalks into halves, lengthwise. Tie into bunches and cook twenty minutes in boiling salted water. Chill. Drain and serve with Vinaigrette Sauce.

Orange in Syrup with Coconut

Peel navel oranges, remove all the skin and membrane by cutting partway down the segments, leaving the orange whole. Prepare a syrup of one cup orange juice, two-thirds cup pineapple juice, one-third cup lemon juice, and one cup sugar. Boil ten minutes; place oranges in it and boil for only one minute, so that oranges do not fall apart. Remove to serving dish. Chill thoroughly and before serving, sprinkle with fresh grated coconut.

Pinwheel Cookies

$\frac{1}{2}$ pound sweet butter
$\frac{1}{2}$ pound cream cheese
2 cups flour

$\frac{1}{4}$ teaspoon salt
Red raspberry jelly
Chopped nuts

Cream butter, add cheese, mix with flour and salt. Place in icebox overnight. Roll thin, spread with jelly, and sprinkle with nuts. Roll as a jelly roll; slice thin. Bake until light brown in a hot oven (400° F.). Ice with Vanilla Icing.

Vanilla Icing

1 tablespoon butter
1 cup confectioner's sugar

Boiling water
$\frac{1}{2}$ teaspoon vanilla

Cream butter; add sugar with sufficient water to make right consistency for spreading; then add flavoring.

Filled Honeydew Melon
Shad Roe Sauté   Broiled Bacon
Mashed Potato Balls
Vegetable Aspic   Cream Dressing
New England Tea Biscuit
Chocolate Soufflé   Marshmallow Mint Sauce
Coffee

Filled Honeydew Melon

Cut honeydew melons into thirds or quarters. Using a French vegetable-cutter, carefully make balls and retain the shells. Cut balls from a watermelon and a cantaloupe. Add a few pitted black cherries, sherry wine and apricot brandy to taste. Chill thoroughly, refill cavities in the melon shell with the assorted fruit balls and cherries. Serve with a slice of lemon.

Shad Roe Sauté

Parboil in salted water; sprinkle with salt and pepper, and sauté in bacon fat two to three minutes on each side. Serve with Maître d'Hôtel Butter (see page 102).

Broiled Bacon

Put thin slices of bacon on a wire broiler. Place over dripping-pan and bake in a hot oven until bacon is crisp and brown, turning once. Drain on unglazed paper.

Mashed Potato Balls

2 cups hot riced potatoes	Dash of cayenne
1 tablespoon butter	1 teaspoon chopped parsley
$\frac{1}{4}$ teaspoon salt	1 egg
$\frac{1}{8}$ teaspoon celery salt	Flour

Add seasonings to the potatoes. Cool, and add the beaten egg. Shape into small balls and roll in flour. Fry in deep fat and drain on unglazed paper.

Vegetable Aspic

2 cups Aspic   Radishes, sliced
Asparagus   Peas, cooked
Cucumber, sliced   Cauliflower, cooked
          String beans, cooked

Line an oiled ring mold with asparagus tips standing on tip ends.
Add remaining vegetables and fill mold to top with aspic. Chill until
firm. Serve with Cream Dressing.

Aspic

2 tablespoons gelatin dissolved in:
    1 cup water $\frac{1}{4}$ cup vinegar
    2 cups of boiling water $\frac{1}{4}$ cup sugar
      with a bouillon cube dissolved in it   1 teaspoon salt
      Juice of 1 lemon

Cream Dressing

1 tablespoon dry mustard   Few grains of cayenne
1 teaspoon salt $\frac{1}{3}$ cup vinegar
2 teaspoons flour   1 egg yolk
$1\frac{1}{2}$ teaspoons powdered sugar   1 tablespoon melted butter
          1 cup whipping cream, or sour cream

Mix dry ingredients together, then slowly add vinegar, egg, and butter.
Cook over boiling water until mixture thickens. Cool and add whipped
cream.

New England Tea Biscuit

2 cups flour $\frac{1}{2}$ cup butter
4 teaspoons baking powder $\frac{3}{4}$ cup milk
$\frac{1}{2}$ teaspoon salt   Loaf sugar
1 tablespoon sugar   Orange marmalade or orange juice

Sift dry ingredients together. Cut in the butter and add enough milk
to form a soft dough, handling as little as possible. Roll one-half inch
thick; cut into small biscuits. Press into the top of each a small piece
of loaf sugar, first dipped in orange marmalade or orange juice. Brush
over top with orange juice or marmalade. Sprinkle with additional
sugar and bake in a hot oven (400° F.) ten to twelve minutes.

Chocolate Soufflé

3 tablespoons butter   1 cup cream
⅓ cup flour   3 eggs, separated
½ cup sugar   2 squares bitter chocolate, melted
                              1 teaspoon vanilla

In top of double boiler, melt the butter, blend in the flour and sugar.
Stir until smooth, then gradually add cream and cook until thickened.
Add well-beaten yolks and cook a minute longer. Remove from fire and
stir in the chocolate. Allow mixture to cool slightly and fold in beaten
whites and vanilla.

Pour into buttered baking-dish. Set it in a pan of hot water and
bake in a moderate oven (350° F.) about thirty minutes.

Marshmallow Mint Sauce

¼ cup water   2 egg whites
½ cup sugar   Essence of peppermint
12 marshmallows   Green fruit coloring

Boil sugar and water slowly for five minutes, then add the marshmallows
and allow to stand until soft. Beat egg whites stiff and slowly add
syrup, drop by drop, beating constantly. Add mint and tint a pale
green. Can be served hot or cold, but must be beaten again just before
serving.

Canapé Honoré
Sweetbreads Italienne
Mushroom Ring   Potato Puffs
Finger Rolls
Grape Compote
Butterscotch Tarts
Coffee

Canapé Honoré

Select large firm tomatoes. Cut into as many thin slices as canapés desired. Cut thin slices of bread into rounds the same size as tomatoes. Toast on one side; spread with caviar. Place the tomato slices on top. Cover with riced hard-cooked egg, seasoned with enough onion juice, salt, paprika, Worcestershire Sauce, catsup, and olive oil to form a paste. In lattice form, put fillets of anchovies on the top; sprinkle with finely chopped parsley.

Sweetbreads Italienne

Cook sweetbreads in salted and acidulated water with a bay leaf for twenty minutes. Put into cold water. Remove membrane, being careful to leave the sweetbreads whole. Sauté in a small quantity of butter, adding enough beef extract to give the sweetbreads a glazed appearance. Serve around mushroom ring with Italienne Sauce.

Italienne Sauce

4 tablespoons butter	1½ cups catsup
4 tablespoons flour	1 tablespoon Worcestershire Sauce
1 cup cream	Salt, paprika

Melt butter, add flour, and, when mixed, gradually add the liquid and seasonings. Cook until thick, stirring constantly. Serve in a bowl in the center of the mushroom ring.

Mushroom Ring

1 pound fresh mushrooms	1 cup milk
1 onion	4 eggs, separated
4 tablespoons butter	Salt
2 tablespoons flour	Pepper

Wash, drain, and put mushrooms and onion through meat-grinder. Sauté in two tablespoons butter for five minutes. Make a white sauce of remaining butter, flour, and milk. Combine with the mushrooms. Cool, and add egg yolks, beaten light; fold in egg whites, beaten stiff. Add seasonings; pour into a well-buttered and floured ring mold. Place in a pan of boiling water and bake until set in a moderate oven (350° F.) thirty to forty minutes.

Potato Puffs

2 eggs, separated	1 teaspoon baking powder
1 cup riced potatoes	1 cup milk
1 cup flour	Salt

Add beaten egg yolks to potatoes. Sift flour and baking powder. Add to the potatoes alternately with the milk. Fold in the egg whites, beaten stiff; season with salt. Drop small portions from a teaspoon into hot fat. Cook until puffed and delicately browned. Drain on unglazed paper.

Finger Rolls (see page 18)

Grape Compote

Fill a mold with seedless grapes. Dissolve a package of Lime Jello in two cups hot water; pour over grapes and allow to congeal.

Butterscotch Tarts

2 cups brown sugar	6 egg yolks
4 tablespoons butter	2 cups milk
2 tablespoons cream	4 tablespoons flour
	⅛ teaspoon flour

Cook sugar, butter, and cream until the sugar is dissolved. Add the egg yolks. Gradually add milk to the flour and salt. Combine the mixtures. Cook in a double boiler until thick. Fill baked individual pie shells with the mixture. Top with either meringue or whipped cream.

Meringue for Tarts

Add two tablespoons of sugar to each stiffly beaten egg white. Spread meringue over tarts and bake a few minutes until delicately browned.

Note: Do not try to make this in a large pie shell, as the custard is so rich that the pie will not slice without running.

Consommé with Egg Puffs
Boiled Fish with Orange Sauce
Berny Potatoes   Countess Salad
Croissants
Raspberry Bombe
Chocolate Drops
Coffee

Consommé with Egg Puffs

2 tablespoons chicken fat or butter	2 eggs
	Salt, pepper
3 tablespoons flour	1 cup fresh peas, cooked
Water	Consommé

Minced parsley

Brown the flour in fat. Add enough water to form a thick paste. Remove from fire and add the eggs, one at a time, beating thoroughly after the addition of each. Cool and season. Add the peas to the consommé and, when boiling, drop in small portions of the batter. Add minced parsley and serve as soon as the puffs rise to the top.

Boiled Fish, Orange Sauce

Wrap a three- to four-pound trout or pike in a napkin or cheesecloth. Boil in two quarts of water with an onion, carrot, stalk celery, bay leaf, cloves, one-fourth cup vinegar, salt and pepper. Boil until the flesh separates from the bones. Drain off all the liquid, place on a serving dish, skin, and pour the following sauce over the fish while hot:

6 egg yolks	1 large lemon, grated rind and juice
$\frac{1}{2}$ cup sugar	
$\frac{1}{2}$ teaspoon vinegar	$1\frac{1}{4}$ cups white wine
3 oranges, grated rind and juice	Salt

Mix all the ingredients together and cook in a double boiler until creamy. Pour over fish and garnish with slices of orange.

Berny Potatoes

2 cups riced potatoes	2 truffles, minced
$\frac{1}{8}$ teaspoon white pepper	1 egg yolk
$\frac{1}{2}$ teaspoon salt	Almonds
2 tablespoons butter	Grated nutmeg

Mix all the ingredients together and beat until light. Shape into small cylinders or cones. Roll in flour, then in beaten egg and then in blanched and finely shredded almonds. Fry in deep hot fat and drain on unglazed paper.

Countess Salad

Line a salad bowl with chicory and romaine. Fill with sliced artichoke bottoms and sliced cucumbers mixed with French Dressing. Garnish with peeled tomatoes cut into quarters.

Croissants

3 cups flour	3 tablespoons lard
$\frac{1}{2}$ teaspoon salt	$\frac{1}{2}$ cake yeast
3 tablespoons sugar	$\frac{1}{2}$ pint scalded milk
$\frac{1}{4}$ pound butter, creamed	

Sift flour, salt, and sugar. Cut in the lard, and add the lukewarm milk with the yeast dissolved in it. Mix, then knead until soft and spongy. Brush with melted butter and allow to rise. Roll the dough out and spread one-third of the creamed butter on it. Fold the dough and roll; repeat three times. Add one-half the remaining butter and repeat the process. Then place dough in refrigerator overnight. Roll out thin and spread with remaining butter. Cut the dough into four inch squares, roll diagonally and shape into crescents. Let rise, brush over with heavy cream, and bake in a hot oven fifteen minutes.

Raspberry Bombe

1 can raspberries	1 quart vanilla ice cream

Put the raspberries into the freezing tray of the refrigerator and, when frozen, cover with the ice cream. Return to the refrigerator for about an hour.

Chocolate Drops

1 cup butter	2 cups flour
1½ cups sugar	2 teaspoons baking powder
3 whole eggs	½ teaspoon cinnamon
2 ounces chocolate, melted	½ teaspoon cloves

½ pound blanched chopped almonds

Cream butter and sugar; add eggs, chocolate, flour, and the rest of the ingredients. Drop on buttered cooky sheet, about a half-teaspoon for each cooky. Flatten with a spatula so they will be very thin. Bake in moderate oven.

Ice with either a vanilla or chocolate uncooked frosting, using a stiff pastry brush to spread it on.

Caviar en Gelée
Toast Melba
Stuffed Mushrooms under Glass
Brandied Peaches
Meringue Cake
Coffee

Caviar en Gelée

Put a thin layer of aspic in an oiled ring and when almost firm, insert slices of pimiento, olives, or truffles cut into fancy shapes. Allow to congeal completely. To the remaining aspic, add two cans of caviar. Fill ring and chill until firm. Serve with Egg Timbales and Thousand Island Dressing (see page 55).

Aspic Jelly

2 tablespoons gelatin	2 cloves
4½ cups cold water	1 bay leaf
2 tablespoons carrots	2 bouillon cubes
2 tablespoons onions	2 tablespoons sherry wine
2 tablespoons celery	Juice of 1 lemon
3 sprigs parsley	Salt, white pepper

Soak the gelatin in one-half cup water. Simmer vegetables, cloves, and bay leaf in remaining water for twenty minutes. Strain; dissolve gelatin and bouillon cubes in three and one-half cups of hot vegetable broth. Add sherry and lemon. Season to taste.

Egg Timbales

Hard-cooked eggs   Stuffed olives with green butter

Rice as many eggs as number of molds desired, separating whites and yolks. Butter small molds. Place in the center of each two stuffed olives. Pack firmly with alternate layers of riced egg yolk and white until molds are filled. Chill.

Stuffed Olives with Green Butter

Pitted olives	½ teaspoon vinegar
2 tablespoons butter	1 teaspoon anchovy paste
½ teaspoon minced parsley	1 teaspoon minced capers
1 minced shallot	1 teaspoon minced pickle

Salt, paprika

Fill olives with paste made by creaming butter, adding seasonings and thoroughly mashing all together.

Stuffed Mushrooms under Glass

Mushrooms	Sherry wine
Salt, pepper	½ teaspoon lemon juice
3 slices French bread	1 pound crab flakes
½ cup milk	2 tablespoons heavy cream
1 tablespoon butter	Thin ham slices
2 egg yolks	English muffins

Select large white mushrooms, allowing three for a portion. Remove stems, wash and dry. Sprinkle with salt and pepper.

Cook the bread and milk together, stirring constantly, until a thick paste is formed. Add butter, egg yolks, sherry, and lemon juice, then the crabmeat. Fill mushrooms, heaping full. Smooth with a spoon dipped in hot water. Brush with cream. Bake in hot oven on oiled pan for ten minutes.

Sauté thin ham slices in butter. Lay on toasted and well-buttered halves of English Muffins, placed in individual Pyrex dishes and top with three stuffed mushrooms. Mask each mushroom wih Maître d'Hôtel butter. Place bell over dish and bake for five minutes.

Maître d'Hôtel Butter

¼ cup butter	½ tablespoon chopped parsley
½ teaspoon salt	1 tablespoon lemon juice
⅛ teaspoon pepper	½ teaspoon Escoffier Sauce

Cream butter, add salt, pepper, and parsley, then the lemon juice and Escoffier Sauce.

Brandied Peaches

Select ripe, uniform peaches. Plunge into boiling water for two minutes, then put into cold water. Peel. Weigh the fruit. For each pound allow one-half pound sugar and one-half cup water. Boil for five minutes. Add the peaches and boil gently until they are tender when pierced with a straw. Remove peaches to hot sterilized jars and place a stick of cinnamon in each jar. Add to the syrup one-half pint brandy for each pound of fruit. Fill jars to overflowing and adjust covers.

Meringue Cake

Ladyfingers
6 egg whites
$\frac{1}{8}$ teaspoon salt

2 cups sugar
1 teaspoon vanilla
1 quart berries

$\frac{1}{2}$ pint whipping cream

Beat egg whites and salt until dry and stiff. Fold in sugar and vanilla. Line the sides and bottom of a spring form with ladyfingers, putting the crust-side next to the pan. Fill with mixture and bake one hour in slow oven (275° F.). When cold, remove from form. Cover with mashed fresh berries or drained canned berries; decorate with whipped cream.

Chicken Broth
Halibut Ring with Sea Food Newburg Sauce
Broiled Mushrooms
Chiffonade Salad
Toast　　　Cherry Conserve
Scotch Cones
Coffee

Chicken Broth

4-5 pound hen	2 stalks celery
Chicken feet	8 peppercorns
4 quarts water	2 bay leaves
1 tablespoon salt	2 cloves
6 sprigs parsley	1 onion

Scald and skin chicken feet. Put chicken and feet on to boil in cold water. Skim thoroughly. Let cook slowly for two hours, then add seasonings and cook until chicken is tender. Strain and cool.
To clarify (see page 43).

Serve with a thin slice of lemon, dashed with paprika or minced parsley.

Halibut Ring

2 pounds halibut	1 tablespoon onion, grated
3 tablespoons butter	1 tablespoon parsley, chopped
2 tablespoons flour	1 teaspoon lemon juice
$\frac{1}{2}$ cup milk	4 eggs, separated
1 teaspoon salt	1 pint whipping cream

Cook halibut until tender in boiling salted water seasoned with onion, bay leaf, clove, parsley, celery, and vinegar. Remove skin and bones and grind fine. Make a white sauce of butter, flour, and milk. Add seasonings and the well-beaten yolks, then the fish and egg whites beaten stiff. Fold in the whipped cream. Pour into a well-greased and floured ring mold. Place in a pan of boiling water. Cook until set, thirty to forty minutes in a moderate oven (350° F.). Fill with Newburg Sauce.

Sea Food Newburg Sauce

3 tablespoons butter
3 tablespoons flour
1 cup cream
1 cup milk

1 teaspoon salt
$\frac{1}{2}$ teaspoon paprika
3 egg yolks, slightly beaten
$\frac{1}{4}$ cup sherry wine

Sea food

Melt butter, add flour, and gradually add cream and milk. Cook until smooth and thick; season with salt and paprika. Add lobster, shrimp, crabmeat, or oysters, alone or in combination, with egg yolks mixed with sherry. Cook in a double boiler until blended and thoroughly heated.

Chiffonade Salad

Mix riced or sliced eggs, sliced cooked beets, chicory and watercress in a salad bowl and marinate with a tart French Dressing.

French Dressing

1 cup salad oil
$\frac{1}{3}$ cup vinegar or lemon juice
$\frac{1}{2}$ teaspoon salt
1 teaspoon Worcestershire Sauce

1 teaspoon dry mustard
1 teaspoon grated onion
$\frac{1}{2}$ clove garlic
$\frac{1}{2}$ teaspoon paprika

Rub bowl well with garlic. Mix ingredients. Chill. Shake or beat well before using.

Cherry Conserve

3 pounds sour cherries
3 pounds sugar
$\frac{1}{2}$ pound seedless raisins

$\frac{1}{2}$ pound English walnut meats
Juice of 2 oranges
Juice of 1 lemon

Wash, stem, and pit cherries. Mix all the ingredients except nuts. Cook slowly until clear and thick, removing scum as it forms. Add nuts and pour into sterilized glasses. When cold, cover with paraffin.

Scotch Cones

$\frac{1}{2}$ cup molasses
$\frac{1}{2}$ cup butter
1 cup flour

$\frac{2}{3}$ cup sugar
1 teaspoon ginger
1 tablespoon brandy

Heat molasses to the boiling point and add butter. Gradually add the sifted dry ingredients, stirring constantly. Add brandy. Drop small portions from the tip of a spoon on a greased baking-sheet, two inches apart. Bake in a slow oven (300°) twelve minutes or until they stop bubbling. Cool slightly and roll over the handle of a wooden spoon into cornucopias. If they become too crisp, reheat in oven for a few minutes. Fill with Vanilla Ice Cream. Serve with Caramel Sauce (see page 184).

Vegetable Broth
Sweetbread Soufflé — Mushroom Sauce
Asparagus Vinaigrette
Tea Biscuits   Strawberry Preserves
Crêpes Suzette or Crêpes aux Marrons
Coffee

Vegetable Broth

1 bunch carrots, diced	Salt
2 stalks celery, diced	2 bay leaves
½ pound spinach	2 cloves
1 bunch parsley	2 quarts water
½ teaspoon peppercorns	1 pint tomato juice
2 onions	Celery salt

Maggi

Simmer the vegetables and spices in the water for two hours. Strain. There should be three pints. Add tomato juice, a dash of celery salt and maggi. Serve hot or cold.

Sweetbread Soufflé

3 pounds sweetbreads	1 tablespoon parsley, minced
2 tablespoons butter	Salt, pepper
2 tablespoons flour	4 eggs, separated
1 cup cream	1 teaspoon baking powder
½ tablespoon grated onion	1 teaspoon lemon juice

Parboil and mince sweetbreads. Combine butter, flour, and cream; cook until thick. Add seasonings and egg yolks beaten light. Beat egg whites with baking powder until stiff. Mix all together lightly. Add lemon juice. Pour into a well-buttered and floured ring mold. Place in a pan of boiling water and bake forty-five to fifty minutes in a moderate oven (350° F.). Serve with mushroom sauce.

Asparagus Vinaigrette

Cut off lower parts of stalks as far as they will snap. Carefully cut away
any thick skin and scales. Tie into bunches. Cook uncovered in boiling
salted water until tender. Drain; remove string. Chill thoroughly.
Serve with Vinaigrette Sauce.

Tea Biscuits

1½ cups flour	1 teaspoon salt
3 teaspoons baking powder	½ pint cream

Sift flour, baking powder, and salt together. Add the cream, stirring as
little as possible to mix it. Drop from a spoon into small greased muffin
pans. Bake in a hot oven (400° F.) ten to twelve minutes.

Strawberry Preserves

1 quart strawberries	3 cups sugar

Juice of ½ lemon

Use firm, ripe strawberries; scald them, leaving them in boiling water
two minutes, then drain. Add two cups sugar, lemon juice and boil for
two minutes, after the entire contents are bubbling. Remove from fire.
After bubbling has stopped, add one more cup sugar and boil for five
minutes. Pour into shallow pans and let stand overnight; pack cold
preserves in sterilized jars and seal at once.

Crêpes Suzette

Follow directions for French Pancakes (see page 11). When baked,
spread with **Suzette Sauce** or **Marron Butter Crème** and roll. Pour
Liqueur Syrup over all.

Suzette Sauce

2 egg yolks	1 cup powdered sugar
1 orange, juice and rind	⅛ teaspoon salt

½ pound sweet butter

Mix all ingredients. Cook in a double boiler until it thickens.

Liqueur Syrup

1 orange, juice and rind	½ cup water
¼ lemon, juice and rind	⅛ teaspoon salt
1 cup sugar	1 jigger Curaçao

1 jigger rum or brandy

Boil orange, lemon, sugar, water and salt gently for ten minutes. Remove from fire and add liqueur.

OR

Marron Butter Crème

¼ pound butter	½ cup chopped maraschino cherries
¼ pound sugar	1 tablespoon apricot jam
1 cup broken marrons or	½ cup rum
½ cup roasted filberts, grated	⅛ teaspoon salt

Cream butter and sugar and mix with remaining ingredients. Fill pancakes, roll and sprinkle with sugar. Place under the broiler or in a hot oven for a few minutes until glacéd.

Hot Tomato Madrilène
Radishes   Olives
Oysters Poulette
Stuffed Artichokes Vinaigrette
Corn Muffins
Krispy Crunch Ring
Coffee

Hot Tomato Madrilène

1 quart chicken stock	2 bay leaves
1 quart tomatoes, fresh or canned	2 teaspoons salt
1 cup diced celery	$\frac{1}{2}$ tablespoon peppercorns
$\frac{1}{2}$ cup diced carrots	Cayenne
$\frac{1}{2}$ cup sliced onion	$\frac{1}{2}$ teaspoon lemon juice
6 sprigs parsley	$\frac{1}{2}$ teaspoon sugar
4 cloves	2 tablespoons sherry

Mix stock, tomatoes, vegetables, cloves, bay leaves, salt, peppercorns, and cayenne. Bring to a boil and simmer for thirty minutes. Strain and cool. Clarify (see page 43). Heat, adding lemon juice, sugar, and sherry.

Oysters Poulette

1 quart oysters	4 egg yolks
2 tablespoons butter	Paprika, salt
1 tablespoon flour	Lemon juice
1 cup cream	Whipped cream

Place oysters in a saucepan and simmer until edges curl. Strain and save liquid. Make a sauce of the butter, flour, oyster liquid, and seven-eighths of the cream. Blend the egg yolks and remaining cream. Gradually add to the sauce. Season with salt, paprika, and lemon juice. Cook until thick in double boiler. Just before serving, add oysters and heat thoroughly. Top with several teaspoons of whipped cream, sprinkled with paprika. Serve with toast points.

Stuffed Artichokes

Remove portion of upper leaves to make a flat surface. Soak for thirty minutes in cold water. Cook thirty to forty minutes in boiling salted, acidulated water. Remove from water and place upside down to drain. Remove choke. Chill and fill with asparagus tips.

Vinaigrette Sauce

½ cup olive oil
4 tablespoons tarragon vinegar
1 tablespoon chopped sweet
   pickle
1 hard boiled egg, riced

1 teaspoon minced chives or
   Bermuda onion
2 tablespoons chopped parsley
½ can pimiento, chopped
Salt, pepper, paprika

Blend oil and vinegar; add remaining ingredients. Chill before serving.

Corn Muffins

1 cup corn meal
1 cup flour
2 tablespoons sugar
3 teaspoons baking powder

¾ teaspoon salt
1 cup milk
1 egg, well beaten
2 tablespoons melted butter

Mix and sift dry ingredients. Add milk, egg and butter. Bake in greased muffin pans twenty minutes in moderate oven (375° F.).

Krispy Crunch Ring

⅓ cup butter
½ pound marshmallows

½ teaspoon vanilla
1 package Rice Krispies (5½ ounces)

Melt butter and marshmallows in double boiler. Add vanilla; beat thoroughly to blend. Put Rice Krispies in large buttered bowl and pour on marshmallow mixture, stirring briskly. Press into a buttered ring mold.

(*Note*: Nut meats and coconut may be added.)

Unmold when cold and set. Serve with a bowl of caramel sauce in the center and vanilla ice-cream balls around it.

> *Lemon Tuna Omelet*
> *Baked Tomatoes with Cucumbers*
> *Toasted English Muffins*
> *Florida Coconut Pie*

Omelet

6 eggs, separated	Salt, pepper
3 tablespoons milk	Butter

Beat yolks until lemon-colored; add milk, salt, and pepper. Fold in, very lightly, the beaten whites. Melt butter in a heavy frying-pan and pour in the omelet. Cook over low flame until puffy. Remove to a 300° oven and bake until omelet is firm to the touch and lightly browned. Remove from the pan and fill with the tuna mixture and fold.

Lemon Tuna Omelet

7-ounce can tuna fish	4 tablespoons butter, melted
2 tablespoons grated American cheese	Juice of 1 lemon
1 cup Medium White Sauce	Minced parsley

Add the tuna fish and cheese to the White Sauce. Pour over omelet before folding. Add lemon juice to butter, pour over omelet and sprinkle with minced parsley.

Baked Tomatoes with Cucumbers

2 cucumbers	4 tablespoons water
2 teaspoons grated onion	Salt, pepper
4 teaspoons lemon juice	Tomatoes
4 tablespoons butter	Buttered bread crumbs

Peel and dice cucumbers; add onion, lemon juice, butter, water, and seasonings; simmer for five minutes. Remove seeds and pulp from the tomatoes and drain. Fill the tomatoes with the cooked cucumbers, sprinkle with bread crumbs and bake in a hot oven until the tomatoes are tender and the crumbs are brown.

Florida Coconut Pie

1 large coconut, grated	1½ cups sugar
2 tablespoons water	2 eggs
⅛ pound butter	

Boil sugar, water, and coconut for fifteen minutes. Remove from fire; add well-beaten eggs and butter. Put into piecrust and bake.

Single Piecrust

1½ cups sifted flour	½ teaspoon salt
3 tablespoons water	½ cup shortening

Make a paste with a quarter cup of the flour and the water. Cut shortening into the rest of the flour and salt, until pieces are the size of small peas. Add flour paste to this and mix thoroughly until dough comes together and can be shaped into a ball. Roll about an eighth of an inch thick.

Almond Tuna Ring — Mushroom Sauce
Peas and Carrots   Fruit Salad
Danish Torte

Almond Tuna Ring — Mushroom Sauce

1 13-ounce can tuna fish	½ cup almonds,
1 jar of chow mein	coarsely chopped
noodles	2 eggs
2 cups thin cream sauce	

Drain off all oil and flake the tuna. Combine with the noodles, almonds, cream sauce, and beaten egg yolks. Fold in beaten whites. Place in a buttered ring mold, set in a pan of hot water, and bake for a half hour (no longer) in a moderate oven.

Chop or grind a pound of mushrooms and sauté in butter. Add this to about two cups of cream sauce. Season to taste. Serve in the center of the ring.

Surround with peas and cooked carrot strips.

Fruit Salad

Arrange orange and grapefruit sections on lettuce. Sprinkle with pomegranate seeds. Serve with French Dressing.

Danish Torte

2½ cups cake flour	2 cups sugar
2½ teaspoons baking powder	4 eggs
6 tablespoons butter	1 cup milk

Sift flour, measure, add baking powder, and sift together three times. Cream butter, add one cup sugar gradually, and cream until light. Add remaining sugar to eggs and beat well; combine with butter. Add flour alternately with milk, beating after each addition.

Butter six cake tins and cover bottoms with waxed paper. Divide batter into pans and bake twelve to fifteen minutes in moderate oven. Remove at once from pans.

Frosting

½ pound bitter chocolate   3 cups sugar
1 cup milk   2 tablespoons butter
4 egg yolks   2 teaspoons vanilla

Melt chocolate in milk. Beat egg yolks with six tablespoons of the sugar; add remaining sugar to the chocolate mixture and cook until sugar is dissolved. Add eggs and butter and cook one minute. Cool, add vanilla and beat until creamy. Spread between layers and over cake.

OR

Spread layers alternately with strawberry jam and custard (see page 321). Cover top with powdered sugar.

> *Chicken-Tongue Ring à la King*
> *Southern Salad*
> *Cherries — Golden Sauce*

Chicken-Tongue Ring

5- or 6-pound chicken,	½ cup celery
boiled	1 pound mushrooms
¼ pound cooked smoked tongue	Salt, pepper
4 eggs, separated	1 cup cream

Grind dark meat of chicken with tongue, celery, and stems of mushrooms. Add beaten yolks, cream, salt, and pepper and fold in stiffly beaten egg whites. Place in buttered ring mold and bake in 350° oven, forty to forty-five minutes.

Chicken à la King

Mushroom caps, sliced	1 cup heavy cream
½ green pepper, sliced	1 cup chicken broth
1 pimiento, sliced	¼ cup butter
Chicken breast	3 tablespoons flour
Sherry	2 egg yolks

Sauté mushrooms and green pepper in a little butter; add pimiento. Make a cream sauce of the remaining butter, flour, chicken broth, and cream, using more cream if necessary to make a thin sauce. Add mushrooms and peppers and chicken breast, cut into large cubes. Reduce heat and add egg yolks; stir and cook until well blended. Season and add sherry to taste.

Serve in the center of ring.

Southern Salad

4 strips bacon, fried crisp	2 slices toasted bread,
4 heads Bib lettuce	cut in cubes

French Dressing

Put lettuce leaves in a bowl. Add toast cubes and bacon, broken into small pieces, French Dressing, and toss. Serve at once.

Brandied Cherries — Golden Sauce

Fresh Bing cherries $\frac{1}{2}$ cup sugar
1$\frac{1}{2}$ cups brandy

Pit cherries carefully so they remain whole. Place in a double boiler with sugar and brandy. Cover with wax paper and place lid on tightly. Heat thoroughly.

Golden Sauce

6 egg yolks   Vanilla
$\frac{3}{4}$ cup thin cream   1 pint whipped cream
$\frac{1}{2}$ cup sugar $\frac{1}{2}$ cup rum

Make a thin custard of yolks, cream, and sugar. When cool, add vanilla, rum, and whipped cream.

Serve cherries hot and pass chilled sauce.

Family Dinner

Oyster and Chicken Soup
Halibut Platter
Potatoes with Caraway Seeds
Chinese Salad
Chocolate Crème Torte
Coffee

Oyster and Chicken Soup

1 pint soup stock	$\frac{1}{2}$ pint oysters
1 pint chicken stock	Minced parsley
Whipped cream	

Combine the two soups and bring them to a boil. Add the oysters and cook until the edges curl. Serve with a little minced parsley, and one teaspoon whipped cream in each plate.

Halibut Platter

2 pounds halibut	$\frac{1}{4}$ pound grated American cheese
4 tablespoons butter	Salt
2 tablespoons flour	Pepper
1 cup milk	Juice of 1 lemon
$\frac{1}{2}$ can tomato soup	1 tablespoon Worcestershire Sauce
$\frac{1}{2}$ pound mushrooms	Cayenne
$\frac{1}{2}$ small can tiny peas, drained	Paprika

Boil the fish. Cool, and break into inch-size pieces. Melt two table-spoons butter; add flour, then the milk and soup. Cook for three minutes. Sauté mushrooms in remaining butter. Combine fish, sauce, mushrooms, peas, and half of the cheese. Season highly with salt, pepper, lemon, Worcestershire Sauce and a dash of cayenne. Spread on an ovenware platter; sprinkle with remaining cheese, top with small pieces of butter and paprika. Bake twenty minutes in hot oven (375° F.).

Potatoes with Caraway Seeds

Boil about eight small potatoes in their jackets until tender; peel while hot. Put two tablespoons of oil in a frying pan. When hot, put in the potatoes and brown well. Drain, sprinkle with salt and one-half teaspoon caraway seeds.

Chinese Salad

2 cups bean sprouts	1 green pepper, minced
½ cup celery cubes	2 tomatoes, cut into small cubes
1 cucumber, sliced thin	French Dressing

Minced chives

Rinse and drain the bean sprouts. Combine all vegetables and toss with French Dressing containing a nip of Soy Sauce. Chill salad for an hour. Drain off any extra dressing and serve with mayonnaise. Sprinkle top with minced chives.

Chocolate Crème Torte

4 ounces bitter chocolate	2 cups sugar
1 cup milk	1 cup pastry flour
5 egg yolks	1 teaspoon baking powder

5 beaten egg whites

Melt chocolate in milk and let cool. Cream egg yolks and sugar, add flour, baking powder, chocolate mixture, and fold in beaten egg whites. Bake in two layers in 325° oven.

Chocolate Cream Filling

5 ounces Mailiard's chocolate	3 tablespoons water
2¾ tablespoons sugar	3 egg yolks
⅛ teaspoon salt	¾ pint whipping cream

Cook chocolate, sugar, salt, and water in a double boiler until it is smooth and thick. Remove from fire and add egg yolks, one at a time. Cool and fold in whipped cream.

Split Pea Soup
Croutons
Stuffed Cabbage with Corned-Beef Hash
Corn and Tomatoes   *Senfgurken*
Bread
Apple Torte
Coffee

Split Pea Soup

1½ cups split peas	1 bay leaf
2½ quarts water	1 clove garlic, grated
1½ teaspoons salt	2 tablespoons butter
⅛ teaspoon pepper	2 tablespoons flour
1 large onion	1 pint soup stock
1 celery root	½ teaspoon lemon juice

Ring sausage

Soak peas for several hours, drain. Add water, salt, pepper, onion, celery, bay leaf, and garlic. Simmer three to four hours and then press through a sieve. Melt butter, add flour and then the soup stock (or water with a bouillon cube). Combine with puréed peas, add lemon and sausage, skinned and cut into half-inch slices.

Serve with croutons.

Stuffed Cabbage

Select a large head of cabbage; soak in salt water one hour; cook uncovered in boiling salted water with one-fourth teaspoon soda until partially soft. Drain, and scoop out the inside. Fill with corned-beef hash. Cover with buttered crumbs and bake for thirty minutes in a hot oven.

Corned-Beef Hash

Combine equal parts of chopped corn beef and diced new potatoes. Season with chopped onion, salt, and pepper to taste; moisten with two or three tablespoons of soup stock. Simmer until potatoes and onions are tender.

Corn and Tomatoes

Peel and cut six large tomatoes into pieces. Cook slowly with one tablespoon grated onion, salt and pepper for twenty minutes, stirring occasionally. Add two cups corn and one-fourth cup butter. Cook slowly for fifteen minutes longer.

Senfgurken

1 dozen ripe cucumbers	4 tablespoons mustard seed
2 pounds sugar	Bay leaves
1 quart vinegar	Slices of fresh horseradish
4 red peppers	2 pieces cinnamon bark
Salt	1 tablespoon cloves

Peel and cut cucumbers into halves or quarters; scrape out seeds. Salt and let stand overnight. Drain and dry. Add to the sugar and vinegar, pepper, mustard seed, bay leaves, horseradish, cinnamon, and cloves, tied in a bag. Boil to a syrup, and add cucumbers. Cook until they are glossy. Remove spice bag. Pack in sterilized jars and seal while hot.

Apple Torte

1 package Zwieback	$\frac{1}{4}$ cup water
$\frac{3}{4}$ cup sugar	4 eggs, separated
$1\frac{1}{2}$ teaspoons cinnamon	1 can Eagle Brand milk
$\frac{1}{2}$ cup butter, melted	Juice of 1 lemon
3 large apples	1 teaspoon vanilla

$\frac{1}{8}$ teaspoon salt

Roll Zwieback and add sugar, cinnamon, and butter. Press three-fourths of this mixture into the bottom and around the sides of a spring form.

Cut the apples into pieces. Add water, cook slowly until tender and then press through a sieve. Beat the egg yolks until light, then add milk, lemon, vanilla, salt, and apples. Fold in stiffly beaten egg whites. Pour into pan, sprinkle remaining crumbs on top and bake thirty minutes in a moderate oven (375° F.).

Potato and Mushroom Soup
Meat Pie
Winter Salad   Vinaigrette Sauce
Banana Puff
Coffee

Potato and Mushroom Soup

2 large potatoes, cubed	2 tablespoons flour
1 onion, finely cut	1 quart soup stock
½ stalk celery, minced	½ pound mushrooms, chopped
2 tablespoons poultry fat	Salt, pepper, celery salt
½ tablespoon minced parsley	Caraway seeds

Cook potatoes, onion, and celery until tender, in enough water to cover. Brown flour in fat. Add the cooked potatoes and liquid in which they were cooked. When mixed, pour into the boiling soup stock. Add mushrooms, salt, pepper, caraway seeds, and a dash of celery salt. Simmer for thirty minutes. Just before serving, add parsley.

Meat Pie

Cut left-over beef into one-inch cubes. Cook slowly in its own gravy or in water to which a bouillon cube is added, for one hour. Add boiled small onions, cubed carrots, and fresh peas. Season with Escoffier Sauce. If gravy is too thin, thicken with flour. Put into a buttered pudding dish, cover with mashed potatoes and brush over top with egg diluted with one tablespoon milk. Bake in a hot oven until brown.

Winter Salad

Celery roots	Asparagus tips
Quartered tomatoes	Chicory
Vinaigrette Dressing	

Wash and pare celery roots; boil in enough salted water to cover. When tender, remove from water, slice and marinate in French dressing. Chill.

and serve on chicory with peeled and quartered tomatoes, asparagus, and Vinaigrette Dressing.

Banana Puff

Allow one banana for each portion. Roll in sugar and cinnamon and wrap in rich piecrust rolled very thin. Bake in very hot oven (450° F.) for fifteen minutes. Serve with Lemon Sauce.

Lemon Sauce

$\frac{1}{2}$ cup sugar	1 cup boiling water or pineapple juice
1 tablespoon flour	Juice and grated rind of $\frac{1}{2}$ lemon
$\frac{1}{8}$ teaspoon salt	1 tablespoon butter
	2 tablespoons raisins

Cook sugar, flour, salt, and liquid over hot water for ten minutes. Add lemon, butter, and raisins. Serve hot.

Mock Turtle Soup
Pork Tenderloin
Brussels Sprouts
Glazed Apple Squares
Coffee

Mock Turtle Soup

1 can Mock Turtle Soup	½ teaspoon lemon juice
1 can Tomato Soup	1 teaspoon Worcestershire Sauce
3 cups soup stock	1 hard-cooked egg, riced
	Sherry wine

Combine soups, add lemon juice and Worcestershire Sauce. Simmer for twenty minutes. Before serving, add egg, and flavor with sherry wine.

Pork Tenderloins (three or four)

Season the tenderloins with salt and pepper. Sauté in butter for five to ten minutes until brown. Add one-fourth cup butter and a small glass of currant jelly. Place in the oven. Bake for forty minutes, basting frequently. Blend one tablespoon flour into one cup of cream and add to the sauce in the pan. Mix well and cook for ten minutes longer.

Brussels Sprouts

Let sprouts stand in cold water for thirty minutes. Put into rapidly boiling salted water and cook uncovered for fifteen to twenty minutes. Drain, add salt, pepper, and butter, and toss them until well seasoned.

Glazed Apple Squares

½ cup butter	2 cups flour
2 tablespoons sugar	⅛ teaspoon salt
2 eggs, well beaten	4 teaspoons baking powder
1 cup milk	Pared, cored, and sliced apples

Topping

½ cup butter   1 cup confectioner's sugar
Vanilla

Cream one-half cup butter with two tablespoons sugar. Add eggs and the sifted dry ingredients alternately with the milk. Pour into a buttered and floured biscuit pan one-half inch thick. Cover with sliced apples and bake in a moderate oven until the apples are tender (forty to forty-five minutes). Cream the remaining butter and sugar, add flavoring, spread over the hot cake. When cold, cut into squares.

> *Black Bean Soup*
> *Liver with Mushrooms*
> *Special Baked Potatoes   Red Cabbage Slaw*
> *Chocolate Pudding — Vanilla Sauce*
> *Coffee*

Black Bean Soup

1 pint black beans	2 teaspoons salt
2 quarts cold water	$\frac{1}{4}$ teaspoon pepper
2 tablespoons chopped onion	Cayenne
1 grated clove garlic	$\frac{1}{4}$ teaspoon mustard
4 tablespoons fat	2 tablespoons flour
1 diced celery root	1 lemon
2 hard-cooked eggs	

Wash beans and soak overnight in water. Drain and rinse. Fry onion and garlic in two tablespoons fat. Add to beans with celery root and two quarts of water. Cook slowly until beans are soft. Add more boiling water as it boils away. Rub through a strainer, add the seasonings and heat. Melt the remaining fat and add flour. Gradually pour on the hot soup; boil for fifteen minutes. Cut lemon and eggs into thin slices and serve in the soup.

Liver with Mushrooms

1 pound calves' liver	$\frac{1}{2}$ cup sour cream
2 tablespoons chopped onion	2 tablespoons flour
3 tablespoons bacon fat	1 teaspoon salt
1 cup mushrooms (cut into pieces and sautéed in butter)	$\frac{1}{4}$ teaspoon pepper
	1 cup meat stock

Cut liver into cubes and brown with onion in hot fat. Simmer for five minutes. Add mushrooms and cream, blended with flour and meat stock. Add seasonings. Add more liquid if needed. Heat thoroughly and serve on toast.

Special Baked Potatoes

6 potatoes	2 tablespoons butter
1 teaspoon salt	½ cup grated American cheese
¼ cup hot milk	Paprika

Select large, uniform potatoes, scrub and bake in a hot oven (450° F.) for fifty to sixty minutes. Cut into halves lengthwise, scoop out the insides, mix with salt, milk, and butter. Beat until creamy. Refill shells; sprinkle with cheese and paprika and bake in a moderate oven (350° F.) from five to ten minutes.

Red Cabbage Slaw

Shred a head of red cabbage. Combine with a small can of pineapple cut into pieces, and one-half cup browned and sliced almonds. Toss together in mayonnaise which has been thinned with the pineapple juice. White cabbage can be used or a combination of both.

Chocolate Pudding

1 cup sugar	2 squares bitter chocolate
2 tablespoons butter	1 cup milk
2 eggs	1 cup flour
2 teaspoons baking powder	

Beat eggs very light, add sugar, melted or soft butter; cream together. Add flour and baking powder, milk, and melted chocolate. Put in buttered custard cups or a large layer pan. Bake in a pan of hot water in a slow oven for forty-five minutes. Serve warm.

Vanilla Sauce

2 egg yolks beaten very light; add, gradually:
 1 cup confectioner's sugar
 1 cup whipped cream
 1 teaspoon vanilla
 Lastly, fold in 2 egg whites, beaten very stiff

Serve the sauce in a bowl placed in the center of a platter with squares or molds of the pudding around it.

Mushroom and Barley Soup
Barbecue Spareribs
Mashed Potatoes   *Sauerkraut*
Pineapple Cottage Cheese Cake
OR
Icebox Cheese Cake
Coffee

Mushroom and Barley Soup

2 quarts soup stock	$\frac{1}{2}$ grated onion
$\frac{3}{4}$ cup pearl barley	2 tablespoons butter
$\frac{1}{2}$ pound mushrooms	1 tablespoon minced parsley

Salt, pepper

Simmer the barley in one-half the soup stock until soft. Sauté the chopped mushrooms and onion in butter. Add to the barley with the remaining soup stock, parsley, salt and pepper. Boil for ten minutes.

Barbecue Spareribs

1 cup vinegar	1 tablespoon Harvey Sauce
1 clove garlic, grated	$\frac{1}{3}$ cup catsup
1 tablespoon olive oil	1 teaspoon dry mustard
$2\frac{1}{2}$ tablespoons Worcestershire Sauce	1 teaspoon salt
Tabasco Sauce	Pepper, paprika
1 tablespoon sugar	1 tablespoon walnut sauce
	Spareribs

Mix all the ingredients together and simmer for fifteen minutes. Cut the spareribs into portions of two bones each, and salt. Place in the broiler under a low flame. Brush with the sauce and turn every ten minutes brushing the ribs each time. Cook until crisp.

Sauerkraut

2 pounds kraut	1 tablespoon bacon fat
Water	$\frac{1}{2}$ red pepper pod
Ends of spareribs	$\frac{1}{2}$ teaspoon caraway seeds
1 green apple, sliced	1 raw potato, grated
Salt	

Cover kraut with water. Put in the meat, apple, fat, pepper, and caraway seeds. Cook slowly for one and one-half hours. Add the potato and salt, if necessary, and continue to cook for thirty minutes.

Pineapple Cottage Cheese Cake

2 cups finely rolled corn flakes	4 tablespoons sugar
$\frac{1}{4}$ pound butter, melted	1 tablespoon cinnamon

Blend all ingredients. Pack three-fourths of the mixture in the bottom and around the sides of a spring mold. Pour in filling, sprinkle with remaining crumbs and place in refrigerator until firm.

Filling

2 tablespoons gelatin	1 pound cottage cheese, riced
2 tablespoons cold water	$\frac{1}{2}$ lemon, juice and grated rind
3 eggs, separated	1 teaspoon vanilla
$\frac{1}{2}$ cup sugar	$\frac{1}{2}$ cup crushed pineapple
$\frac{1}{8}$ teaspoon salt	$\frac{1}{4}$ cup maraschino cherries
1 cup milk	$\frac{1}{2}$ cup whipping cream

Soak the gelatin in cold water. Beat egg yolks with sugar and salt. Add milk and cook in double boiler until creamy, stirring constantly. Dissolve the gelatin in hot custard. Add cheese, lemon, vanilla, pineapple, and cherries; fold in stiffly beaten egg whites and whipped cream. Pour into crust.

OR

Icebox Cheese Cake

1 package Zwieback, rolled	$\frac{1}{4}$ pound butter, melted
1 teaspoon cinnamon	

Melt butter and mix with Zwieback and cinnamon. Press three-fourths of the mixture on the bottom and around the sides of the spring form.

Pour in cheese filling, sprinkle remaining crumbs on top, and place in the refrigerator until firm.

Cheese Filling

1 cup sugar	3 tablespoons cornstarch
$\frac{1}{8}$ teaspoon salt	2 pints cottage cheese
3 eggs, separated	Grated rind of 1 lemon
Juice of 2 lemons	$\frac{1}{2}$ teaspoon vanilla

Beat sugar, salt, and egg yolks until light. Blend lemon juice and cornstarch. Add to the egg mixture with the cheese. Cook in a double boiler until thick. Cool and add lemon rind, vanilla, and stiffly beaten egg whites.

Soup with Farina Balls
Brisket of Beef   Horseradish Sauce
Bouillon Potatoes
Kohlrabi
Poppyseed Cake
Coffee

Farina Balls

1 cup hot milk	1 tablespoon butter
½ teaspoon salt	½ cup farina
Pepper	2 eggs, separated

Cook milk, salt, pepper, and butter in a double boiler. When hot, add farina. Cook until smooth and thick. Cool. Add well-beaten egg yolks and fold in stiffly beaten egg whites. Form into small balls and drop into boiling soup ten minutes before using. (If desired, add one-fourth cup grated almonds and a little nutmeg to farina mixture.)

Brisket of Beef

4 to 5 pounds brisket of beef	5 carrots
2 onions, sliced	Salt, pepper
1 bay leaf	Boiling water
1 stalk celery	

Place the meat in a kettle, add seasonings, vegetables, and enough boiling water to cover. Bring to a boil and cook slowly until tender (three to four hours). Remove meat from broth, slice and serve in Horseradish Sauce.

Horseradish Sauce

1 large onion, chopped fine	1 cup vinegar
4 tablespoons butter	2 cloves
2 tablespoons flour	2 bay leaves
2 cups soup stock	1 teaspoon salt
1 cups fresh grated horseradish	Pepper
½ cup granulated sugar	

Fry onion in melted butter until brown. Add flour and soup stock gradually, then add remaining ingredients. Boil ten minutes. Heat the sliced meat in the sauce. Serve with minced parsley sprinkled over the top.

Bouillon Potatoes

Pare and quarter eight medium-sized potatoes. Add one and one-half cups soup stock and six minced shallots. Bring to a boil and then simmer until almost tender. Add two tablespoons butter, a little flour mixed with stock, minced parsley, and additional seasoning if necessary. Cook for a few minutes longer.

Kohlrabi

Wash, peel, and slice kohlrabi. Chop the leaves. Melt two tablespoons sugar in three tablespoons butter. Add kohlrabi and leaves, salt and pepper, with enough soup stock or water to half-cover them. Cover the kettle. Cook slowly until the kohlrabi are tender and the liquid evaporated. Add one tablespoon flour, blended with one tablespoon liquid, and more seasoning if desired.

Poppyseed Cake

$\frac{1}{2}$ cup poppyseed	$\frac{1}{8}$ teaspoon salt
1 cup milk	1 teaspoon vanilla
$\frac{1}{2}$ cup butter	2 cups flour
$1\frac{1}{2}$ cups granulated sugar	2 teaspoons baking powder

4 egg whites, stiffly beaten

Grind poppyseed and soak in the milk for one hour. Cream butter and sugar thoroughly. Add poppyseed, salt, and vanilla. Add sifted dry ingredients. Fold in egg whites. Pour into well-greased tube pan and bake one hour in moderate oven (350° F.). Cool. Sprinkle with confectioner's sugar.

OR

Bake in two layers, put a custard between, and top with whipped cream.

Deviled Roast Beef
Escalloped Potatoes and Mushrooms
Braised Celery   Chow-Chow
Apple Dumplings
Coffee

Deviled Roast Beef

Spread slices of cold roast beef on both sides with mustard. Sprinkle with buttered white bread crumbs and broil in a hot oven until brown. Serve with Deviled Sauce.

Deviled Sauce

1 tablespoon flour	1 tablespoon A-1 Sauce
½ cup catsup	1 teaspoon Worcestershire Sauce
	1 cup soup stock

Mix flour and seasonings; gradually add boiling soup stock. Cook for about three minutes.

Escalloped Potatoes and Mushrooms

1 quart sliced potatoes	¼ teaspoon pepper
1 teaspoon salt	Can of mushroom soup
	Buttered bread crumbs

Peel and slice potatoes. Place in buttered baking-dish in alternate layers with mushroom soup. Season. Sprinkle top with crumbs and bake one hour or longer until potatoes are soft.

Braised Celery Hearts

8 or 10 celery hearts	Salt, pepper
1 tablespoon chopped onion	Beef stock
½ cup butter	½ teaspoon beef extract

Trim off the outer stalks and leaves of celery, split the hearts in half.

Cook the onion in half of the butter for a few minutes, then arrange the celery on top, season with salt and pepper, and moisten with beef stock. Cover the pan and simmer for about twenty minutes or until the celery is tender. Blend the beef extract with the liquid in the pan and baste the celery with it. Add the remaining butter. Place the pan, uncovered, in a moderate oven and bake until the celery has absorbed most of the liquid. Baste the celery once or twice while it is in the oven.

Chow-Chow

2 quarts green tomatoes	2 cups salt
12 small cucumbers	1 gallon vinegar
3 red peppers	$\frac{1}{4}$ pound mustard seed
1 cauliflower	2 ounces tumeric
2 bunches celery	$\frac{1}{2}$ ounce allspice
1 pint small onions	$\frac{1}{2}$ ounce pepper

$\frac{1}{2}$ ounce clove

Clean vegetables and chop into small pieces. Cover with salt and let stand for twenty-four hours. Drain and press dry. Heat vinegar and spices to the boiling point; add vegetables and simmer until tender. Fill jars and seal while hot.

Apple Dumplings

2 cups flour	$\frac{3}{4}$ cup milk
4 teaspoons baking powder	1 stick cinnamon
$\frac{1}{2}$ teaspoon salt	1 lemon rind
$\frac{1}{3}$ cup lard and butter	6 apples

Sift flour, baking powder, and salt. Cut in the shortening. Add the milk. Roll dough one-fourth inch thick; cut into six-inch squares. Place a peeled and cored apple in the center and sprinkle with one tablespoon sugar. Bring up the corners of the dough and press firmly together. Put into a well-greased casserole dish, with cinnamon and lemon rind; pour over the following syrup:

2 cups white sugar	$\frac{1}{2}$ teaspoon salt
$\frac{1}{2}$ cup brown sugar	2 cups boiling water
2 tablespoons cornstarch	$\frac{1}{2}$ cup butter

Combine sugars, cornstarch, and salt in a saucepan. Mix well and stir in boiling water to make a smooth paste. Add butter and let simmer, stirring constantly until thickened and smooth.

Pour over dumplings, cover tightly, and bake in a 425° oven for about thirty minutes. Remove cover and baste dumplings with sauce occasionally. Continue baking uncovered until dumplings are a golden brown.

Serve hot in the sauce they were baked in.

> *Fish Chowder*
> *Grilled English Lamb Chops*
> *Eggplant and Tomatoes*
> *Cucumber Relish*
> *Cherry Sponge Torte*
> *Coffee*

Mrs. Appleyard's Fish Chowder

A 4-pound haddock, cut for chowder, head and all	3 large onions, finely sliced
3 cups milk	6 medium potatoes
1 cup cream	1 teaspoon salt
8 pilot crackers	¼ teaspoon black pepper
½ pound salt pork, diced	½ teaspoon paprika

Slice the potatoes. Fry the pork dice till they are a delicate cracker brown. Dip them out with a skimmer and put them on a saucer. Fry the onion in the pork fat until it is a light straw color. Lay the fish in a large kettle. Add potatoes, onions, pork, and seasonings and hot water to cover the fish and potatoes. Cover the kettle and let the fish cook slowly for forty minutes.

Add milk and cream. Let it come to the boil but not boil, and season. Remove large pieces of bone and head. Serve in tureen with broken pilot crackers dropped into the chowder.

Grilled English Lamb Chops

Select one-and-one-half-inch thick loin chops with the kidneys attached. Remove bone, roll chop, wrap with a slice of bacon and fasten with a small skewer or toothpick, and broil. Remove skewer before serving, and season.

Eggplant and Tomatoes

Peel and slice an eggplant; soak in cold, salted water for an hour; drain. Peel and slice tomatoes. Place layers of eggplant and tomatoes alternately in baking-dish with seasoning and grated cheese (Swiss or Parmesan) between layers. Sprinkle top with bread crumbs and cheese and dot with butter. Bake in a slow oven for one hour.

Cucumber Relish

12 large cucumbers	2 tablespoons mustard seed
4 large onions	2 red peppers
1 cup salt	$\frac{1}{2}$ cup sugar
1 tablespoon celery seed	2 cups vinegar
4 bay leaves	$\frac{1}{2}$ cup water

Peel and slice cucumbers and onions very thin. Add salt and soak overnight. Drain and press dry. Combine spices with sugar, vinegar, and water and boil for three minutes. Add cucumbers and onions; boil for two minutes. Fill sterilized jars and seal at once.

Cherry Sponge Torte

Two 9-inch baked pie shells

Filling

1 cup sugar	$\frac{1}{2}$ teaspoon cinnamon
2 tablespoons cornstarch	Juice of $\frac{1}{2}$ lemon
2 cans pitted sour cherries	

Blend sugar, cornstarch, cinnamon, and lemon juice with juice from cherries. Cook until creamy. Add cherries. Boil for one minute. Pour into the hot pie shells. Cover with sponge batter and bake ten to fifteen minutes in a moderate oven (375° F.). Sprinkle with confectioner's sugar.

Sponge Batter

2 tablespoons sugar	$\frac{1}{16}$ teaspoon salt
2 eggs, separated	2 tablespoons water
2 tablespoons flour	$\frac{1}{2}$ teaspoon vanilla

Beat sugar and egg yolks until thick and lemon-colored. Sift flour and fold in alternately with the stiffly beaten egg whites and water. Add vanilla.

Onion Soup
Wiener Schnitzel
Tomato Pudding   *Cole Slaw*
Bundt Kuchen
OR
Thin Coffee Cake
Coffee

Onion Soup

6 large white onions, sliced	Salt, pepper
4 tablespoons butter	8 thin slices toast
1 quart soup stock	Grated Parmesan cheese

1 teaspoon Worcestershire Sauce

Sauté onions in butter until they are light brown. Add the soup stock and simmer one-half hour. If too thick, add water and season. Serve with a piece of toast generously sprinkled with cheese, on top of each portion.

Wiener Schnitzel

Have veal steak cut a half-inch thick. Pound with wooden masher until thinner. Cut in pieces for serving; salt and pepper. Dip in flour, then beaten egg, and then fine bread crumbs. Let stand about fifteen minutes. Fry slowly completely covered in deep fat (preferably butter) for ten to twelve minutes. (Butter should be hot but not brown.)

Serve garnished with quartered lemons, capers, anchovies, and a fried egg.

Tomato Pudding

1 large can tomatoes	$\frac{1}{2}$ cup melted butter
6 slices soft white bread	$\frac{3}{4}$ cup brown sugar

Salt, pepper

Press tomatoes through sieve and season. Fill buttered baking-dish with very small broken pieces of bread (no crusts). Pour butter over bread and sprinkle with sugar. Add strained tomatoes and bake in a covered casserole about thirty minutes. Stir occasionally while baking, so that bread is absorbed by tomato.

Cole Slaw

Shred cabbage. Soak in cold water until crisp; drain and dry. Add one-half chopped green pepper, one diced cucumber, one tablespoon grated onion, and one tablespoon chopped parsley. Marinate with French Dressing.

Bundt Kuchen

1 cup scalded milk	1 cup butter
1 cup flour	1 cup sugar
1 teaspoon salt	6 eggs, beaten
1 tablespoon sugar	Grated rind of 1 lemon
1 yeastcake	Grated rind of half an orange
	Flour

Mix one cup flour with salt and sugar. When milk is lukewarm, dissolve yeast in it and beat into flour. Set aside in a warm place to rise (two hours). Cream butter and sugar, add eggs, yeast mixture, orange and lemon peel, with sufficient flour to form a heavy batter. Beat until it blisters. Fill a greased and floured bundt form one-half full. Cover and let it rise slowly (about four hours), then bake in a moderate oven (350° F.) for one hour.

Thin Coffee Cake

Fill cake pans with one-third-inch layer of bundt dough. Spread with butter, cover, and set aside to rise. Before baking, sprinkle with Streusel. Bake fifteen to twenty minutes in moderate oven.

Streusel

2 tablespoons butter	2 tablespoons flour
5 tablespoons sugar	Cinnamon or vanilla

Mix together, by rubbing well with the fingertips, until small crumbs are formed. Add a few chopped nuts.

Meat Roll with Green Pea Sauce
Baked Tomatoes Vertis
Pepper, Cucumber, and Radish Salad
Apples Bonne Femme
Sugar Cookies
Coffee

Meat Roll with Green Pea Sauce

2 cups flour	¾ cup milk
4 teaspoons baking powder	2 cups ground meat (cooked)
½ teaspoon salt	Catsup
4 tablespoons shortening	Worcestershire Sauce
	Gravy

Sift dry ingredients, cut in shortening and add milk. Roll dough one-third inch thick in rectangular shape. Season meat with catsup and Worcestershire Sauce. Moisten to a paste with gravy and spread over the dough. Roll (like a jelly roll) and cut into slices one and one-half inches thick. Place on a buttered pan and bake fifteen to twenty minutes in a moderately hot oven (375° F.). Serve with a small amount of pea sauce on each roll and pass remaining sauce.

Green Pea Sauce

2 tablespoons butter	1 cup cooked peas
2 tablespoons flour	1 tablespoon chopped pimiento
1½ cups milk	1 egg yolk
Salt, pepper	1 tablespoon water

Melt butter, add flour. Gradually pour on milk, stirring constantly. Season, add peas and pimiento. Cook until smooth and thick. Stir in the egg yolk mixed with the water. Heat thoroughly but do not boil.

Baked Tomatoes Vertis

8 tomatoes	3 sprigs parsley
2 medium carrots	3 tablespoons butter
1 small green pepper	1 egg, beaten
1 onion	1 cup dried bread crumbs
3 large stalks celery	½ cup milk
2 cups raw spinach	½ teaspoon salt

⅛ teaspoon pepper

Select firm tomatoes, wipe and cut a thin slice from the stem end. Scoop out seeds and pulp. Wash remaining vegetables and put through a food-chopper. Melt butter, add vegetables, and simmer until they are brown. Add the remaining ingredients and mix thoroughly. Fill tomatoes and sprinkle with grated cheese. Place in a buttered pan and bake in a hot oven (400° F.) twenty minutes or until tomatoes are tender.

Pepper, Cucumber, and Radish Salad

2 cucumbers	1 bunch radishes
2 green peppers	French Dressing

Peel cucumbers, slice very thin and soak in salted ice water. Drain, dry, and place on a platter. Slice peppers and radishes very thin and lay over cucumber slices. Cover with French Dressing and allow to stand about fifteen minutes before serving.

Apples Bonne Femme

8 baking apples	Water
1 cup sugar	

Peel apples; core and place in a baking-dish. Sprinkle with sugar and cover two-thirds with water. Bake slowly forty minutes, basting occasionally. Serve with Apricot Sauce poured over them.

Apricot Sauce

½ pound dried apricots	½ cup sugar
3 cups water	1 stick cinnamon

1 lemon, juice and rind

Wash apricots; soak in water for several hours, add sugar, cinnamon, and lemon. Cook slowly until apricots are very soft. Press through a sieve.

Sugar Cookies

¾ pound butter
3 cups sugar
2 eggs, well beaten
Grated rind of one lemon
1 teaspoon vanilla

6 cups pastry flour
4 teaspoons baking powder
¼ teaspoon salt
¾ cup cream
Chopped blanched almonds

Cream butter and sugar. Add eggs, flavoring, and the sifted dry ingredients, alternately with the cream. Place in the refrigerator overnight. Roll a small quantity of the dough very thin. Cut; brush cookies with additional beaten egg. Sprinkle with sugar and chopped blanched almonds. Bake in a slow oven (300° F.) until delicately brown.

Noodle Soup
Paprika Schnitzel
Sponge Dumplings   Wax Beans
Lemon Soufflé
Coffee

Noodle Soup

Add fine-cut noodles and a dash of maggi to rapidly boiling soup stock. Boil five minutes. Add minced parsley.

Paprika Schnitzel

3 pounds veal steaks	Salt, pepper
Bacon drippings	Egg yolks
Paprika	Flour
2 onions, sliced	1 pint sour cream

Melt fat in frying-pan, add paprika until red. Add onion and brown. Cut veal into pieces for serving and sprinkle with salt and pepper. Dip in slightly beaten egg yolks, then in flour. Sauté in the fat until brown. Add the cream, cover and cook slowly one-half hour or until tender. If sauce is too thick, dilute with a little water.

Sponge Dumplings

1 cup milk	1 teaspoon salt
$\frac{1}{2}$ cup butter	1 tablespoon farina
1 cup flour	4 eggs

Bring milk to a boil, add butter. When melted, mix in flour and salt. Cook until it leaves the sides of the pan clean. Cool. Add farina and one egg at a time, beating vigorously after each one. Drop from a teaspoon into boiling salted water; cook eight minutes. Serve covered with buttered bread crumbs.

Wax Beans

Shred beans and parboil in salt water.   Simmer a can of tomatoes or use
fresh ones; strain.   Melt two tablespoons butter, add two teaspoons
flour, add strained tomato juice, then add beans and finish cooking until
tender.   Season and serve.

Lemon Soufflé

1 cup sugar	2 tablespoons butter
$\frac{1}{16}$ teaspoon salt	2 lemons, juice and rind
2 tablespoons flour	3 eggs, separated

1 cup milk

Mix sugar, salt, and flour.   Add butter, lemon juice and rind, and beaten
egg yolks, blended with the milk.   Beat well.   Fold in stiffly beaten egg
whites.   Pour into a buttered casserole, place in a pan of boiling water,
and bake for twenty minutes in a moderate oven (350° F.).   Be accurate
as to baking time, as bottom remains a thick liquid, which serves as a
sauce.

Ragout of Beef
Noodle Ring   Peas and Carrots
Pickled Tomatoes
Palatschinken
Coffee

Ragout of Beef

4 pounds beef, cut into two-inch
    cubes
¼ cup dried mushrooms
2 large onions, chopped
½ cup poultry fat or butter
2 bay leaves
2 sliced Bermuda onions
1 green pepper, chopped

2 tomatoes, peeled and sliced
½ pound mushrooms, sliced
2 cloves garlic, grated
Salt
Pepper
Paprika
Flour
½ teaspoon kitchen bouquet

Soak dried mushrooms overnight. Brown onions in fat. Add meat,
dried mushrooms, and the water in which they were soaked, and bay
leaves. Cover and simmer for an hour. Add remaining vegetables,
season and simmer until the meat is tender. Thicken gravy with flour
blended with water and kitchen bouquet.

Noodle Ring

1 package broad noodles
4 eggs
1 cup cream
2 tablespoons Worcestershire Sauce

½ cup catsup
½ cup grated American cheese
Salt
Paprika

Cook noodles ten minutes in boiling salted water. Drain and rinse in
cold water. Beat eggs until light, add remaining ingredients, season,
and mix with the noodles. Pour into a buttered and floured ring mold
and place in a pan of boiling water. Cover with a lid and bake in a
moderate oven (350° F.) for thirty minutes until firm. Fill center
with vegetables.

Peas and Carrots

2 tablespoons butter   1 cup cooked carrots, diced
2 cups cooked peas   Salt, pepper
Minced parsley

Melt butter, add vegetables, salt and pepper. Toss until well mixed, sprinkle with parsley.

Pickled Tomatoes

4 tomatoes, sliced thin   Vinegar
1 Bermuda onion, sliced thin   Salt, pepper
Paprika

Mix lightly together. If vinegar is strong, dilute with water. Serve cold.

Palatschinken

3 eggs $\frac{1}{8}$ teaspoon salt
1 cup flour   1 tablespoon sugar
$\frac{1}{4}$ teaspoon baking soda $\frac{3}{4}$ cup milk
Sour cream

Beat eggs until light; add sifted dry ingredients with milk and beat thoroughly. Make thin pancakes on a well-greased pan, using sweet butter. Spread the filling on each cake, roll and place in a buttered ovenware dish. Pour sour cream over them and heat in a hot oven. Sprinkle with powdered sugar before serving.

Filling

1 tablespoon butter   1 tablespoon Sultana raisins
$\frac{1}{2}$ cup sugar   1 pound cottage cheese
3 egg yolks $\frac{1}{8}$ teaspoon salt
3 tablespoons sour cream

Cream butter and sugar, add remaining ingredients. Mix well.

Tomato Bisque
Roast Crown of Lamb — Apple Fritters
Red Cabbage, Sweet and Sour
Almond Blitz Torte
Coffee

Tomato Bisque

1 quart tomatoes	2 tablespoons butter
½ cup water	2 tablespoons flour
1 onion, sliced	1½ cups scalded milk
1 bay leaf	1 teaspoon salt
2 cloves	1 teaspoon sugar
1 stalk celery, diced	Pepper, minced parsley

¼ teaspoon soda

Simmer first six ingredients for twenty minutes. Press through a strainer. Melt butter, add flour, gradually pour on milk, and add the seasonings. Cook three minutes. When ready to serve, add the soda to the hot tomatoes and pour gradually into the cream sauce, stirring constantly. Add parsley and serve at once.

Roast Crown of Lamb

Protect each bone of the roast from charring, by covering with a cube of salt pork. Season meat with salt and pepper; place in a moderate oven (350°) and allow thirty to thirty-five minutes to the pound. An hour before cooking is completed, remove from oven and fill center with ground sausage meat or a bread and sausage stuffing. Remove salt pork before serving roast.

Prepare the gravy by browning three tablespoons of flour in three tablespoons of the drippings; add:

2 cups water	1 teaspoon Worcestershire Sauce
3 tablespoons vinegar	mixed with ½ teaspoon
½ teaspoon sugar	mustard
1 tablespoon catsup	⅛ teaspoon paprika

Simmer until well blended.

Apple Fritters

Apple fritters (see page 159) may be used as a garnish around roast pork. Serve with a dab of currant jelly in the center of each fritter.

Red Cabbage, Sweet and Sour

2 tablespoons poultry fat	1 finely chopped onion
$\frac{1}{4}$ cup sugar	Salt, pepper
1 finely chopped red cabbage	1 tablespoon flour
2 apples, pared and sliced	$\frac{1}{4}$ cup vinegar

Melt fat and sugar. Add cabbage, apples, onion, salt and pepper. Simmer for two hours, adding boiling water as necessary to prevent burning. Blend the flour with the vinegar, add to the cabbage, and cook until well blended.

Almond Blitz Torte

$\frac{1}{2}$ cup butter	1 teaspoon baking powder
$\frac{3}{4}$ cup sugar	$\frac{1}{8}$ teaspoon salt
4 eggs, separated	5 tablespoons milk
1 cup grated almonds	1 teaspoon vanilla
1 cup pastry flour	1 cup sugar
$\frac{1}{2}$ pint whipping cream	

Cream butter and three-fourths cup sugar. Add the well-beaten egg yolks, three-fourths cup nuts, and the sifted dry ingredients alternately with the milk and flavoring. Beat vigorously. Pour into two buttered and floured layer-cake tins. Fold cup of sugar into stiffly beaten egg whites. Spread over the batter in the tins and sprinkle with remaining nuts. Bake in a moderate oven (350° F.) for twenty to twenty-five minutes. When cool, spread Chocolate Custard or the whipped cream between layers.

Chocolate Custard

$1\frac{1}{2}$ ounces chocolate	$\frac{1}{4}$ teaspoon salt
1 cup milk	1 egg yolk, slightly beaten
6 tablespoons granulated sugar	$\frac{1}{2}$ teaspoon vanilla
$1\frac{1}{2}$ tablespoons flour	$\frac{1}{3}$ cup whipping cream

Melt chocolate and heat milk in double boiler. Add sugar, flour, and salt, and cook until thickened, stirring constantly. Stir in egg yolk, cook two minutes. Remove from heat, add vanilla. Cool, and fold in whipped cream.

> *Lentil Soup*
> *Stuffed Green Peppers*
> *Salad Dufour*
> *Dampf Noodles — Cherry or Caramel Sauce*
> *Coffee*

Lentil Soup

1 cup lentils	1 finely chopped onion
2 quarts water	1 cup strained tomatoes
A piece of smoked meat	1 teaspoon salt
½ cup diced celery	⅛ teaspoon pepper

Soak lentils for 12 hours; drain. Simmer them with a ham bone or the end of a tongue, in the water for about three hours. Add vegetables and simmer for another hour. Put through a colander and skim off grease. Heat one tablespoon butter, add one tablespoon flour and some of the soup, gradually. Mix with the remaining soup. Season and serve with pieces of the smoked meat or slices of fried sausage and croutons.

Stuffed Green Peppers

6 or 8 green peppers	1 cup boiled rice
2 tablespoons butter	1 tablespoon minced parsley
2 tablespoons grated onions	1 teaspoon celery seed
1 pound ground beef	Salt, pepper
	Tomato soup

Remove stems and seeds of peppers. Cover with boiling water and simmer for five minutes; drain and cool. Sauté onions and beef in butter; combine with rice and seasonings and fill peppers. Cover with tomato soup and bake in a moderate oven (350°) for twenty to thirty minutes.

(Dilute tomato soup with half the usual amount of water.)

Salad Dufour

Mix three cups diced beets with two cups potatoes and marinate well. Just before serving, add one-half cup each, of shredded cooked ham and Swiss cheese. Toss until well mixed. Serve in a salad bowl lined with lettuce leaves.

Dampf Noodles

1 yeast cake	2 egg yolks
1¾ cups lukewarm milk	4 tablespoons sugar
6 cups flour	1 teaspoon salt
Melted butter (about ¾ cup)	1 tablespoon sherry wine
	1 teaspoon vanilla

Dissolve yeast in three-fourths cup milk and add gradually to two cups flour. Beat until smooth. Set in a warm place to rise. Mix the remaining ingredients together. Add the sponge. Beat until mixture blisters. Cover and allow to rise. Roll out one inch thick and cut with a small round cutter. Place in a warmed Dutch oven with melted butter one-half inch deep. Cover and allow to rise again. Add one cup cherry sauce, cover and bake in a hot oven (400° F.) until it sizzles. Turn out on a serving platter upside down and serve hot with remaining cherry sauce. *Or*, bake dumplings without sauce in the hot oven (400° F.) and, ten minutes before removing from oven, pour boiling hot Caramel Sauce over them. Turn out on the platter upside down and serve hot with Vanilla Sauce.

Cherry Sauce

½ cup sugar	½ cup water
1 tablespoon cornstarch	1 can cherries
⅛ teaspoon cinnamon	Juice of ½ lemon

Mix sugar, cornstarch, and cinnamon with the water. Add to cherries and cook for three minutes. Add lemon juice.

Caramel Sauce

2 cups sugar	½ cup maple syrup
½ cup boiling water	½ cup cream
1 tablespoon butter	Vanilla

Caramelize sugar in an iron pan, add water and cook until smooth. Add remaining ingredients and boil until thick.

Vanilla Sauce

2 tablespoons butter	$\frac{3}{4}$ cup sugar
2 tablespoons flour	Vanilla
$\frac{1}{16}$ teaspoon salt	4 egg yolks
1 cup milk	$\frac{1}{2}$ pint whipping cream

Rum

Melt butter, add flour and salt, and gradually pour on milk. Cook until smooth and thick, stirring constantly. Add sugar and vanilla. When cool, add egg yolks, cream, and flavor with rum.

Vegetable Soup
Stuffed Breast of Veal
Franconia Potatoes   Beets with Orange Sauce
Date Pecan Pie
Coffee

Vegetable Soup

1½ quarts soup stock	½ cup lima beans
1 tablespoon uncooked rice	1 large can tomatoes
½ cup diced carrots	¼ pound okra, sliced
½ cup diced celery	1 cup corn kernels
½ cup diced potatoes	½ teaspoon sugar
½ cup shredded beans	Salt and pepper

½ tablespoon minced parsley

Put rice in boiling soup stock and let cook ten to fifteen minutes. Add vegetables and seasoning and cook until all are tender. Add parsley before serving. (If canned okra and canned corn are used, add later than other vegetables.)

Stuffed Breast of Veal

Rub meat with salt, mixed with grated garlic, pepper, paprika, and ginger. Fill the pocket with dressing and close with skewers. Place in a roasting-pan with two tablespoons each of diced celery, carrots, green pepper, tomato, onion, a teaspoon lemon juice, and a bay leaf. Spread with six tablespoons chicken fat. Cover and roast two to three hours, basting every half-hour. Serve with brown gravy.

Dressing

2 or 3 slices bread	2 crackers, rolled
Cold water	Milk or cream
3 tablespoons chicken fat	1 tablespoon minced parsley
1 small onion, grated	½ cup minced celery
2 eggs beaten	Few grains ginger

Salt, pepper

Soak bread in cold water and press dry. Melt fat and add onion and bread. Cook until fat is absorbed. Add to egg with seasonings and crackers and sufficient liquid to moisten.

Brown Gravy

3 tablespoons fat $\frac{1}{4}$ teaspoon kitchen bouquet
3 tablespoons flour $\frac{1}{2}$ tablespoon Escoffier Sauce
$2\frac{1}{2}$ cups soup stock   Salt, pepper

Use fat from drippings in baking-pan, add flour and brown. Add liquid and seasonings. Cook for few minutes and strain.

Franconia Potatoes

Wash, peel medium-sized potatoes. Soak in cold water for one-half hour. Parboil for ten minutes, drain and place in the pan in which the meat is roasting. Bake until soft (about forty-five minutes), basting with fat in the pan.

Beets with Orange Sauce

1 tablespoon butter $\frac{3}{4}$ cup orange juice
4 tablespoons brown sugar   Slivered orange peel
$1\frac{1}{2}$ tablespoons flour $\frac{1}{8}$ teaspoon salt and paprika
$2\frac{1}{2}$ cups diced cooked beets

Melt butter in double boiler; add sugar mixed with flour, and orange juice; cook until thick, stirring constantly. Add seasonings, and beets; heat thoroughly.

Date Pecan Pie

1 cup corn syrup $\frac{1}{2}$ teaspoon vanilla
3 tablespoons sugar   2 eggs, separated
2 tablespoons flour   1 cup chopped pecans
$\frac{1}{4}$ teaspoon salt $\frac{1}{2}$ cup chopped dates
$\frac{1}{2}$ teaspoon cinnamon   Pastry shell
3 tablespoons melted butter   Sweetened and flavored whipped cream

Mix corn syrup with sugar, flour, salt, cinnamon, melted butter, and vanilla. Add well-beaten egg yolks; fold in beaten egg whites. Add pecans and dates. Pour into pastry shell and bake about fifteen minutes in a hot oven (450° F.). Reduce heat to 325° F. and bake in slow, moderate oven thirty to thirty-five minutes. Cover with sweetened and flavored whipped cream.

Clam and Tomato Broth
Braised Oxtails   *Green Salad*
April Fritters
Coffee

Clam and Tomato Broth

Combine equal quantities of clam broth and tomato bouillon. Season to taste with celery salt, onion salt, dash of Worcestershire Sauce and cayenne. Heat, and top with salted whipped cream.

Braised Oxtails

3 pounds oxtails, disjointed	2 cups canned tomatoes
6 tablespoons fat	2 cloves
2 tablespoons flour	1 bay leaf, crushed
1½ teaspoons salt	1 cup sliced mushrooms
¼ teaspoon pepper	1 cup diced celery
½ teaspoon chili powder	1 cup diced carrots
3 onions, sliced	Potato balls
1 large clove of garlic, grated	Kitchen Bouquet
1 cup soup stock	Minced parsley

¼ cup sherry

Parboil oxtails for about ten minutes. Drain, dry, and dredge with flour mixed with seasonings. Sauté in four tablespoons fat, with onions and garlic, until well browned. Add stock, tomatoes, cloves and bay leaf, and bring to a boil. Place in a covered baking-dish and bake at 325° for two and one-half hours. Add more stock if needed. Remove the oxtails, strain the sauce and skim off excess fat. Combine oxtails and strained sauce in baking-dish. Sauté mushrooms, celery, and carrots in remaining fat ten minutes. Add to the oxtails with the potatoes and a few drops of Kitchen Bouquet. Cover and bake until potatoes are done. If sauce is too thin, add one tablespoon flour blended with one tablespoon water. Add sherry just before serving, and sprinkle with minced parsley.

Apple Fritters

1 cup flour	2 eggs, separated
¼ teaspoon salt	1 tablespoon melted butter
⅔ cup milk	Sliced apples

Powdered sugar

Sift flour. Add milk gradually with the beaten egg yolks and butter. Fold in the stiffly beaten egg whites. Pare, core, and slice apples crosswise. Dip in the batter and fry in deep hot fat until brown. Drain on unglazed paper. Sprinkle with sugar mixed with cinnamon or serve with Melba Sauce.

Melba Sauce

1 cup canned raspberries	½ tablespoon cornstarch
½ cup currant jelly	1 tablespoon cold water
¼ cup sugar	1 teaspoon lemon juice

Combine berries, jelly, and sugar; bring to a boil. Add cornstarch blended with water and lemon juice; cook, stirring constantly, until clear. Press through a sieve.

Note: Apples soaked two hours in lemon juice and powdered sugar before being coated with the batter give an extra fine flavor.

Veal Roulade (Mock Squab)
Risi Bisi   *Cole Slaw Singapore*
Lemon Fluff Pie
Coffee

Veal Roulade or Mock Squab

Cut thin slices of veal from the leg. Remove skin and bones; pound until only one-fourth inch thick and cut into pieces four inches square. Add three slices of chopped and sautéed bacon to the beaten yolks of three eggs and one egg white, with one-fourth cup grated cheese and one-fourth cup cracker crumbs. Moisten with milk or soup stock and season highly with salt, pepper, cayenne, ginger, lemon juice, onion juice, and chopped parsley. Spread each piece of veal with the mixture. Roll and tie or fasten with skewers. Sprinkle with salt, paprika, and pepper. Dredge with flour and brown in butter. Add three sliced tomatoes, one bay leaf, one clove, one-half onion, and one-fourth cup of butter. Cook slowly for thirty minutes. Add one-half cup cream. Cover and continue cooking until tender. Serve on small slices of toast, straining pan gravy over the birds.

Risi Bisi

1 cup rice	1 small onion
1 quart boiling water	Small bunch parsley
1 teaspoon salt	1 cup cooked fresh peas
2 tablespoons butter	

Wash and rinse rice. Add to boiling salted water with the onion and parsley. Cook slowly for twenty minutes. Remove the onion and parsley. Add peas and butter; mix well. Simmer for ten minutes or until the water is evaporated. Salt and pepper to taste.

Cole Slaw Singapore

1 cucumber, sliced
½ onion, grated
1 cabbage, finely shredded
1 pimiento, chopped
1 green pepper, chopped

1½ cups chili sauce
1 bottle rich cream
Juice of 1 lemon
1 tablespoon minced chives
Salt, pepper

Soak cucumber in salted ice water one-half hour. Press and add to cabbage and onion. Parboil pimiento and green pepper for two minutes. Strain, chill, and add to cabbage. Combine remaining ingredients and add to cabbage mixture just before serving.

Lemon Fluff Pie

6 eggs, separated
1½ lemons (juice)
1 grated lemon rind

3 tablespoons boiling water
⅛ teaspoon salt
1 cup confectioner's sugar
Baked pie shell

Beat egg yolks until lemon-colored. Add juice and rind of lemon, water, salt, and sugar. Cook in double boiler until thick. Cool and fold in three of the egg whites, stiffly beaten. Beat the other three whites with six tablespoons of sugar to make a meringue for top. Fill baked pie shell, cover with the meringue and place in a hot oven (450° F.) to brown.

Lamb Stew   *Potato Dumplings*
Green Beans au Gratin
Corn Relish
Rice Pudding, Balbrook
Custard Sauce
Coffee

Lamb Stew

3 pounds lamb shoulder, cut into pieces for serving	1 teaspoon paprika
	Salt, pepper
3 onions, sliced	2 cups tomatoes
3 tablespoons butter	1 cup thick sour cream
½ cup minced parsley	

Simmer the onions in the butter until light brown. Add the well-seasoned meat, and sear. Add the tomatoes; cover and cook slowly for two
hours, adding water if necessary to prevent burning. Just before
serving, add the cream and parsley and cook a few minutes more.

Potato Dumplings

8 potatoes (medium size)	1 tablespoon salt
2 eggs, slightly beaten	Flour
Few grains of nutmeg	Shredded onions

Boil the potatoes in their jackets. Chill thoroughly. Peel and grate.
Add eggs, seasonings, with enough flour to hold potatoes together.
Form into balls, drop into boiling salted water and simmer for twenty
minutes. Drain, serve with shredded onions which have been sautéed
in a generous amount of butter, or bread crumbs Polonaise.

Toasted bread croutons may be rolled into the balls.

Green Beans au Gratin

1½ pounds string beans   ¾ cup grated cheese
¾ cup milk   Salt, paprika
2 tablespoons butter   Few grains cayenne
Buttered bread crumbs

Shred beans and combine with milk, butter, one-half cup cheese, and seasonings. Pour into a buttered baking-dish, cover and bake slowly at 350° F. for one hour. Stir several times during baking and, when nearly done, sprinkle over the top the remaining cheese mixed with a few bread crumbs. Continue baking until brown.

Corn Relish

6 to 8 cucumbers   ½ dozen green peppers
2 onions   3 red peppers
1½ dozen green tomatoes   ½ cup salt

Grind above ingredients; add salt and set in refrigerator overnight. Drain off all the liquid that has formed and add the following:

3 dozen ears of corn   1 cup water
6 cups sugar   1 tablespoon celery seed
5 tablespoons flour   1 tablespoon mustard seed
3 cups vinegar   1 tablespoon turmeric

Mix all together and cook fifty minutes, stirring frequently. Pack in sterilized jars and seal.

Rice Pudding, Balbrook

¾ cup rice   ¼ cup butter
1 quart milk (or half cream)   Salt, mace, cinnamon
½ cup sugar (generous   1 teaspoon vanilla
    (measurement)   3 egg whites

Heat oven to 325° F. Wash the rice thoroughly. Put the rice in the milk and bake in a slow oven, covered until soft (about one hour). Stir occasionally and add more milk as rice absorbs it. Cool slightly; add the sugar, pinch of salt, speck of mace, a little cinnamon, the butter and vanilla and more milk to make a soft mixture. Fold in the stiffly beaten egg whites and bake in a pudding dish about twenty minutes (325° F.). Serve with Custard Sauce (page 164).

Custard Sauce

3 egg yolks	2 cups milk
4 tablespoons sugar	1 tablespoon butter
1 teaspoon cornstarch	1 teaspoon vanilla

Whipped cream

Make a paste of the egg yolks, sugar, and cornstarch. Thin out with the milk that has been scalded and cooled. Cook until thick; add butter, cool, and add vanilla and a little whipped cream.

```
Celery Root Appetizer
Veal Cutlets with Chestnuts
Cauliflower — Pimiento Sauce
Grilled Cheese Apple Pie
Coffee
```

Celery Root Appetizer

Boil three celery roots. Peel and mash. Season with salt, pepper, onion juice, English mustard, and enough mayonnaise to form a paste. Shape into two inch pyramids. Make an indentation in the top, fill with caviar or an anchovy, and make a border of cooked riced egg yolks. Serve on a slice of marinated beet, on shredded lettuce.

Veal Cutlet with Chestnuts

Select eight one-inch loin chops. Remove bone, roll chop, and hold in place with a small skewer or toothpick. Rub with salt, pepper, and paprika. Brown two large sliced onions in one-half cup butter in a Dutch oven; then remove onions and brown the cutlets in the same fat. Add two pounds boiled and skinned chestnuts and one cup veal soup stock (made from the veal bones). Cover and bake slowly for one and one-half hours. Turn meat and baste frequently so that it does not burn, and if necessary, add more stock. Just before serving, remove skewers and add one-half cup Madeira wine.

Cauliflower — Pimiento Sauce

2 tablespoons flour	2 tablespoons butter
½ teaspoon salt	1 cup hot milk
Pepper	4 tablespoons pimiento (purée)
1 head cooked cauliflower	

Blend flour, salt, and pepper with melted butter. Gradually pour on the milk. Cook until creamy, stirring constantly. Add pimiento purée (pimientoes forced through sieve). Pour over cauliflower.

Grilled Cheese Apple Pie

Rich pie pastry	½ cup sugar
5 or 6 apples	⅛ teaspoon salt
Juice of 1 lemon	½ teaspoon grated cinnamon
Few gratings lemon rind	American cheese

Pare, core, and slice the apples; add lemon, cover and let stand one hour. Line pie plate with rich pie pastry. (See page 51.) Fill with apples; sprinkle with sugar mixed with salt and cinnamon; dot with butter. Wet edges of under crust and cover with upper crust, and press edges together. Bake forty to forty-five minutes in a moderate oven. Just before serving, place thin slices of cheese over pie, place under broiler until cheese melts.

Soup Maigre
Italian Steak with Tomatoes
Celery Root with Potato
Lettuce   *Chiffonade Dressing*
French Strawberry Pie
Coffee

Soup Maigre

⅓ cup diced **carrots**	3 cloves
1 cup peas	Salt
½ cup beans	Pepper
½ cup celery	3 quarts water
1 can tomatoes	1 cup okra
1½ cups diced potatoes	Dash of maggi
2 chopped onions	2 tablespoons butter
1 bay leaf	1 tablespoon chopped parsley

Simmer carrots, peas, beans, celery, tomatoes, potatoes, onions, barley, spices, salt, and pepper in the water for two and one-half hours. Add the okra, cook one-half hour longer. Just before serving add the maggi, butter, and parsley.

Italian Steak

Cut three-fourths-inch thick slices of round steak into pieces for serving. Season with salt and pepper. Dip in beaten egg, then bread crumbs, and brown quickly in olive oil. Remove from pan. Place in tomato sauce and bake slowly forty-five minutes or until meat is tender.

Tomato Sauce

2 tablespoons butter	2 cloves
1 onion, finely chopped	1 bay leaf
2 cloves garlic, minced	1 can tomatoes
6 sprigs parsley, minced	Salt, pepper, paprika

Simmer vegetables in butter; add tomatoes and seasonings. Cook five minutes. Then add the meat.

Celery Root with Potato

2 tablespoons butter	2 cups potatoes, diced
6 chopped shallots	1 tablespoon flour
1 clove garlic, grated	2 tablespoons water
2 cups celery root, diced	$\frac{1}{2}$ cup minced parsley
Soup stock	Salt, pepper

Melt butter, add shallots and garlic, and simmer until they begin to change color. Add the celery root with enough soup stock (or water with a bouillon cube) to cover. Cook for twenty minutes; add potatoes with more liquid if necessary and boil until tender. Add flour mixed with water, the parsley, and seasoning. Cook about 3 to 5 minutes longer.

Chiffonade Dressing

1 cup French Dressing	1 tablespoon minced pimiento
1 hard-cooked egg, riced	2 tablespoons cooked minced beet
2 teaspoons minced parsley	1 teaspoon chives
	Lettuce

Combine ingredients and serve over quartered heads of lettuce.

French Strawberry Pie

1 baked pie shell (9-inch)	1 quart strawberries
1 3-ounce package	1 cup sugar
cream cheese	3 tablespoons cornstarch
Cream	$\frac{1}{2}$ pint whipped cream

Soften cream cheese to a fluffy consistency with cream and spread on bottom of piecrust. Select best half of berries and arrange whole on top of cheese. Mash and cook remaining berries and put through sieve to extract juice. Combine sugar and cornstarch and add juice, stirring to prevent lumping. Cook until clear and thick. Cool and pour over berries in the crust. Chill, and when ready to serve, top with whipped cream.

Clam-Juice Cocktail
Pork Chops Creole
Sautéed Okra   Fried Apple Rings
Chocolate Pie
Coffee

Clam-Juice Cocktail

2 cups clam juice	Dash Tabasco sauce
½ cup strained catsup	Crushed ice
Celery salt	Nutmeg

Combine ingredients; shake well. Sprinkle a few grains of nutmeg over each glass.

Pork Chops Creole

Salt and pepper thick chops. Place in a pan with a one-fourth-inch slice of Bermuda onion and a half-inch ring of green pepper on each. Put into each pepper ring one teaspoon washed rice. Add one can tomato soup. Bake in a moderate oven (350° F.) one and one-half hours. Baste frequently. If necessary, add a small quantity of water to prevent chops from becoming dry.

Sautéed Okra

Wash and dry okra. Cut off stem ends and slice crosswise. Melt two tablespoons of butter (for a pound of okra) and add okra; cover and cook gently for ten minutes, stirring frequently. Remove cover and continue cooking until brown and tender.

Fried Apple Rings

Core and slice apples crosswise. Put into a frying-pan one cup sugar, one tablespoon butter, and three tablespoons water. When the sugar is melted, add apples, cover and cook slowly, adding more water as necessary. Brown on both sides.

Chocolate Pie

1 tablespoon gelatin	4 eggs, separated
¼ cup cold water	¾ cup sugar
2 ounces chocolate	¼ teaspoon salt
½ cup boiling water	1 teaspoon vanilla

9-inch baked pie shell

Soften gelatin in cold water; mix chocolate with boiling water until smooth; dissolve gelatin in the hot mixture. Add beaten egg yolks, one-half of the sugar, salt, and vanilla. Cook over hot water about one minute; cool, and when mixture begins to thicken, fold in stiffly beaten egg whites, to which has been added the remaining sugar. Fill pie shell and chill. Garnish with whipped cream.

Chicken Gumbo
Tomato Ciboulettes
Liederkranz Cheese, Toasted Wafers
Raspberry Pie
Coffee

Chicken Gumbo

2 stewing chickens	1 large can tomatoes
Flour	1 bunch carrots, diced
Salt, pepper	1 pound green peas
Paprika, ginger	$\frac{1}{2}$ pound cut string beans
3 large onions, sliced	1 pound okra, sliced
2 green peppers, diced	$1\frac{1}{2}$ cups corn
2 stalks celery, diced	1 tablespoon parsley, chopped
2 cloves grated garlic	Cooked rice

Remove surplus fat from chickens and cut into pieces. Dip in flour mixed with salt, pepper, and ginger, and brown quickly in hot chicken fat. Put in a large soup kettle. Sauté the onions, peppers, celery, and garlic in the same fat for fifteen minutes. Add to chicken with the tomatoes, cover and simmer for one hour. Add the carrots, peas, and beans, with enough boiling water to cover. Season and cook slowly until the chicken is nearly tender, adding more boiling water as necessary. Twenty minutes before serving, skim off the fat and add the okra, corn, and parsley. Serve from a tureen. Place a spoonful of boiled rice in each plate.

Tomato Ciboulettes

Remove skins from small tomatoes, cut into halves crosswise, and marinate for an hour. Serve on a bed of lettuce leaves and watercress. Cover lightly with mayonnaise and sprinkle with finely chopped chives. Serve with Liederkranz Cheese and toasted crackers.

Raspberry Pie

2 baked pie shells $1\frac{1}{4}$ cups sugar
$\frac{1}{2}$ cup water   2 to 3 boxes raspberries
1 cup whipping cream

Boil sugar and water until it forms a heavy syrup. Add one-half the berries and cook until soft. Place uncooked fruit in pie shell, cover with cooked fruit and syrup. Decorate with whipped cream. Do not fill crusts until ready to serve.

> *Mushroom Bisque*
> *Smoked Tongue   Purée of Peas*
> *Beet and Horseradish Relish*
> *Savoy Cabbage*
> *Pecan Pie*
> *Coffee*

Mushroom Bisque

½ cup dried mushrooms	3 tablespoons butter
1 pound fresh mushrooms, ground	3 tablespoons flour
1 pint water	1 pint milk
1 large onion, sliced	1 pint cream
½ cup tomato purée	Salt, pepper

Soak the dried mushrooms overnight; drain and grind. Cook with water and onion for thirty minutes. Brown fresh mushrooms in butter, add flour; blend. Add milk, cream, and tomato purée. Combine mixtures, season, and cook slowly for ten minutes.

Smoked Tongue

Cover tongue with cold water and cook slowly until tender, adding more boiling water when necessary, to keep tongue covered. When tender, remove from water, skin, and let cool in the water in which it was cooked. If served hot, reheat in the same liquid. Serve with Purée of Peas or Egg Sauce.

Purée of Peas

2 cups dried peas	3 tablespoons butter
2 pints water	1 teaspoon salt
1 clove garlic	Pepper
2 tablespoons flour	1 onion, chopped

Soak the peas for one hour; drain. Add water and garlic and cook slowly

until soft. Press through a strainer, add flour browned in two tablespoons butter, with salt and pepper, and cook until thick. When
ready to serve, put onion which has been browned in remaining butter
on top.

Egg Sauce for Hot Tongue

Mix three hard cooked egg yolks with three tablespoons of olive oil and
three tablespoons prepared mustard, one teaspoon sugar, and salt and
pepper to taste. Chop whites. Add to yolk mixture and blend.

Beet and Horseradish Relish

Add one-third cup grated cooked beets to one cup grated horseradish.
Moisten with vinegar.

Savoy Cabbage

1 head curly cabbage	1 cup soup stock
1 tablespoon poultry fat	Salt
1 tablespoon flour	Pepper
Hard-cooked egg	

Cook cabbage in boiling salted water. Drain and chop fine. Brown
flour in melted fat, add soup stock, cabbage, and seasonings. Cook
slowly for ten minutes. Garnish with hard-cooked egg.

Pecan Pie

1 unbaked pie shell	1 cup dark Karo syrup
3 eggs	1 cup pecan nuts, chopped
$\frac{1}{2}$ cup granulated sugar	$\frac{1}{2}$ teaspoon salt
1 teaspoon vanilla	

Beat the eggs slightly; add the sugar, syrup, nuts, salt, and vanilla.
Pour into an unbaked pie shell and bake for ten minutes in a 450° F.
oven, then forty minutes in a moderate oven.

Green Kern Soup
Hamburgers de Luxe
Boiled Potatoes with Dill
Sweet and Sour Beans
Chocolate Sponge Pudding
Coffee

Green Kern Soup

Soak a half cup of green kern in water overnight. Have ready a soup stock made of two oxtails, a soup bone, a veal bone, and soup greens. Drain water from green kern and cook in some of the soup stock until soft. Add more soup stock to make the desired number of servings.

Hamburgers de Luxe

1 pound ground round steak	1 teaspoon salt
2 eggs, unbeaten	Pepper
1 tablespoon flour	$\frac{1}{4}$ cup catsup
$\frac{1}{2}$ grated onion	Sautéed onions or mushrooms

Bacon

Mix the meat with the eggs, flour, and seasonings; beat thoroughly (the longer the mixture is beaten, the better). Form into thin cakes: spread a layer of onions or mushrooms between two cakes and press the edges together; place a strip of bacon around the edge; fasten with a toothpick and fry on a hot greased skillet.

Boiled Potatoes with Dill

Cook small potatoes in boiling salted water until tender. Drain and shake gently over the fire, uncovered, until dry. Add two tablespoons butter and one tablespoon minced dill.

Sweet and Sour Beans

1 pound wax beans	$\frac{3}{4}$ cup sugar
2 eggs	$\frac{1}{2}$ cup vinegar
$\frac{1}{2}$ pint thick sour cream	Salt, pepper

Cut beans lengthwise and simmer until tender, in as little water as possible. Drain. Mix the remaining ingredients. Pour over the beans, season, and heat thoroughly but do not boil.

Chocolate Sponge Pudding

1 tablespoon gelatin	3 eggs, separated
$\frac{1}{4}$ cup cold water	$\frac{1}{2}$ cup sugar
$\frac{3}{4}$ cup boiling water	$\frac{1}{8}$ teaspoon salt
2 squares bitter chocolate	1 teaspoon vanilla
Whipped cream	

Soak gelatin in cold water; dissolve in boiling water. Melt chocolate in a double boiler. Beat egg yolks, sugar, and salt until thick and lemon-colored. Add gelatin, chocolate, and flavoring. When mixture begins to stiffen, fold in stiffly beaten egg whites. Pour into a mold; chill until firm. Garnish with whipped cream.

> *Beef Stew, Gaston*
> *Potato Pudding* *Wilted Salad*
> *French Bread*
> *Banana Cake*

Beef Stew, Gaston

Cut a 4- to 5-pound piece of bottom round in large squares. Brown on all sides in hot fat and add four tablespoons of hot sherry or red wine. Remove meat and to the pot (Dutch oven) add the following vegetables:

3 or 4 zucchini squash, sliced and peeled	½ pound shelled peas
4 or 5 carrots, sliced	½ pound green beans, cut in pieces
2 dozen baby onions, whole	½ pound of mushrooms, cut up

Cook all briskly for ten minutes. Add one tablespoon of tomato paste and four tablespoons of flour, and blend well. Stir in four cups or more of water and cook until it boils. Replace meat in pot with the vegetables. Season to taste and add two bay leaves.

Cover and cook very slowly until meat is tender, about two hours. Add one or two tablespoons of red wine every fifteen minutes during cooking. When nearly done add four or five tomatoes, peeled and diced.

Potato Pudding

5 or 6 potatoes	1 egg
Small amount of onion	3 tablespoons beef fat
2 tablespoons flour	Salt, pepper

Grate the raw potatoes and onion. Add flour, beaten egg, and melted beef fat. Place in greased muffin tins and bake about an hour in 300° to 350° oven.

Wilted Salad

3 slices of bacon, diced

½ cup vinegar

½ teaspoon salt

2 teaspoons sugar

½ teaspoon mustard

Freshly ground pepper

1 tablespoon chives

1 sprig dill

2 hard cooked eggs, sliced

Leaf lettuce

Sauté bacon until crisp; remove from pan. To the bacon fat, add vinegar, salt, sugar, mustard, and pepper; simmer about two minutes. Pour over lettuce, add chopped chives, dill, bacon, and eggs. Toss and serve immediately.

Banana Cake

1½ cups brown sugar

Pinch of salt

½ cup butter

3 eggs, separated

2 cups flour

1 teaspoon baking soda

½ cup buttermilk

1 cup banana pulp, riced

Cream butter and sugar; add yolks one at a time. Add alternately flour sifted with baking soda and buttermilk. Fold in banana and beaten whites. Bake in a single layer in a moderate oven for twenty-five to thirty minutes. Frost with caramel frosting.

Caramel Frosting

3 cups light brown sugar

½ cup white sugar

1 small can Pet
condensed milk

1 tablespoon butter

Cook slowly to a soft ball stage. Cool and beat until consistency to spread.

Braised Sweetbreads and Ham
Noodles Polonaise   Green Salad, Maurice
Orange Custard

Braised Sweetbreads and Ham

3 pounds sweetbreads	2 tablespoons flour
¼ cup sherry	3 cups soup stock or water
½ pound mushrooms sliced	1 cup cooked ham, shredded
1 tablespoon tomato paste	Bay leaf, salt, pepper

Parboil sweetbreads (see page 78). Brown on each side in butter, using Dutch oven or iron skillet and add the hot sherry. Remove sweetbreads and to the pan add more butter and the mushrooms. Cook briskly a few moments, covered. Turn off flame, add tomato paste and flour and pour on stock, stirring and scraping pan until well blended. Stir over fire until it comes to a boil, adding more stock if necessary to make a gravy consistency. Add ham, salt, pepper, bay leaf, and sweetbreads. Cover and cook very slowly, about twenty-five minutes.

Noodles Polonaise

Brown bread crumbs in butter and sprinkle over boiled noodles.

Green Salad, Maurice

4 tablespoons salad oil	1½ tablespoons Heinz
2 tablespoons vinegar	light yellow mustard
Salt	Freshly ground pepper

Blend ingredients, add to lettuce and toss.

Orange Custard

½ cup sugar
3 tablespoons cornstarch
Few grains salt
1 pint milk, scalded

2 egg yolks
2 tablespoons cream
½ teaspoon almond extract
3 oranges

Mix sugar, cornstarch, and salt; add milk and cook in a double boiler. When thick add egg yolks blended with the cream and cook one minute. Remove from fire; add almond extract. Place orange sections in a shallow casserole, pour custard over fruit, and cover with meringue. Bake in a hot oven (425° F.) until browned. (Meringue is made by adding a third cup sugar to two beaten egg whites.) Serve chilled.

Friends for Dinner

Grapefruit Ring

1 tablespoon gelatin	1 cup boiling water
¼ cup cold water	1½ cups grapefruit pulp
¼ cup lemon juice	Green coloring
½ cup sugar	Avocado pears
½ teaspoon salt	Persimmons

Soften gelatin in cold water; mix the lemon juice, sugar, salt, and boiling water. Bring all to the boiling point and add gelatin. When the mixture begins to thicken, add grapefruit pulp and a little green coloring. Turn into mold and chill. Invert on a bed of lettuce, surround with sections of avocado pears and persimmons, and serve with Lorenzo Dressing (page 78).

Chicken Fricassée

2 chickens	4 tablespoons chicken fat
Salt, pepper, ginger	4 tablespoons flour
Water	2 egg yolks
½ cup each — onion, carrot, and celery	2 tablespoons minced parsley
1 bay leaf	1 can mushrooms

Cut chickens into pieces for serving; sprinkle with salt, pepper, and a few grains of ginger. Cover with water and cook slowly for one hour. Add the vegetables and bay leaf and continue cooking until chicken is tender. Blend flour and melted chicken fat. Gradually add about three cups of the hot chicken broth; season and cook until smooth. Pour onto the beaten yolks; add mushrooms and parsley and pour over chicken.

Baking Powder Dumplings

2 cups flour
4 teaspoons baking powder
½ teaspoon salt

2 tablespoons butter
2 eggs, well beaten
Milk

Sift flour, baking powder, and salt; cut in the butter and add eggs with enough milk to form a heavy drop batter. Drop quickly by the spoonful into chicken broth or boiling water. Cover closely and cook ten minutes without removing the lid.

Creamed Spinach

1 peck spinach
4 tablespoons butter or poultry fat
4 tablespoons flour
1 tablespoon onion, grated

2 cups soup stock or milk
1 teaspoon salt
¼ teaspoon pepper
Hard-cooked eggs

Wash the spinach several times in cold water to remove all sand. Put in kettle without water. Cover and simmer fifteen to twenty minutes until tender. Drain and chop very fine. Heat fat in a frying-pan. Add flour and onion, and cook until brown. Gradually add soup stock or milk, stirring constantly. Add spinach and seasonings, and simmer several minutes. Garnish with slivered egg whites and riced yolks.

Fresh Coconut Pudding

1 pint cream
2 tablespoons gelatin
1 cup sugar

1 teaspoon almond extract
2 cups grated fresh coconut
1½ pints whipping cream

Let cream come to a boil; add the gelatin, which has been soaked in a little cold water, and the sugar. When dissolved add flavoring and coconut and fold in the whipped cream. Pour into a mold to chill until firm. Remove from mold, sprinkle with coconut, and serve with Caramel Sauce.

Caramel Sauce

1 tablespoon butter
1 pound light brown sugar
2 egg yolks

1 cup cream
⅛ teaspoon salt
1 teaspoon vanilla

Combine butter and sugar. Add yolks, cream, and salt. Cook in a double boiler until smooth and creamy. Cool and add vanilla.

Avocado Ring
Pumpernickel Melba Toast
Planked Steak with Duchess Potatoes
Stuffed Tomatoes   Stuffed Peppers
Cherry Torte
Coffee

Avocado Ring

1 package Lime Jello	$\frac{3}{4}$ cup cream, whipped
1 cup hot water	$\frac{3}{4}$ cup mayonnaise
3 tablespoons minced parsley	$\frac{1}{2}$ teaspoon salt
2 cups avocado, mashed	1 tablespoon lemon juice

Dissolve the Jello in the hot water. Chill until it begins to congeal; fold in remaining ingredients. Fill oiled ring mold and chill until firm. Surround with fresh fruits and serve with Lorenzo Dressing.

Planked Steak

Broil a sirloin steak two inches thick for five minutes on each side. Sprinkle with salt and pepper. Butter a wooden plank. Arrange a border of Duchess Potatoes close to the edge, using a pastry bag and a rose tube. Place steak on plank and bake until it is done and the potatoes are brown. Spread steak with one-fourth cup melted butter mixed with one-half tablespoon each of minced parsley and lemon juice. Garnish plank with stuffed tomatoes and stuffed peppers.

Duchess Potatoes

3 cups hot riced potatoes	3 tablespoons butter
1 teaspoon salt	Yolks of 3 eggs, slightly beaten

Mix all the ingredients. After potato border is made, brush over with an additional beaten egg yolk, blended with one teaspoon water.

Stuffed Tomatoes

6 tomatoes	2 egg yolks
1 cup grated rye bread	1 tablespoon chopped parsley
2 tablespoons butter	$\frac{1}{4}$ teaspoon grated onion

Salt, pepper

Slice off stem ends of tomatoes and remove pulp. Cook bread crumbs in butter, add onion juice, tomato pulp, parsley and seasoning. Remove from fire, add yolks and fill tomatoes. Sprinkle tops with buttered cracker crumbs. Place on a buttered tin and bake for thirty minutes in a moderate oven.

Stuffed Peppers

6 peppers	1 cup corn
1 onion, grated	1 cup tomato sauce
2 tablespoons butter	1 cup bread crumbs

Salt, pepper

Remove the blossom end of peppers and seeds. Cook in boiling salted water for five minutes, and drain. Sauté onion in butter until golden brown; add corn, tomato sauce, and bread crumbs. Fill peppers and sprinkle with buttered crumbs; bake in a moderate oven (350° F.) for thirty minutes.

Cherry Torte

$\frac{1}{2}$ pound butter	1 teaspoon baking powder
4 tablespoons sugar	$1\frac{1}{2}$ cans drained cherries
$\frac{1}{2}$ teaspoon salt	$\frac{1}{2}$ cup chopped and blanched
$2\frac{1}{4}$ cups flour	almonds

Cream butter and sugar; add sifted dry ingredients. Chill dough a few hours before baking. Press dough on the bottom and around the sides of a buttered spring form. Bake fifteen minutes or until brown in a hot oven. Fill with one-half the custard, then cherries, and spread remaining custard on top. Cover with meringue, sprinkle with chopped nuts, and bake in a slow oven (325° F.) until meringue is brown.

Custard

3 teaspoons cornstarch	1 cup milk
5 tablespoons sugar	5 egg yolks, slightly beaten
$\frac{1}{8}$ teaspoon salt	$1\frac{1}{2}$ teaspoons vanilla

Mix cornstarch, sugar, and salt; add the milk gradually, then egg yolks. Cook in a double boiler, stirring constantly until smooth and thick. Add vanilla.

Meringue

5 egg whites	$\frac{1}{2}$ teaspoon baking powder
5 tablespoons sugar	$\frac{1}{8}$ teaspoon salt

Mix sugar and baking powder. Fold into the salted and stiffly beaten egg whites.

Bouillon with Pancake Strips
Cheese Dreams
Roast Turkey   *Chestnut Dressing*
Giblet Sauce   *Cranberry Sherbert*
Sweet Potatoes and Apples
White Asparagus Polonaise
Pumpkin Pudding
Coffee

Pancake Strips

3 tablespoons flour   ¼ cup water
⅛ teaspoon salt   1 egg
1 tablespoon minced parsley

Mix and beat all ingredients together. Make thin, well-browned pancakes in an oiled frying-pan; stack and cut into strips an eighth-inch wide. Serve strips in bouillon.

Cheese Dreams

1½ cups grated cheese   ½ tablespoon Worcestershire Sauce
2 tablespoons melted butter Salt
¼ cup milk   Paprika
½ teaspoon dry mustard   1 egg

Mix to a smooth paste. Spread between rounds of bread. Fry in butter, browning both sides. Drain on unglazed paper. Serve with bouillon.

Roast Turkey

Clean turkey and rub inside and out with salt. Fill cavity loosely with dressing and sew or close with skewers. Cover breast with butter and flour. Place the bird, breast up, in a roasting-pan and roast uncovered in 300° oven until tender. Allow eighteen to twenty minutes per pound. Baste every half-hour with pan drippings or use more butter if necessary.

Chestnut Dressing

3 cups peeled and skinned chestnuts
½ cup butter
1 teaspoon salt
1 cup bread crumbs

⅛ teaspoon pepper
¼ cup minced celery
½ cup seeded raisins
Sherry wine

Cook chestnuts in boiling salted water until tender. Mix with the remaining ingredients. Flavor with sherry. If too dry, moisten with hot milk. (Double this for a large bird.)

Giblet Gravy (see pages 230, 234)

Sweet Potatoes and Apples

Pare, core, and cut the apples into thick slices. Place a layer in a buttered baking-dish, cover with slices of boiled sweet potatoes and top with apples. Sprinkle with sugar and dot with butter. Repeat until all the ingredients are used. Bake slowly (325° F.) one hour.

White Asparagus Polonaise

Heat the asparagus in the liquid from the can and drain. Serve covered with bread crumbs, browned in butter. At either end of the platter place cooked lima beans, well seasoned with salt, pepper, and butter.

Cranberry Sherbet

1 pound cranberries
1½ cups water
1 cup sugar

18 marshmallows
¼ cup orange juice
2 teaspoons lemon juice

Cook cranberries in water until tender. Press through a sieve, add sugar, and stir until dissolved. Heat marshmallows in one-half cup of the cranberry juice until they are half-melted. Combine with the remaining cranberry and fruit juices, and blend well. Place in a freezing tray in the refrigerator and stir several times during freezing.

Pumpkin Pudding

4 cups steamed, mashed pumpkin	Dash of nutmeg
2 cups brown sugar	1½ teaspoons salt
1 cup granulated sugar	2 tablespoons melted butter
2 tablespoons molasses	2 tablespoons brandy
3 teaspoons cinnamon	6 eggs, well beaten
3 teaspoons ginger	4 cups cream

Mix pumpkin with one cup brown sugar, granulated sugar, and molasses. Add the seasonings, butter, eggs, and cream. Butter two small casseroles or one large one. Spread remaining sugar on the bottom and pour in the pumpkin mixture. Place in a pan of boiling water and bake in moderate oven (350° F.) for fifty minutes or until set. Chill until ready to serve, then remove to serving platter. Pass with Kirsch and cream.

Sea Food 'Patio'
Whole Wheat Toast
Baked Steak Palais
Hashed-Brown Potatoes
Lima and String Beans
Rolls
Nesselrode Pudding
Coffee

Sea Food 'Patio'

1 tablespoon Gulden mustard	½ cup chili sauce
½ teaspoon English mustard	Salt, pepper
1 teaspoon Worcestershire Sauce	½ chopped green pepper
1 cup mayonnaise	Sea food

Make a paste of the mustards and Worcestershire Sauce. Add the mayonnaise and chili sauce and season to taste. Mix with shrimps, crabmeat, and lobster. Serve in a bowl; sprinkle with green pepper.

Baked Steak Palais

Place a sirloin steak three to four inches thick in a baking-pan. Place on the broiler, sear both sides, and drain off the fat. Sprinkle with salt and pepper. Add one large grated Bermuda onion, one sliced green pepper, three tablespoons melted butter, two tablespoons Worcestershire Sauce, and three-fourths cup catsup. Bake three-quarters of an hour, basting several times. Skim off fat.

Rub a frying-pan well with garlic. Sauté one pound of halved mushrooms in two tablespoons butter. Add one tablespoon Worcestershire Sauce, one-half cup catsup, one cup cream, mixed with two tablespoons flour, and salt and pepper to taste. Cook five minutes. Pour over steak and mix well with the seasoning in the pan. Bake for ten minutes longer before serving.

Hashed-Brown Potatoes (see page 11)

Lima and String Beans

Cook separately, then mix equal parts of lima and string beans. Season with butter, salt and pepper, and toss until well mixed.

Nesselrode Pudding

6 eggs, separated	¼ cup crystallized cherries,
6 tablespoons sugar	chopped
⅛ teaspoon salt	1 cup broken pecans
1¼ cups sherry wine	12 macaroons, crushed
1 tablespoon gelatin	Ladyfingers
1 tablespoon cold water	Whipped cream

Beat egg yolks, sugar, and salt. Add one cup wine. Cook in a double boiler until thick. Soak gelatin in cold water; dissolve in hot custard. Cool and add cherries, nuts, and macaroons. Fold in the stiffly beaten egg whites. Line a mold with ladyfingers. Pour remaining sherry over them and fill with pudding. Place in refrigerator until firm. Remove from mold, and garnish with whipped cream.

> *Bisque of Shrimp*
> *Crown of Lamb with Force Meat*
> *Currant Mint Sauce*
> *Broccoli au Gratin*
> *Sherry Almond Cream*
> *Coffee*

Bisque of Shrimp

2 pounds shrimps	3 cups chicken stock
3 tablespoons butter	1 cup white wine
¼ cup mushrooms	1 cup cream
2 tablespoons chopped carrots	Salt, cayenne

Chop raw shrimps, mushrooms, and carrots; sauté in butter over a slow fire for two or three minutes. Season with salt and cayenne; add chicken stock and boil until shrimps are thoroughly cooked. Press through a coarse sieve; add wine and cream. Reheat almost to the boiling point and serve immediately.

Crown of Lamb

Wrap each rib bone with a thin strip of salt pork; rub meat, inside and out, with salt mixed with paprika, pepper, and a few grains ginger. Fill center with Force Meat. Roast according to rules for Leg of Lamb (see page 231). Remove pork from bones before serving.

Force Meat

Grind the meat cut from the ribs of the lamb, add an equal amount of sausage meat and one cup chopped mushrooms. Season to taste with salt, pepper, onion juice; add enough soup stock to moisten. Mix well and place in center of the crown.

Currant Mint Sauce

With a fork soften a glass of currant jelly but do not beat it. Add one and one-half tablespoons finely chopped mint leaves and grated rind of one-fourth of an orange.

Broccoli au Gratin

2 tablespoons minced onion	1 egg yolk
1 tablespoon butter	1 cup grated Parmesan cheese
1 cup medium white sauce	3 tablespoons buttered crumbs
Cooked broccoli	

Brown onion lightly in butter. Mix with white sauce; add egg yolk and one-half cup of cheese. Pour some of the sauce into a buttered baking-dish. Put the hot broccoli in the sauce and top with remaining sauce, cheese, and buttered bread crumbs. Brown in oven.

Sherry Almond Cream

1 tablespoon gelatin	6 egg whites
$\frac{1}{4}$ cup cold water	$\frac{1}{2}$ teaspoon almond extract
1 cup boiling water	$\frac{1}{3}$ cup sherry
$1\frac{1}{4}$ cups sugar	1 cup blanched, chopped almonds

Soak gelatin in cold water; add boiling water and sugar, and stir until dissolved. Chill the mixture until it begins to stiffen, then beat until frothy. Add stiffly beaten egg whites to the gelatin mixture and blend. Add the almond extract and the sherry. Pour into a mold, alternating layers of the mixture and the chopped almonds. Chill in refrigerator for two hours. Serve with Sherry Custard Sauce.

Sherry Custard Sauce

1 pint milk	$\frac{1}{8}$ teaspoon salt
6 egg yolks	$\frac{1}{2}$ teaspoon vanilla
$\frac{1}{4}$ cup sugar	$\frac{1}{2}$ pint whipping cream
3 tablespoons sherry	

Scald milk in double boiler. Beat the egg yolks lightly and add the sugar and salt. Pour milk slowly into the egg mixture, then return to the double boiler and cook until the mixture coats a spoon. When cool, add the vanilla, whipped cream, and sherry.

Shrimps en Coquille
Baked Broilers with Sweetbread Stuffing
Oranges Filled with Orange Ice
New Potatoes   *Beans Almondine*
Peppermint Chocolate Roll
Coffee

Shrimps en Coquille

2 pounds cooked shrimps	$\frac{1}{8}$ teaspoon pepper
1 clove garlic	Paprika
2 tablespoons flour	$\frac{1}{2}$ cup catsup
2 tablespoons butter, melted	$1\frac{1}{2}$ tablespoons Worcestershire
1 cup cream	Sauce
$\frac{1}{2}$ teaspoon salt	Buttered bread crumbs

Rub pan well with garlic, add flour to melted butter, pour the cream on gradually and cook, stirring constantly until smooth and thick. Add seasonings and shrimps. Fill shells or ramekins. Sprinkle with crumbs; place in a hot oven (400° F.) to brown — ten to twelve minutes.

Baked Stuffed Broilers

Season halved chickens with salt and pepper. Fill cavities with dressing and tie two together. Place in a roasting-pan with a sliced onion and two tablespoons chicken fat or butter over each chicken. Bake in a hot oven (400° F.) until tender, basting frequently (one hour).

To four tablespoons of the fat in which the chickens were cooked, add four tablespoons of flour and brown. Pour on gradually hot chicken stock or two and one-half cups of boiling water. Cook until smooth and thick. Season, and add two tablespoons of sour cream. When ready to serve, cut chickens into halves, garnish platter with orange shells, filled with orange ice.

Sweetbread Stuffing (for Three Broilers)

4 slices dry bread	1 egg white
Water	Chicken livers
3 tablespoons chicken fat	½ pound boiled sweetbreads
1 onion, sliced	1 tablespoon minced parsley
2 egg yolks	Salt, pepper, paprika

Soak the bread in water. Squeeze dry. Brown onion in fat. Add bread and cook until the fat is absorbed. Cool. Add slightly beaten egg yolks and white, puréed livers, sweetbreads broken into small pieces, and seasonings.

Oranges with Orange Ice

Oranges	¼ cup lemon juice
1 cup water	2 cups orange juice
1½ cups sugar	Grated rind of two oranges

Cut oranges into halves, remove fruit and scallop edges. Boil sugar and water until it forms a syrup; cool, add fruit juices and rind, and freeze in freezer. Serve in the orange shells.

Beans Almondine

Cut beans lengthwise and cook until tender in enough boiling water to cover. Place on serving platter, and pour over them blanched and sliced almonds which have been browned in butter.

Chocolate Peppermint Roll

5 eggs, separated	2 tablespoons cocoa
¾ cup powdered sugar	1 tablespoon flour

Beat egg yolks and sugar until thick and lemon-colored. Add stiffly beaten egg whites. Sift dry ingredients and fold into egg mixture. Pour into a large baking-pan lined with oiled paper (batter should not be more than one-half inch thick) and bake in a moderate oven (350° F.) for twenty minutes. Turn out on a damp hot cloth. Remove crust from all four sides, and roll while still warm. Let stand until ready for use; unroll, spread with filling, re-roll, and ice.

Peppermint Filling

To $\frac{1}{2}$ pint whipped cream add $\frac{1}{2}$ cup crushed peppermint-stick candy

OR

Chocolate Filling

$\frac{1}{2}$ pint whipping cream	2 tablespoons Droste's chocolate
$\frac{1}{2}$ cup confectioner's sugar	1 teaspoon vanilla

Add sugar, chocolate, and vanilla to whipped cream. Place in refrigerator for several hours before using.

Icing

$\frac{1}{2}$ cup confectioner's sugar	$\frac{1}{2}$ teaspoon vanilla
1 tablespoon cocoa	2 tablespoons cream

Mix sugar and cocoa. Add flavoring and enough cream to make the right consistency for spreading.

> *Oyster Soup*
> *Minute Steaks*   *Patio Mustard Sauce*
> *French Fried Potatoes*
> *Minted Peas*   *Filbert Torte*
> *Coffee*

Oyster Soup

2 tablespoons onion, grated	1 tablespoon flour
2 tablespoons celery, minced	1 pint bouillon
1 tablespoon parsley, minced	Salt, pepper
2 tablespoons butter	Dash of cayenne

1 pint oysters

Simmer the vegetables in the butter. Add the flour and brown. Gradually add the liquor from the oysters and bouillon. Season and boil for five minutes. Just before serving, add oysters (either whole or cut into small pieces) and cook until they are well heated.

Pan-Broiled Minute Steaks

Trim off the extra fat and use it to grease a hot frying-pan. Sear steak on both sides. Cook three to five minutes, depending on thickness. Sprinkle with salt and pepper. Serve with mustard sauce.

Patio Mustard Sauce

Melt scant one-half cup butter in a hot frying-pan. Add two teaspoons dry mustard, three tablespoons Escoffier Diable Sauce, salt, and black pepper. When thoroughly heated and mixed, remove from flame, add about one-quarter cup cream and blend.

French Fried Potatoes

Wash, pare, and cut potatoes into eighths lengthwise. Soak one hour in cold water; dry; fry in deep hot fat until brown. Drain on unglazed paper. Sprinkle with salt.

Minted Peas

Cook green peas in a small quantity of boiling water. Add salt when nearly tender. Remove lid and allow water to evaporate. Add butter and minced mint leaves. Toss until well mixed.

Filbert Torte

12 eggs, separated	Juice and rind of one orange
⅛ teaspoon salt	1 pound shelled and grated filberts
2 cups sugar	12 stale ladyfingers, grated

Beat egg yolks, salt, and sugar until thick and lemon-colored; add orange. Alternately fold in nuts combined with ladyfingers, and the stiffly beaten egg whites. Bake in a buttered and floured ten-inch spring form in a slow oven (325° F.) for about one hour. When cool, ice with raspberry jelly. Cover with sweetened whipped cream.

Sautéd Goose Liver   *Rye Toast*
Roast Goose
Toulouse Ragout   *Brussels Sprouts*
Cinnamon Apples
Sponge Cake Ring — Peach Melba
OR
Sponge Cake Ring au Rum
Coffee

Sautéd Goose Liver

Carefully remove gall from liver and soak in cold salted water for several hours. Drain and wipe dry. Sprinkle with salt and pepper, a few grains of sugar and ginger. Sauté in hot goose fat and brown on both sides

Roast Goose

Rub goose well inside and out with salt mixed with grated garlic, pepper, paprika, and a few grains of ginger. Stuff and place in a roasting-pan with a sliced onion and diced celery. Prick the skin on breast. Cover closely and roast three to four hours until the meat is tender, basting every fifteen minutes. When tender, remove goose, skim off all but four tablespoons of the fat in the pan, add four tablespoons flour, and brown well. Gradually pour on three cups boiling water, season and cook ten minutes. Strain before serving.

Goose Stuffing

6 slices stale bread	1 teaspoon salt
1 grated onion	Pepper, ginger
2 tablespoons fat	2 tablespoons minced parsley
Gizzard and heart, chopped	1 stalk celery, diced
½ cup tomato purée	1 egg

Soak bread in water and press dry. Sauté onion in fat, add bread, and cook until it has absorbed all the fat. Mix with remaining ingredients.

Toulouse Ragout

Leg and second joint of goose	1 soup bunch
1 pound navy beans	Salt, pepper
3 cloves garlic, grated	1 can tomato purée
¼ pound garlic sausage	Goose fat
Bread crumbs	

Soak beans overnight in cold water. Remove leg and second joint of
goose before it is roasted. Brown in goose fat (or the fat from fried-out
salt pork), garlic, and one-half tablespoon salt. Cover beans and goose
with water and cook slowly for one hour. Add the peeled and sliced
sausage, soup bunch, salt, pepper, tomato purée, and continue cooking
until the skins of the beans burst. If necessary, add more boiling water
to prevent burning. If the goose gets too tender, remove it from the
pot. Grease a deep casserole, place the goose in it, and pour the beans
and sausage over it. Cover with crumbs, well moistened with goose fat,
and bake in a slow oven (325° F.) one hour, until dry and the crumbs
brown.

Brussels Sprouts

Cook Brussels sprouts uncovered in boiling salted water until tender.
Drain and add butter, pepper, and additional salt, if necessary.

Cinnamon Apples

Core and pare apples. Make a syrup of one cup sugar, one and one-half
cups water, and three tablespoons red cinnamon drops. Place apples in
syrup, cover and cook slowly, basting frequently until apples are tender.

Sponge Cake Ring — Peach Melba

6 eggs, separated	Grated rind, ½ orange
1 cup sugar	1 cup pastry flour
1 tablespoon lemon juice	1 teaspoon baking powder
¼ teaspoon salt	

Beat egg yolks and sugar until thick and lemon-colored. Add lemon
juice and orange rind. Sift dry ingredients and fold in alternately with
stiffly beaten egg whites. Pour into a buttered and floured ring mold
and bake in a moderate oven (350° F.) twenty-five to thirty minutes.
Remove from ring. When cold, glaze with melted raspberry jelly, fill
center with vanilla ice cream. Place whole canned peaches around and
tint each with jelly. Serve with Melba Sauce.

Melba Sauce

Mix one cup raspberry pulp and juice, fresh or canned, with one-half cup currant jelly and one-half cup sugar, and bring to boiling point. Add one-half tablespoon arrowroot or cornstarch mixed with one table-spoon cold water. Boil, stirring to prevent burning, until mixture becomes thick and clear. Strain and cool.

OR

Sponge Cake Ring au Rum

When cake ring has been removed from pan, insert a sharp knife at intervals along the top and pour in a little Jamaica rum and apricot brandy. Glaze with jelly. Just before serving, sprinkle with ground pistachio nuts. In the center and outside of the ring, pile fresh strawberries. Serve with a cold boiled custard to which has been added an equal quantity of whipped cream and vanilla or almond flavoring.

Chow-Chow Ring — Thousand Island Dressing
Melba Toast
Baked Fillet of Beef Italienne
Succotash, Haricots
Browned Potato Balls
Pyramid Pudding
Coffee

Chow-Chow Ring

11 hard-cooked eggs	½ cup water
⅔ cup chopped ripe olives	1 tablespoon Worcestershire Sauce
⅔ cup chopped chow-chow	Salt, pepper, paprika
1 cup mayonnaise	Rolled anchovies
1 bottle pearl onions	Halves of peeled tomatoes
1 tablespoon gelatin	Caviar

Rice the eggs and set aside one-fourth cup. Mix remaining part with olives, chow-chow, mayonnaise, and onions. Soak the gelatin in the water. Dissolve over hot water and add to chow-chow mixture with Worcestershire Sauce, salt, pepper, and paprika. Pour into an oiled ring mold and chill. Serve on a bed of lettuce leaves, garnish with rolled anchovies, and place halves of small peeled tomatoes around it. Put the remaining riced egg and caviar in the center of each tomato. Serve with Thousand Island Dressing.

Baked Fillet of Beef Italienne

1 bottle chili sauce	1 pound onions, sliced
1 tablespoon Worcestershire Sauce	

Sprinkle a larded fillet of beef with salt and pepper. Place in a hot oven, cover with chili sauce, onions, and Worcestershire Sauce, and bake twenty-five minutes, basting several times.

Remove the vegetables and juice from the pan in which the fillet was baked, and press through a sieve. Skim off the fat. Brown two tablespoons flour in three tablespoons of the fat, add the juice from the pan with enough soup stock to make two cups. Cook five minutes. Season with salt, pepper, Kitchen Bouquet, and sherry.

Succotash, Haricots

Cook separately equal parts of fresh, frozen or canned corn niblets, baby lima beans, and half the quantity of string beans. Cut beans in very thin slices, crosswise. Combine the vegetables with butter, salt and pepper to taste.

Pyramid Pudding

½ cup sugar	1½ cups white wine
1 tablespoon cornstarch	2 dozen macaroons
⅛ teaspoon salt	Juice of 1 lemon
7 eggs, separated	1 teaspoon grated lemon rind
Blanched almonds	

Mix sugar, cornstarch, and salt, and add the egg yolks and wine. Cook in a double boiler until smooth and thick. Cool. When nearly set, mound on macaroons placed on an ovenware platter. Beat the egg whites until stiff, fold in two tablespoons additional sugar, the lemon juice and rind. Cover custard with meringue and stick in almonds à la porcupine. Brown in the broiler. Serve cold.

Lobster à l' Américaine
Broiled Chicken
Rice and Mushroom Ring
Tutti-Frutti
Burnt Almond Torte
Coffee

Lobster à l'Américaine

2 large onions, chopped	6 cups soup stock
$\frac{1}{2}$ cup butter	4 $1\frac{1}{2}$-pound live lobsters
Paprika	6 tablespoons tomato pulp
Salt	4 tablespoons cognac
6 cups white wine	6 tablespoons sherry

Sauté onion in butter with a little paprika and salt. When deep yellow, add the white wine and soup stock. Cook in skillet until liquid is reduced to half the original amount. Meanwhile, cut the live lobsters in pieces, remove intestinal vein, and cover with salt and pepper. Place the lobsters into the liquid and cook, covered, until it is red. Add the tomato pulp, cognac, and sherry. Cook slowly for fifteen minutes. Remove shells from soup before serving.

Broiled Chicken

Select chickens weighing one and three-fourths to two pounds. Split in half, and sprinkle with salt and pepper. Spread with chicken fat. Place in broiler, skin side down, with a slice of tomato on each. Broil until brown, then turn and brown the other side, basting several times. Reduce the heat and broil until tender (twenty to twenty-five minutes). Strain pan drippings and pour over chickens.

Rice and Mushroom Ring

1 pound mushrooms	1 cup rice
2 tablespoons butter	Salt

Boil rice and rinse in cold water. Put mushrooms through meat-grinder;

sauté in butter. Add rice and seasoning and let simmer fifteen minutes. Put mixture in buttered ring mold; set in pan of boiling water and bake in moderate oven (350° F.) about three-quarters of an hour. Serve with buttered peas in center.

Tutti-Frutti

Select firm, perfect fruit such as strawberries, cherries, red and black raspberries, blackberries, gooseberries, apricots, peaches, pineapples, grapes, and pears.

Start in the spring and place each fruit as it comes in season in a stone crock with a proportion of one pound fruit to one pound sugar. Fruit must be covered with brandy and alcohol in the proportion of one pint brandy to each quart of alcohol. Press down with a weight and cover. Stir carefully every few days to keep sugar from settling on the bottom of the crock. After the last fruit is added, the mixture should stand six to eight weeks and may then be canned.

Note: There will be a great deal of extra juice which may be bottled separately and used for sauces or wine.

Burnt Almond Torte

8 eggs, separated	½ pound blanched and grated almonds
½ pound confectioner's sugar	⅛ teaspoon salt

Beat egg yolks and sugar until light and lemon-colored; add nuts. Fold in stiffly beaten egg whites and salt. Pour into two buttered and floured cake pans. Bake in a moderate oven twenty minutes.

Filling and Frosting

6 ounces sweet butter	3 teaspoons coffee essence
2 cups confectioner's sugar	(or more to taste)
4 egg yolks	Halved browned almonds

Cream butter and sugar. Add yolks separately, then flavoring. Spread between layers and frost cake. Cover with browned halves of almonds, placed in circles, as closely together as possible. Put in the refrigerator for several hours before serving.

> Crabmeat Cocktail
> Roast Beef   Yorkshire Pudding
> Broccoli Ring
> Horseradish Hollandaise Sauce
> Scotch Apple Pie
> Coffee

Crabmeat Cocktail

3 hard-cooked eggs (separated)   ¼ cup vinegar
1 tablespoon butter   Sugar
1 tablespoon prepared mustard   ¼ cup whipped cream
¾ cup Durkee Salad Dressing   Crabmeat

Blend mashed egg yolks with butter. Add remaining ingredients, using a small amount of sugar to taste, and blend all together. Serve over crabmeat and garnish with chopped egg whites.

Roast Beef

Allow meat to stand at room temperature for several hours before roasting. Set oven at 300° about fifteen minutes before meat is to be put in. Place roast beef, fat side up, in roaster. Salt and pepper generously; slice one or two onions over the meat. (Toothpicks will hold them on.)

Roast according to the following timetable:

> *Rare* — about twenty minutes per pound.
> *Medium* — about twenty-five minutes per pound
> *Well done* — about thirty minutes per pound.

Increase oven heat to 425° F. the last fifteen minutes of roasting, to get beef browned.

There will be very little drippings in the roaster, but gravy can be made by following the usual procedure and adding Kitchen Bouquet and Escoffier Sauce for flavor.

Yorkshire Pudding

1½ cups flour	1½ cups milk
¼ teaspoon baking powder	3 eggs
½ teaspoon salt	⅓ cup beef drippings

Mix dry ingredients. Add milk gradually, then the eggs, and beat very well. Place hot drippings from Roast Beef in oblong pan. Pour in batter one inch deep. Bake in moderate oven (350° F.) for twenty to thirty minutes, gradually decreasing the heat. Cut in squares; serve at once around Roast Beef.

Broccoli Ring

2 pounds broccoli	1 cup cream
1 clove garlic	4 eggs, separated
2 tablespoons butter	Salt
2 tablespoons flour	Pepper

Cook broccoli in boiling salted water with the garlic until tender. Remove garlic, drain, and chop broccoli into small pieces. Melt butter, add flour, and gradually pour in the cream. Cook until thick; add beaten egg yolks and broccoli. Fold in the stiffly beaten egg whites, and season. Pour into a buttered and floured ring. Place in a pan of boiling water and bake in a moderate oven (325° F.) thirty minutes.

Horseradish Hollandaise

To Hollandaise sauce (see page 58), just before serving, add one-half cup grated horseradish.

Scotch Apple Pie

Pared and sliced apples	¼ teaspoon salt
1½ cups brown sugar	½ cup butter
1 cup flour	¾ cup chopped nuts

Arrange apples in Pyrex pie plate. Add one-half the sugar. Mix remaining ingredients together; spread over the apples, pressing down around the edge. Bake one hour in moderate oven (350° F.). Serve warm with hard sauce flavored with sherry wine.

Crab Bisque
Melba Toast
Roast of Spring Lamb   Mint Sauce
Braised Onions
Lettuce and Cress Salad
Cherries à la Russe
Marble Cup Cakes

Crab Bisque

1 can tomato soup	$\frac{1}{2}$ pound crab meat
1 can pea soup	$\frac{1}{2}$ cup cream
2 cups beef broth	Sherry

Salt, pepper

Mix soups, bring to a boil, add crab meat and cream. Season with salt, pepper, and sherry.

Roast Lamb

Season the meat with salt and pepper; cover it with sliced onions. (Toothpicks will hold them on.) Place in a pre-heated 300° oven, uncovered, and allow thirty to thirty-five minutes per pound for roasting. Increase to 425° oven the last half-hour, to brown the meat.

Mint Sauce

$\frac{1}{4}$ cup chopped mint leaves   1 tablespoon powdered sugar
$\frac{1}{2}$ cup vinegar

Heat vinegar, add sugar and pour over mint leaves. Let stand thirty minutes. If vinegar is very strong, dilute with water.

OR

Mint Syrup

1 cup sugar
1 tablespoon light corn syrup
$\frac{1}{4}$ cup chopped mint leaves

$\frac{1}{16}$ teaspoon salt
$\frac{1}{2}$ cup water

Add the sugar, syrup, and salt to the water. Cook slowly, stirring constantly until sugar is dissolved, then cook without stirring until it will form a thread. Remove from fire and add mint leaves.

Braised Onions

Peel small silver-skinned onions and cook in boiling water fifteen minutes. Drain and put in a buttered casserole. Add enough highly seasoned soup stock to cover bottom of dish. Sprinkle lightly with sugar and bake until soft, basting with stock.

Lettuce and Cress Salad

Shred outside leaves of lettuce. Quarter the hearts, place on the shredded lettuce, and pile cress high in the center. Sprinkle with chopped egg and serve with Lorenzo Dressing. (Page 78.)

Cherries à la Russe

Drain the juice from two cans pitted black Bing cherries. Add to the cherries one teaspoon lemon juice, two tablespoons sugar, and a few grains cinnamon. Put in a Pyrex pie plate, cover with a glass of currant jelly, sprinkle with blanched and shredded almonds. Bake for ten minutes. Pour a wineglass of Kirsch over cherries and serve lighted.

Marble Cup Cakes

$\frac{1}{2}$ cup butter
$1\frac{1}{2}$ cups sugar
3 eggs, well beaten
2 cups flour

4 teaspoons baking powder
$\frac{1}{4}$ teaspoon salt
$\frac{1}{2}$ cup milk
2 tablespoons cocoa

1 teaspoon vanilla

Cream butter and sugar. Add eggs. Sift flour, baking powder, and salt together and add alternately with the milk. Add vanilla. Divide the batter into two parts. Add cocoa to one. Into small buttered muffin pans put alternate spoons of white and dark batter. Bake in a hot oven (375° F.) for fifteen to twenty minutes. Frost with chocolate or vanilla icing.

Thousand Island Ring with Sea Food
Russian Dressing   *Melba Toast*
Chicken Marengo
Eggplant Fritters   *Baked Alaska Pie*
Coffee

Thousand Island Ring

2 tablespoons gelatin	1 can pimiento, diced
½ cup cold water	½ teaspoon sugar
1 cup chili sauce	Dash of Tabasco Sauce
1½ cups mayonnaise	1 teaspoon Worcestershire Sauce
6 hard-cooked eggs, diced	½ cup catsup
1 cup celery, diced	Sea food (shrimps, crabmeat, or lobster)

Soak gelatin in cold water; place over hot water until dissolved. Mix the remaining ingredients (excepting sea food) and add the gelatin. Pour into an oiled ring mold and chill until firm. Invert on a bed of lettuce and fill the center with sea food. Serve with Russian Dressing and Melba toast.

Chicken Marengo

Cut fryers in quarters or desired size pieces; sprinkle with salt and pepper and dredge with flour; sauté. When tender, remove from pan and keep warm. Using the same pan, make a brown sauce of two tablespoons flour, two tablespoons butter, and a cup of soup stock. (Double according to number of chickens.) Add to this sliced mushrooms, cut-up tomatoes, sliced green olives, and a little white wine to taste. Let simmer about ten minutes and pour over chicken.

Serve with chow mein noodles in the center of the platter, cooked peas sprinkled over the chicken, and a generous amount of browned almonds tossed over all.

Eggplant Fritters

Cook eggplant until tender; mash and season with salt and pepper. Add one egg, two teaspoons baking powder, and enough flour to hold together. Form into round cakes, dredge with flour, and fry in deep fat.

Baked Alaska Pie

1 pastry shell, baked and cooled	3 egg whites
1 pint ice cream, frozen hard	$\frac{1}{4}$ teaspoon cream of tartar
Fruit, fresh or canned	$\frac{1}{2}$ cup sugar

Add cream of tartar to egg whites and beat until stiff. Fold in the sugar gradually. Line pastry shell with sliced peaches or other fruit in season. Sweeten if fruit is tart. Cover fruit with ice cream and top with a few peach slices. Cover with meringue. This must cover the entire surface and must be thick enough to keep the ice cream from melting. Place in hot oven (425° F.) and brown quickly.

Beet and Horseradish Ring
Russian Dressing
Toasted Rye Bread
Broiled Fillet of Beef
Garlic Sauce
Sauté Zucchini *Broiled Tomatoes*
Chocolate Apricot Pudding
Coffee

Beet and Horseradish Ring

1 package lemon Jello	Salt
2 cups boiling water or beet juice	4 tablespoons prepared horseradish
Juice of 1 lemon	Crabmeat or cooked shrimps
1 can beets, riced	Avocado pears

Russian Dressing

Dissolve Jello in water and lemon juice. Chill and allow to congeal partially. Add beets, salt and horseradish. Pour into an oiled ring mold and chill until firm. Invert on shredded lettuce. Surround with halved avocado pears filled with either crabmeat or shrimps well mixed with dressing. Serve additional dressing in the center of ring.

Broiled Fillet of Beef

Season an unlarded fillet of beef with pepper only. Broil twenty to twenty-five minutes, basting constantly with butter. Make a sauce of grated garlic, salt, pepper, paprika, chopped parsley, and melted butter. Pour this on serving platter and roll fillet in it several times so that flavor permeates meat.

Sauté Zucchini

Peel Italian squash as you would cucumbers. Parboil in salted water, drain carefully and dry. When cold, slice lengthwise within an inch of the end, then press gently with hand to make them open like a fan. Sprinkle lightly with flour, salt, and pepper and sauté in butter to a delicate brown on both sides. Place on a hot platter; add lemon juice to the butter in the frying-pan and pour on Zucchini. Sprinkle with finely chopped parsley and serve at once.

Broiled Tomatoes

Cut tomatoes in halves crosswise. Cut off a thin slice from the bottom of each half; sprinkle with salt and pepper. Dip in crumbs, slightly beaten egg, and crumbs again. Place on a buttered broiler and broil six to eight minutes.

Chocolate Apricot Pudding

Crust:
½ cup butter	1 egg
1½ cups flour	2 tablespoons cream

Mix butter and flour; add egg beaten with cream. Line a casserole with a thin layer of the dough; chill. Bake until light tan but not completely done.

Filling:
¾ pound dried apricots	7 eggs, separated
1½ cups sugar	3 ounces bitter chocolate
4 ounces sweet chocolate	

Cook apricots with one-half cup of the sugar; drain well. Beat yolks with remaining sugar. Melt chocolate with a little water; cool. Combine chocolate and egg yolks and fold in beaten whites. Place apricots in crust, pour the chocolate mixture over them and bake in a hot oven (400°) about twenty minutes. Trim off excess crust. Serve with whipped cream.

Baked Shad and Roe
Dill Cucumber   *Melba Toast*
Chicken Florentine
Strawberry Compote
Macaroon Soufflé
Coffee

Baked Shad and Roe

Split and clean a three-pound shad; place in a buttered baking-pan or on a plank. Sprinkle with salt and pepper, and brush with melted butter. Bake twenty-five minutes in a hot oven, basting several times. Spread with Shad Roe mixture.

Roe

3 tablespoons butter	$\frac{1}{3}$ cup cream
1 teaspoon minced chives	2 egg yolks
1$\frac{1}{2}$ tablespoons flour	Salt, pepper, lemon juice

Parboil roe in salted, acidulated water for twenty minutes, remove outside membrane and mash. Melt butter and mix with chives and flour. Pour this very gradually over cream; add roe and cook slowly five minutes. Add egg yolks and season highly with salt, pepper, and lemon juice. Spread over the fish, cover with buttered crumbs, and return to the oven to brown the crumbs slightly. If cooked on a plank, garnish with Duchess potatoes (see page 185) before browning the crumbs. Serve with slices of lemon and sprinkle with minced parsley.

Dill Cucumber

Marinate cucumbers in French Dressing and add finely chopped dill to taste. Serve in a salad bowl on a bed of lettuce.

Chicken Florentine

Chickens   Creamed spinach

Cut fryers in serving portions; sprinkle with salt and pepper and
dredge with flour. Sauté in butter until brown. Add one cup of spinach
broth; cover and cook slowly until the chicken is tender, basting several
times. Cover the bottom of a buttered casserole with creamed spinach,
add the chicken, and bake fifteen to twenty minutes, basting several
times.

Strawberry Compote

Dissolve one package strawberry Jello in one pint hot water. Chill until
slightly thickened, then fold in one quart fresh strawberries. Turn into
a mold and chill until firm. Garnish with whole canned nectarines and
whole peeled apricots.

Macaroon Soufflé

2 tablespoons flour   6 egg whites
4 tablespoons sugar   2 teaspoons vanilla
¼ teaspoon salt   Chopped glacé fruits, soaked in
1 cup milk   brandy
4 egg yolks, beaten   12 macaroons
2 tablespoons butter   1 ounce chocolate, grated

Mix flour, sugar, and salt; gradually add milk and egg yolks. Cook in
a double boiler until thick. Add butter. Cool; and fold in the stiffly
beaten egg whites and the vanilla. Pour half the mixture into a buttered
pudding dish. Cover with fruit, macaroons, and grated chocolate; add
the remaining custard. Place in a pan of boiling water and bake thirty
minutes.

Fish Ring with Lobster Sauce
Broiled Steak, Victor Hugo
Potatoes Anna   Eggplant Garnish
Lettuce — Roquefort Cheese Dressing
Rolled Wafers with Ice Cream
Fudge Sauce
Coffee

Fish Ring

2 tablespoons butter	Salt
2 slices bread	Pepper, paprika
Milk	1 tablespoon minced parsley
5 eggs, separated	1 tablespoon grated onion
2 cups boiled, shredded fish	2 teaspoons lemon juice

Cream butter, add bread soaked in as much milk as it will absorb, egg yolks beaten until light, fish, and the seasonings. Mix thoroughly, and fold in the stiffly beaten egg whites. Pour into a well-buttered and floured ring, with the cover also buttered and floured. Place in a steamer and steam one and one-half hours. Serve with Lobster Sauce.

Lobster Sauce

2 tablespoons butter	Salt
2 tablespoons flour	White pepper
1 teaspoon paprika	Meat from 2 pounds boiled lobster
½ cup milk	½ cup sliced truffles
1 cup cream	Sherry wine

Melt butter. Add flour and paprika. Gradually add milk and cream. Cook until thick and smooth. Add seasonings, lobster meat, truffles, and wine to taste. Heat thoroughly.

Broiled Steak, Victor Hugo

Use a club, porterhouse or sirloin cut of beef. Set the oven for broiler heat (550° F.) and preheat it for 10 minutes with the rack and broiler in position so that it heats up too, along with the oven. Oil the wires of the rack with a piece of suet and place the steak in the center of rack, inserting the broiler pan and rack about 2 or 3 inches below the rack.

If ½ to 2 inches thick place 3 inches below heat. If 1 inch or less use 2 inches.

It will take the following time to cook:

Thickness	Rare (140° F.)	Medium (160° F.)	Well Done (165° F.)
1 inch steak	15 min.	20–25	30 min.
1½ inch steak	25 min.	35 min.	50 min.
2 inch steak	30 min.	40–50	65 min.
Patties (1 inch)	12 min.	15–18	20 min.

When the steak is half done (that is has cooked one-half this time) put a fork into the fatty edges and turn over to brown the other side. Never insert the fork into the lean meat of the steak, for if you do you will lose fine meat juices through the pierced hole. Serve the finished steak broiled the exact time given, on a hot platter brushed with butter. Serve with Sauce Victor Hugo.

Sauce Victor Hugo

1 tablespoon minced shallots
1 tablespoon tarragon vinegar
⅓ cup butter
2 egg yolks
1 teaspoon lemon juice
1 teaspoon meat extract
1 tablespoon grated horseradish

Simmer the shallots in vinegar for three minutes. Add one-third of the butter, the egg yolks, lemon juice, and meat extract. Cook over hot water (not boiling), stirring constantly. As soon as the butter is melted, add one-half the remaining part and when it is melted, add the last part. When the mixture thickens, add the horseradish and salt to taste.

Eggplant Garnish

Pare and slice eggplant. Sprinkle with salt. Stack slices on a plate; cover with a weight and let stand one hour to draw out juice. Dredge with flour and sauté slowly in butter. Serve half a broiled tomato on each slice and top with a broiled mushroom.

Potatoes Anna

Arrange thinly sliced potatoes in layers in a well-buttered iron frying-pan. Season each layer with salt and pepper and brush with melted butter. Bake in a moderate oven until soft and well browned. Turn onto a round serving platter. Sprinkle with minced parsley and place eggplant garnish around potatoes.

Lettuce — Roquefort Cheese Dressing

$\frac{1}{4}$ pound Roquefort cheese	$\frac{1}{2}$ tablespoon Worcestershire
6 tablespoons olive oil	Sauce
$\frac{1}{4}$ teaspoon paprika	$\frac{1}{2}$ teaspoon dry mustard
1 tablespoon lemon juice	1 teaspoon brandy
1 tablespoon tarragon vinegar	Salt

Rub cheese through a sieve. Mix gradually with oil, then add the remaining ingredients and stir until well blended and smooth. Serve over quartered heads of lettuce.

Rolled Wafers

3 eggs	1 cup cake flour
$\frac{3}{4}$ cup sugar	1 teaspoon vanilla, or
1 teaspoon baking powder	1 teaspoon almond extract

Beat eggs until very light; add sugar gradually and beat well. Sift flour, baking powder, and a pinch of salt. Fold into egg mixture; add flavoring.

Drop by spoonfuls on greased cooky sheet about three inches apart. Spread with a spatula so they are about five inches in diameter. Bake at 375° about eight minutes. While warm, roll into cornucopia shapes. (If wafers become too brittle while shaping, place in oven to soften.) Fill with ice cream and serve with either hot or cold Fudge Sauce.

Fudge Sauce

$\frac{1}{3}$ cup boiling water	1 cup sugar
1 ounce grated bitter chocolate	2 tablespoons Karo syrup
1 tablespoon melted butter	$\frac{1}{2}$ teaspoon vanilla
$\frac{1}{8}$ teaspoon salt	

Gradually add water to chocolate and butter; stir until dissolved. Add sugar and syrup; boil five minutes; add vanilla and salt.

Eggs Alpine   *Rye Melba Toast*
Chicken Paprika
Noodles with Caraway Seeds
Beans and Mushrooms
Spiced Apple Balls
Banana Ice Cream
Chocolate Brownies
Coffee

Eggs Alpine

Cut small slices from the flat end of hard-cooked eggs, remove yolks, being careful that whites are not broken. Make a paste of yolks, anchovy paste, and lemon juice to taste. Moisten with mayonnaise. Refill egg whites. Stand upright on slices of tomato placed on shredded lettuce. Garnish tomato slices with rings of green pepper. Blend boiled salad dressing with whipped cream or sour cream and cover egg entirely. Rice egg whites which have been removed and sprinkle over top.

Chicken Paprika

2 young hens	½ cup butter
Flour	2 cups chicken stock or water
2 teaspoons salt	1 pint sour cream
Pepper	1 grated onion
1 teaspoon paprika	2 tablespoons chili sauce
Ginger	1 tablespoon Worcestershire Sauce

Cut chickens into pieces for serving. Sprinkle with flour mixed with salt, pepper, paprika, and ginger, and sauté in butter until brown. Add stock, one-half the cream and seasonings. Cover and cook slowly for one and one-half hours. Skim off any surplus fat and add remaining sour cream. Cook until the chicken is tender. If necessary, thicken gravy with a tablespoon flour mixed with one tablespoon water.

Noodles with Caraway Seeds

Sprinkle buttered noodles (medium width) with poppyseed or caraway seed.

Beans and Mushrooms

1 pound mushrooms   2 pounds string beans

Cut string beans lengthwise; cook and season. Slice mushrooms and sauté in butter. Just before serving, combine and add a little thick cream.

Spiced Apple Balls

4 cups sugar	12 cloves
1 cup white Karo syrup	Cinnamon bark
1 cup white vinegar	Red coloring
$\frac{1}{2}$ cup water	Pippin apples

Cook sugar, syrup, vinegar, water, spices, and apple parings until they form a heavy syrup. Tint red. Cut apples into balls, using a French vegetable-cutter. Drop into syrup and simmer gently until tender and transparent. Place in refrigerator and let stand in the syrup for three or four days. Pack into jars.

Banana Ice Cream

1 cup banana pulp	Grated rind of $\frac{1}{2}$ orange
$1\frac{1}{3}$ tablespoons lemon juice	1 pint whipping cream
$\frac{1}{16}$ teaspoon salt	Confectioner's sugar

Fold the banana, lemon juice, salt, and orange rind into the whipped cream; sweeten to taste. Freeze in ice-cream freezer.

Chocolate Brownies

2 ounces bitter chocolate	$\frac{1}{2}$ cup pastry flour
$\frac{1}{2}$ cup butter	$\frac{1}{3}$ teaspoon salt
2 eggs	1 teaspoon vanilla
1 cup sugar	1 cup chopped pecans

Melt the chocolate and butter over hot water. Cool. Beat eggs and sugar until thick and lemon-colored. Add flour, salt, flavoring, and nuts. Pour into a buttered and floured pan (seven inches by eleven) and bake in a moderate oven twenty to twenty-five minutes. Ice while warm with chocolate frosting (see page 29) and cut into squares.

Salad Laurent
Cheese Puffs
Baked Ham　　　　Sauce Piquante
Spoon Bread
Sweet Potatoes Brulé
Spinach Ring with Creamed Radishes
Coffee Porcupine
Coffee

Salad Laurent

Garlic	Spiced or canned fruit juice
10 fillets anchovies	1 head lettuce, cubed
1 scallion	1 sliced cucumber
1 tablespoon minced parsley	3 tomatoes, cubed
Tarragon vinegar	1 stalk celery, cubed
Worcestershire Sauce	$\frac{1}{2}$ pound French endive, cubed
2 cups mayonnaise	1 bunch radishes, sliced

4 hard-cooked eggs

Rub a salad bowl well with garlic. Grind the anchovies and scallion. Add parsley, a little vinegar, and Worcestershire Sauce. Mix with mayonnaise and add vinegar, diluted with the juice of spiced fruit, until the dressing is somewhat thinner than Thousand Island Dressing. Put vegetables in salad bowl; pour dressing over them and toss until well mixed. Garnish with egg slices.

Cheese Puffs

1 egg yolk	Salt
$\frac{1}{2}$ cup grated American cheese	Paprika
$\frac{1}{4}$ teaspoon dry mustard	Bread

To beaten egg yolk, add cheese, mustard, salt, and paprika. Toast small rounds of bread on one side; spread cheese thickly on untoasted side. Broil in the oven until puffed and brown; about five minutes.

Baked Ham

To roast ham, use no water and place the ham fat side up on a rack. Bake at 325° according to cooking schedule. When glaze is added, the temperature may be increased to 400°.

Cooking Schedule

Weight of Ham	Cooking Time	
16–18 lbs.	4–4½ hours	(15 minutes per lb.)
12–15 lbs.	3½–4 hours	(16 minutes per lb.)
10–12 lbs.	3–3½ hours	(18 minutes per lb.)
8–10 lbs.	2½–3 hours	(20 minutes per lb.)
5– 7 lbs.	2–2½ hours	(22 minutes per lb.)

If the ham is very cold when cooking is started, allow about 5 additional minutes per pound. If a meat thermometer is used, bake to 150 degrees F. internal temperature before glazing, then raise to an internal temperature of 162 degrees F. When nearly done, remove skin, score fat, and cover with brown sugar. Cut diamond-shaped pieces of orange skin; insert a whole clove in each and press into scored section of fat on top of ham. Return to oven and baste several times with orange juice until glazed. Serve surrounded with watercress.

Sauce Piquante

1 glass currant jelly   1 jar Heinz Prepared Mustard

Combine the two; heat thoroughly over hot water.

Spoon Bread

2 cups white corn meal	1½ cups milk
2 cups boiling water	4 tablespoons melted butter
3 eggs	4 teaspoons baking powder
1 teaspoon salt	

Pour the water over the corn meal; mix well. Add the egg yolks, milk, butter, baking powder, and salt. Beat thoroughly. Fold in the stiffly beaten egg whites. Pour into a well-buttered and heated casserole. Bake thirty minutes in a moderate oven (350° F.).

Sweet Potatoes Brulé

Boil sweet potatoes, mash, add butter, and seasonings to taste. Place in a casserole and cover with chopped marrons. Spread lightly with molasses and brown in oven. Pour rum over top and light just before serving. (These may be made into individual balls.)

Spinach Ring with Creamed Radishes

1 peck raw spinach, finely chopped
3 eggs, separated
1 tablespoon butter
1 tablespoon flour
½ cup milk
Salt, pepper

Melt butter, add flour, and blend. Add milk slowly, stirring constantly until thick. Add beaten egg yolks and spinach. Fold in stiffly beaten egg whites and season. Pour mixture into a well-greased ring mold. Bake covered, in a pan of hot water in a moderate oven (350° F.) for thirty-five minutes. Invert and serve creamed radishes in center of ring.

Creamed Radishes

Peel whole young radishes. Boil gently in salted water until tender, but do not allow them to get too soft. Prepare a white sauce and mix with drained radishes.

Coffee Porcupine

1½ dozen ladyfingers
½ pound butter
½ cup sugar
5 egg yolks
5 tablespoons roasted powdered almonds
2 teaspoons vanilla
½ cup strong coffee (scant)
Whipped cream
Toasted almonds

Cream butter, add sugar and blend thoroughly; add egg yolks, one at a time, creaming each time. Add powdered almonds, vanilla, and the cold coffee, drop by drop. Stir the entire mixture until perfectly smooth.

Line a two-quart melon mold with ladyfingers. Spread with coffee mixture and alternate mixture and ladyfingers until all are used. Chill for 12 hours. Invert and cover with whipped cream. Stick the whole surface with toasted almond strips (these strips should be cut before toasting). Make a porcupine face with pieces of chocolate.

Avocado Cocktail
Chicken Valencienne
Asparagus Polonaise   Bibb Lettuce Salad
Chocolate Profiterolles
Coffee

Avocado Cocktail

2 cups diced avocado $\frac{1}{4}$ cup mayonnaise
1 cup diced celery $\frac{1}{2}$ cup chili sauce
1 tablespoon minced chives   Juice of $\frac{1}{2}$ lemon
                Chopped bacon

Sauté bacon until crisp; drain. Mix avocado, celery, and chives
with the mayonnaise, chili sauce, and lemon. Serve in cocktail glasses
and sprinkle the bacon over the top.

Chicken Valencienne

3 chickens, quartered   2 green peppers, chopped fine
Salt, pepper, paprika   2 cloves garlic, grated
Dash of cayenne   2 tomatoes, peeled and cut
Ginger   1 pimiento
1 stalk celery, chopped fine   2 pounds fresh peas
Bay leaf   1 pound mushrooms
2 large onions, chopped fine $\frac{1}{3}$ teaspoon saffron
1 cup butter, melted   1 cup soup stock
2 cups rice   Hard-cooked egg
$\frac{1}{2}$ cup olive oil   Minced parsley

Rub chicken with salt, pepper, paprika, cayenne, and a few grains of
ginger. Put in a greased baking-pan with celery, bay leaf, onion, and
butter. Place in a hot oven and brown quickly. Cover and bake slowly
for forty-five minutes, basting frequently.

Wash rice, add olive oil, remaining vegetables, and enough water to
cover. Cook slowly, covered, for twenty minutes. Boil saffron in soup

stock three minutes; add to the rice and season to taste. Continue cooking twenty-five minutes longer. Place one-half of this mixture in a large casserole, add the chicken, and cover with the remainder of the rice mixture. Sprinkle with the chopped hard-cooked egg and minced parsley. Bake in a slow oven twenty minutes.

Asparagus Polonaise

Brown bread crumbs in butter. Pour over cooked asparagus.

Bibb Lettuce Salad

1 cup salad oil	Dash of tarragon vinegar
⅓ cup lemon juice	Small amount of sugar, to taste
	Salt, pepper

Beat ingredients until well blended. Pour over a bowl of bibb lettuce and toss until leaves are lightly coated with dressing.

Chocolate Profiterolles

½ cup butter	4 eggs
1 cup boiling water	Vanilla ice cream
1 cup flour	Chocolate sauce
	Chopped nuts

Heat to the boiling point butter and water and add the flour all at once; stir vigorously; remove from fire as soon as mixed, and add unbeaten eggs, one at a time, beating after the addition of each egg. Drop by spoonfuls on a buttered sheet, one and one-half inches apart, making them as circular as possible. Bake in a hot oven (400° F.) for a half-hour. Remove one from the pan; if it does not fall, they are done. Cool, and cut open on one side. Fill with ice cream, cover with chocolate sauce, and sprinkle with nuts. Make puffs small and allow about three for a portion.

Petite Marmite
Roast Duck, Giblet Gravy
Wild Rice and Mushroom Stuffing
Apple Compote   *Torte Elysée*
Coffee

Petite Marmite

Add cooked peas, string beans, chopped onion, and small cubes of breast of chicken to clear bouillon. Serve in individual casseroles. Place in each a slice of French bread, sprinkle with grated Parmesan cheese, and place in oven for two minutes.

Roast Duck

Rub duck, inside and out, with salt mixed with a grated clove of garlic, pepper, paprika, and a few grains ginger. Fill with stuffing and roast in an uncovered pan in a slow oven (325° F.), allowing twenty to thirty minutes per pound. Prick the fat skin with a fork from time to time. Serve with giblet gravy (see page 230).

Wild Rice and Mushroom Stuffing

½ pound mushrooms, sliced	Salt, pepper
1 cup wild rice	2 tablespoons butter

Cook rice in boiling water until not completely tender. Sauté mushrooms in the butter. Add to the rice and season.

Apple Compote

6 apples	1 cup white wine
Cold water	Stick of cinnamon
1 cup water	½ lemon — rind and juice
	½ cup sugar

Pare and core apples; cover with cold water. Drain. Simmer parings with one cup water, wine, lemon rind, and cinnamon for fifteen minutes. Strain through a cheesecloth. Add sugar and boil slowly for three minutes. Put in the apples, cover, and cook slowly until tender. Remove apples, boil juice until it is a heavy syrup. Add lemon juice. Replace the apples and cool. Pyramid the apples in a fruit dish and pour the syrup over them.

Torte Elysée

6 eggs, separated	1 teaspoon baking powder
1¼ cups sugar	3 tablespoons lemon juice
¼ teaspoon salt	1 teaspoon vanilla
1 cup pastry flour	2 cups whipping cream

Beat the egg yolks, sugar, and salt until thick and lemon-colored. Fold in the sifted flour and baking powder, alternately with the six stiffly beaten egg whites, lemon juice, and vanilla. Pour into two buttered and floured layer-cake pans. Spread over layers a meringue made by beating four egg whites until stiff and folding in four tablespoons of sugar. Sprinkle one layer with shredded blanched almonds, the other with coconut. Bake in a moderate oven (350° F.) twenty minutes. Spread whipped cream between layers and around sides of cake. Sprinkle sides with shredded, blanched almonds, browned in butter.

> *Crabmeat en Coquilles*
> *Rolled Asparagus Sandwich*
> *Roast Capon*
> *Peas in Casserole*   *Brandied Peaches*
> *Marron Mousse*
> *Coffee*

Crabmeat en Coquilles

1 pound crab flakes	Worcestershire Sauce
½ cup cream sauce	2 tablespoons catsup
1 egg, beaten	Salt, pepper
2 tablespoons minced parsley	1 tablespoon horseradish
½ tablespoon lemon juice	Buttered bread crumbs

Combine crabmeat and other ingredients lightly together. Fill shells, or ramekins, sprinkle with crumbs and bake until they are brown, ten to twelve minutes.

Rolled Asparagus Sandwich

Cut wafer-thin slices of bread, remove crusts, and spread lightly with mayonnaise. Place an asparagus tip on each and roll.

Roast Capon

Season capon inside and out with salt, pepper, paprika, and a few grains of ginger. Fill with Russian Poultry Stuffing, and place in a roasting pan with one-fourth cup chicken fat, an onion, celery, carrot, and parsley. Roast in a slow oven (325°) from twenty-two to thirty minutes to the pound. Baste frequently with drippings and more butter if necessary.

Russian Poultry Stuffing (for two capons)

1 pound calves' liver	Salt, pepper, paprika
3 tablespoons butter	1 teaspoon sugar
½ pound walnut meats	2 tablespoons grated onion
2 cups soft bread crumbs	2 tablespoons minced parsley
3 eggs, beaten	½ teaspoon lemon juice
1 cup cream	Sherry wine

Sauté liver in butter, put through a food-chopper with the walnuts. Add the other ingredients and flavor with sherry.

Giblet Gravy

Pour off liquid from pan in which capon has been roasted. Brown four tablespoons fat in four tablespoons flour; add two cups stock in which giblets, neck, and tip of wings have been cooked. Cook five minutes; season with salt and pepper, add chopped giblets and serve hot with the capon.

Peas in Casserole

2 cups peas	1 cup cream sauce
1 can mushrooms, *or*	1 tablespoon butter
1 cup sautéed mushrooms	1 small onion, grated
4 hard-cooked eggs, sliced	1 can tomato soup
1 cup diced celery	Salt, pepper
Buttered bread crumbs	

Fill casserole with alternate layers of peas, mushrooms, eggs, celery, and cream sauce. Melt butter and sauté onion in it. Add soup and season. Pour over vegetables, cover with crumbs, and bake in a hot oven for fifteen minutes.

Brandied Peaches (see page 102)

Marron Mousse

1½ cups blanched almonds	1½ pint whipping cream
¼ cup sugar	2 bottles marrons
Vanilla or Rum	

Chop almonds medium fine. Caramelize sugar; add almonds and brown. Pour into mold while hot. Whip cream and sweeten to taste. Add one teaspoon vanilla or two teaspoons rum. Cut marrons fine and add to cream. Pour into mold over caramelized almonds. Pack in ice and salt for four hours.

Egg and Avocado Salad Bowl
Leg of Lamb, Southern Style
Boston Baked Potatoes
Pea and Mushroom Soufflé
Date Pudding
Coffee

Egg and Avocado Salad Bowl

1 clove garlic, cut
1 thin slice Roquefort cheese, crumbled
2 avocado pears, cut in Julienne strips

1 head lettuce, shredded
3 hard-cooked eggs, sliced
French Dressing

Rub a salad bowl with the garlic. Toss the remaining ingredients lightly with French Dressing and serve from bowl.

French Dressing

1 cup salad oil
⅓ cup vinegar or lemon juice
½ teaspoon salt
1 teaspoon Worcestershire Sauce

1 teaspoon dry mustard
1 teaspoon grated onion
½ clove of garlic
½ teaspoon paprika

Rub bowl well with garlic. Mix ingredients and chill. Shake or beat well before using.

Leg of Lamb, Southern Style

Season leg of lamb with salt and pepper. Rub with a clove of garlic and put a few slices of onion on the roast. Place in a preheated 300° F. oven, uncovered, and allow thirty to thirty-five minutes per pound for roasting. (For roast weighing less than five pounds, increase roasting time about ten minutes per pound.)

One half-hour before it has finished roasting, increase heat to 425° to brown meat; pour over the following sauce and baste several times. Scrape sauce from roaster, strain, and serve as gravy.

Sauce

| 2 tablespoons butter | 1 cup catsup |
| Juice of 1 lemon | 2 tablespoons vinegar |

Worcestershire Sauce to taste

Melt butter in skillet, add other ingredients, blend and pour over meat.

Boston Baked Potatoes

Wash, pare, and soak medium-sized potatoes for half-hour. Drain, dry, and sprinkle with salt. Place on a rack in the oven and bake thirty-five to forty minutes.

Pea and Mushroom Soufflé

$\frac{1}{2}$ pound mushrooms	1 cup cream
1 teaspoon grated onion	5 eggs, separated
2 tablespoons butter	1 can French peas
2 tablespoons flour	Salt, pepper, paprika

Chop three-fourths of the mushrooms. Sauté with onion in melted butter and add the flour. Add the cream gradually. Cook until thick. When cool, add to the beaten egg yolks with the drained peas and seasonings. Fold in the stiffly beaten egg whites. Pour into a buttered casserole. Top with remaining mushrooms. Place in a pan of boiling water in a moderate oven (350° F.) and bake until set.

Date Pudding

6 eggs, separated	3 tablespoons flour
1 cup sugar	1 teaspoon baking powder
$\frac{1}{2}$ pound dates, chopped	$\frac{1}{8}$ teaspoon salt
$\frac{1}{2}$ pound walnut meats, chopped	1 teaspoon vanilla

Beat egg yolks and sugar until thick and lemon-colored. Mix dates, nuts, and flour. Add to the eggs and sugar. Fold in the stiffly beaten egg whites mixed with the baking powder, salt, and flavoring. Bake in two buttered and floured tins in a moderate oven (350° F.) for fifteen to twenty minutes. Serve warm with whipped cream between layers and on top.

> *Chow-Chow Fish*
> *Broiled Duckling*
> *Kumquat Jelly   Beets Huszar*
> *Chocolate Angel Pie*

Chow-Chow Fish

Place in a fish boiler or wrap in a cheesecloth a salmon trout weighing four to five pounds. Do not remove the head and tail. Add water to cover, in which an onion, carrot, cut stalk of celery, parsley, bay leaf, clove, one-fourth cup vinegar, one lemon, sliced, salt and pepper have been cooked ten minutes. Boil fish until the flesh separates from the bone; remove to serving platter. Before serving, remove skin, pour over the sauce, and surround with Tomatoes Filled with Cucumbers.

Sauce

1 large bottle chow-chow, chopped very fine
½ cup chili sauce
6 hard-cooked eggs, riced
1½ cups mayonnaise
1 tablespoon minced parsley
1 tablespoon minced green pepper

Combine all ingredients.

Broiled Duckling

3 ducklings
Duck fat or butter
Salt, pepper, paprika
¼ teaspoon ginger

Cut each duckling into quarters, removing backbone. Rub entire surface with fat and sprinkle with seasonings. Place, skin side up, on broiler rack in a moderate oven (350° F.) and broil until brown, fifteen to twenty minutes on each side. Baste several times with drippings from the pan or additional melted fat. Serve with Giblet Gravy.

Giblet Gravy

Simmer giblets and backbones of ducklings in two cups of water until tender. Brown two tablespoons flour in two tablespoons of the drippings in the broiler pan. Gradually add one and one-half cups stock from giblets. Cook for three minutes, strain, and add a few drops Kitchen Bouquet.

Kumquat Jelly

3 cups kumquats	2 cups sugar
Juice of ½ lemon	¾ cup sauterne
3 cups water	Gelatin

Cold water

Cut kumquats into thin slices and add to lemon juice, water, and sugar, which have been cooked together five minutes. Cook slowly until kumquats are tender. Cool, add sauterne and measure. For each pint, add one tablespoon gelatin softened in two tablespoons cold water and dissolved over hot water. Chill until partially congealed; stir and pour into mold rinsed with cold water; chill until firm. Remove to serving dish and garnish with Candied Kumquats.

Candied Kumquats

Add one cup sugar to one cup kumquats, cover with water and simmer until tender. Remove from syrup; when almost dry roll in granulated sugar.

Beets Huszar

6 medium-sized beets, cooked	¼ teaspoon pepper
1 tablespoon flour	2 tablespoons vinegar
2 tablespoons sugar	1 tablespoon lemon juice
½ teaspoon salt	2 tablespoons salad oil

½ cup thick sour cream

Shred beets. Mix dry ingredients; add vinegar, lemon juice, and oil. Cook slowly until thick, stirring constantly. Mix with shredded beets and heat thoroughly. Add sour cream and bring to the boiling point.

Chocolate Angel Pie

2 egg whites	½ cup sugar
⅛ teaspoon salt	½ cup chopped nuts
⅛ teaspoon cream of tartar	½ teaspoon vanilla

Beat egg whites until foamy; add salt and cream of tartar. Beat until mixture stands in soft peaks. Add sugar and beat until very stiff. Fold in nuts and vanilla. Turn into a lightly greased eight-inch pie plate, building up sides and leaving center as a shell for the filling. Bake in a slow oven (300° F.) fifty-five minutes. Cool.

Filling

1 bar Baker's Sweet Chocolate	3 tablespoons hot water
(¼ pound)	1 teaspoon vanilla
1 cup cream, whipped	

Melt chocolate in double boiler. Add the hot water and blend. Cool add vanilla and fold in whipped cream. Fill shell and chill.

Shrimp Avocado Cocktail
Broiled Chicken, Vanderbilt
Noodle Timbales   Eggplant Shelburne
Ils Flottante Pralinée

Shrimp Avocado Cocktail

36 shrimps, cooked and cleaned	26 small pearl onions
1½ large avocado	Juice of 1½ large limes

1¼ cup Russian dressing, well chilled

Cut each shrimp into three pieces; dice avocado into one-half inch squares. Combine shrimps, avocado, and onions and squeeze lime juice over all. Mix with Russian dressing and serve in chilled cocktail glasses.

Broiled Chicken, Vanderbilt

4 broilers, split	1 cup sauterne
1 onion, sliced	Garlic, lemon juice
1 carrot, sliced	Salt, pepper, paprika
2 cups water	Butter

1 tablespoon flour

Simmer necks, giblets, onions, and carrots in water until tender. Add wine and strain. Chop giblets fine. Rub chicken with a cut clove of garlic and sprinkle with salt, pepper, paprika, and a few drops of lemon juice. Place skin side down in a shallow pan, brush with butter, and place under broiler. Baste with the wine sauce frequently and turn occasionally. When chickens are tender and brown (thirty minutes) remove from pan. Thicken remaining sauce with the flour and a few drops of Kitchen Bouquet. Add chopped giblets, cook until thickened, and pour over chicken.

Noodle Timbales

1 package fine noodles	½ cup milk
(8 ounces)	Salt
2 eggs	Pepper

Beat eggs until light, add milk and seasoning. Mix with the boiled noodles and pack in well buttered, individual timbale molds. Bake in a moderate oven about thirty minutes. Serve on the platter with the chicken.

Eggplant Shelburne

Peel eggplant and cut in slices about an inch thick. Scoop out some of the center of each slice, fry in deep fat until brown. Fill with creamed spinach (see page 184) and garnish with riced egg.

Ile Flottante Pralinée

Custard:

5 egg yolks	1½ cup milk
5 tablespoons sugar	1 tablespoon rum
3 tablespoons whipped cream	

Beat egg yolks and sugar; add milk and stir over fire until thick. Cool, flavor with rum; add whipped cream.

Meringue:

7 egg whites	3 tablespoons water and
2 tablespoons gelatin	lemon juice, mixed
5 tablespoons sugar	

Melt gelatin in water and lemon juice and dissolve over heat. Fold carefully into stiffly beaten egg whites, add sugar and stir over ice or cold water until set. Scoop egg shaped balls of meringue by using two large oiled spoons.

Caramel:

½ cup sugar	1 tablespoon white corn syrup
¼ cup water	

Cook to a light caramel without stirring.

Place custard in bowl; cover with meringue balls. Dip fork into caramel and shake back and forth over meringue.

Summer Dinners

```
        Crème Vichyssoise
Filet Mignon              Sauce Béarnaise
          Spanish Corn
  Spring Salad    California Cheese Cake
                Coffee
```

Crème Vichyssoise

4 leeks	Pinch of cayenne
1 small onion, thinly sliced	5 medium potatoes, thinly sliced
2 tablespoons butter	1 quart veal or chicken stock
½ teaspoon salt	3 cups cream

Chopped chives

Cut white part of leeks into fine strips. Add sliced onion and brown lightly in butter. Add potatoes, soup stock, and seasoning. Cover and simmer gently for half an hour. Pass through a fine strainer, forcing as much vegetable pulp through as possible. Cool and add cream. Chill, and when ready to serve, garnish each cup with finely chopped chives.

Sautéed Filet Mignon

Cut beef tenderloins in slices, one inch thick. Bind with bacon around the edge and fasten with a small skewer or toothpick. Season with salt and pepper and broil six minutes in a hot buttered frying-pan. Serve each on a heated heart of artichoke.

Sauce Béarnaise

2 tablespoons tarragon vinegar	4 tablespoons butter
1 tablespoon water	¼ cup soup stock
1 teaspoon onion, grated	½ teaspoon salt
4 egg yolks	⅛ teaspoon paprika

½ tablespoon minced parsley

Heat vinegar, water, and onion; cool. Add yolks, one at a time, and

stir. Cook in a double boiler, stirring constantly until smooth. Gradually add the butter, soup stock, and seasoning.

Spanish Corn

¼ cup olive oil	1 cup catsup
4 cups corn kernels	2 tablespoons Worcestershire Sauce
1 chopped green pepper	Salt, pepper
2 tablespoons butter	1 teaspoon paprika

Heat oil, add the corn and green pepper, and sauté for three minutes. Add remaining ingredients and cook in a double boiler twenty minutes.

Spring Salad

Watercress	Tomatoes
Scallions	Radishes
French Dressing	

Toss together with French Dressing.

California Cheese Cake

Crust:

¾ package Zwieback	½ cup melted butter
¼ cup sugar	1 teaspoon cinnamon

Mix ingredients. Press three-fourths of mixture on bottom and sides of a ten-inch spring form. Pour in Cheese Filling.

Cheese Filling:

2 pounds cream cheese	1 tablespoon lemon juice
⅛ teaspoon salt	1 pint sour cream
1 cup sugar	4 tablespoons sugar
4 eggs, well beaten	1 teaspoon vanilla

Cream the cheese. Beat eggs and one cup sugar until thick and lemon-colored; add to the cheese with the lemon juice and salt. Beat well with rotary beater. Pour into lined spring form; bake in a moderate oven (375° F.) for twenty minutes. Blend the cream, four tablespoons sugar and vanilla; spread over partially baked cake, sprinkle with remaining Zwieback crumbs, and bake in a hot oven (475° F.) ten minutes. When cool, place in refrigerator for several hours. Remove an hour before serving.

Vegetable Platter
Sour-Cream Dressing
Caraway Crisps
Chicken Louisiane
Corn on Cob   *Clover-Leaf Rolls*
Fruited Orange Ice   *Petit Fours*
Frosted Grapes
Coffee

Vegetable Platter

Head of cauliflower   Cherry tomatoes
Asparagus tips   Lettuce
Sour cream dressing

Cook cauliflower until partially tender. Drain and chill. Serve on a bed of lettuce with asparagus tips, cherry tomatoes, and sour-cream dressing.

Sour-Cream Dressing

1 cup sour cream   1 tablespoon horseradish
½ cup mayonnaise   Dash of cayenne
1 teaspoon lemon juice   Salt, paprika
¼ teaspoon dry mustard

Mix all together.

Caraway Crisps

2 cups flour   ½ cup shortening
2 teaspoons salt   1 cup grated cheese
4 to 6 tablespoons water

Sift flour with salt and cut in shortening. Add cheese, mix well, and add water gradually. Mix into a dry crumbly dough. Toss on lightly floured board and roll and fold until smooth. Roll about one-eighth inch thick and cut into diamond-shaped pieces. Brush with milk and sprinkle with caraway seeds. Bake in 425° oven for fifteen minutes.

Chicken Louisiane

Frying chickens
Salt, pepper, paprika, ginger
Fat from salt pork, or butter
½ pound mushrooms, sliced
4 artichoke hearts, sliced

3 tablespoons butter, melted
3 tablespoons flour
2 cups soup stock
Stoned olives
Chopped chives

Sherry wine

Cut chicken into pieces for serving; season with salt, pepper, paprika, and a few grains ginger. Sauté with butter or salt pork fat; cover and cook until brown and tender. Remove chickens. Using same pan, sauté mushrooms and artichokes in the melted butter, add the flour, gradually pour on the soup stock. Add olives, chives, salt, and paprika, cook for five minutes; flavor with sherry. Before serving pour over the chicken.

Corn on Cob

Cook in boiling water five to ten minutes. Serve with melted butter, salt, and pepper.

Clover-Leaf Rolls

Grease muffin pans. Roll refrigerator dough (see page 18) into one-inch balls, place three in each muffin cup. Brush all sides with melted butter. Cover and let rise. Bake fifteen to twenty minutes at 400° F.

Fruited Orange Ice

3 cups sugar
1 cup water
5 cups orange juice

½ cup lemon juice
Grated rind ½ orange
3 bananas, sliced

½ cup maraschino cherries, sliced

Make a syrup of sugar and water; cool. Mix orange juice, lemon juice, and grated orange rind; add syrup and sweeten to taste. Freeze in freezer. When half-frozen, add bananas and cherries and continue freezing. Serve on a large platter in a mound surrounded by summer fruits such as Bing cherries, melon balls, strawberries, and raspberries.

OR

Frosted Grapes

Dip clusters of purple or seedless grapes in slightly beaten egg white. When nearly dry, shake finely granulated sugar over them.

Petit Fours

5 eggs, separated	$\frac{3}{4}$ cup sugar
$\frac{1}{2}$ grated lemon rind	$\frac{2}{3}$ cup pastry flour
$\frac{1}{8}$ teaspoon salt	

Beat egg yolks, lemon rind, and sugar until thick and lemon-colored. Alternately fold in sifted dry ingredients and the stiffly beaten egg whites. Bake in small buttered and floured muffin pans (one and one-half inches wide) in a moderate oven. When cold, remove a small section from the top, scoop out center, fill with custard, re-cover and ice. Decorate with bits of candied cherries, colored pineapple, angelica, or pistachio nuts.

Custard

3 tablespoons sugar	4 egg yolks
$\frac{1}{16}$ teaspoon salt	1 cup milk
1 tablespoon cornstarch	1 tablespoon butter
2 teaspoons vanilla	

Mix sugar and salt with cornstarch; add to the beaten egg yolks and gradually pour on the cream. Cook in a double boiler until thick, stirring constantly. Add butter and vanilla, and cool.

Uncooked Icing

2 tablespoons butter	Cream
2 cups confectioner's sugar	Vanilla

Cream butter, add sugar with sufficient cream to make the right consistency for spreading. Flavor and color as desired.

Borsht, Standard Club   Toast Melba
Stuffed Baked Fish   Lattice Potatoes
String Bean Salad
Allegretti Cake   Fresh Berries

Borsht, Standard Club

2 bunches of beets (or 1½ pounds)
1 medium size onion
1 quart water
2 quarts milk, part cream
3 eggs
3 egg yolks

Juice of 2 lemons
Rind of 1 lemon
Worcestershire Sauce
Salt, pepper
2 teaspoons sugar
Sour cream

Peel and chop raw beets and onion very fine. Boil in the water until thoroughly cooked. Simmer grated lemon rind and juice for a few minutes and strain into beets. Heat milk; beat eggs and carefully add to milk and cook to 180°, stirring constantly. Add a dash of Worcestershire, sugar, salt and pepper to taste. Strain and combine with beets. Chill and serve very cold with a teaspoon of sour cream on each portion.

Stuffed Baked Fish

4 to 5 pounds pike
¾ teaspoon salt, pepper, paprika
Ginger
2 cups tomatoes
1 cup water
1 onion

3 cloves
1 bay leaf
½ tablespoon sugar
3 tablespoons butter
2 tablespoons flour
4 strips bacon

Season a boned fish, inside and out, with salt, pepper, paprika, and ginger. Stuff and sew. Cook tomatoes, water, onion, cloves, bay leaf, and sugar for twenty minutes. Melt butter, add flour, and mix with hot liquid. Cook ten minutes and strain. Pour one-half over the fish, place bacon on top, and bake one hour, basting often. Serve with remaining sauce.

Stuffing

1 pound shrimp	1 small glass truffles
1 can mushrooms	1 small glass capers

Juice of $\frac{1}{2}$ lemon

Mix all together.

Lattice Potatoes (see page 24)

String Bean Salad

1 pound green beans	2 tablespoons vinegar
2 tablespoons pearl onion	1 cup bean liquid
2 tablespoons olive oil	$\frac{1}{2}$ tablespoon sugar

Salt, paprika

Cook beans in boiling salted water until tender; drain, reserving one cup of the liquid. Mix bean broth with the remaining ingredients. Pour over the beans while hot. Serve cold, garnished with pearl onions.

Allegretti Cake

3 ounces chocolate	3 teaspoons baking powder
6 ounces butter	$\frac{1}{8}$ teaspoon salt
3 eggs	$\frac{3}{4}$ cup milk
$1\frac{1}{2}$ cups sugar	1 teaspoon vanilla
$1\frac{1}{8}$ cups pastry flour	Marshmallows

Melt chocolate and butter. Beat eggs and sugar until light; add chocolate and sifted dry ingredients alternately with the milk and vanilla. Beat vigorously. Bake in two layers in a moderate oven.

Marshmallow Filling

$1\frac{1}{2}$ cups white Karo syrup	Pinch of salt
2 egg whites	Vanilla

Have water boiling in lower part of double boiler. Put syrup in upper part of double boiler first, then unbeaten egg whites and salt. Start beating immediately, with electric beater preferably, and cook for six or seven minutes, beating constantly. Remove from fire, fill lower part of double boiler with cold water, and continue beating until filling seems thick enough to spread on cake — about five minutes; add vanilla.

A square of bitter chocolate melted with a small amount of butter can be dripped over the cake after the marshmallow filling is on.

Salmon Mousse with Cucumber Sauce
Melba Toast
Potted Pigeon
Corn Pudding   Finger Rolls
Whipped Cream Raspberry Ice   Pecan Balls
Coffee

Salmon Mousse

2 pounds salmon	1 tablespoon Worcestershire Sauce
2 tablespoons gelatin	1 teaspoon lemon juice
½ cup cold fish stock	1 tablespoon onion juice
1 cup boiling fish stock	Salt, pepper
¾ cup mayonnaise	¾ pint whipping cream

Cook fish in seasoned vegetable water. Soak gelatin in cold fish stock. Add the boiling stock and stir until dissolved; cool. When mixture begins to thicken, add mayonnaise. Beat until frothy; add finely minced salmon (or any fish), and seasonings. Fold in the whipped cream. Turn into a fish-mold. Chill until firm. Serve on shredded lettuce leaves with Cucumber Sauce.

Cucumber Sauce

Peel and grate a large cucumber. Combine with one cup mayonnaise, one-half teaspoon prepared mustard, one tablespoon lemon juice, and one tablespoon minced chives.

Potted Pigeon

8 pigeons	½ cup soup stock
Salt, pepper, paprika, ginger	1 cup celery, cut in thin strips
Flour	1 cup carrots, cut in thin strips
1 large onion, sliced	1 cup onions, cut in thin strips
1 cup poultry or bacon fat	½ pound sliced mushrooms

3 tablespoons flour

Rub pigeons inside and out with salt, pepper, paprika, and a few grains

ginger; dredge with flour. Brown the sliced onion in the melted fat,
then remove the onion. Place the pigeons in the fat; add the soup stock
and cook slowly two hours, basting and turning the pigeons every fifteen
minutes. Add celery, carrots, onions, and mushrooms. Cook an hour
longer or until tender. For gravy pour off all the liquid and skim.
Brown two tablespoons flour in three additional tablespoons of fat.
Gradually add the liquid in which the pigeons were cooked, with enough
water to make two cups. Season and boil five minutes.

Corn Pudding

1 can corn kernels *or*	1 cup cream
2 cups fresh corn	1 teaspoon salt, dash of pepper
4 eggs, separated	1 tablespoon sugar
1 tablespoon flour	

Score fresh corn before cutting off cob. Drain off any liquid. Add the
well-beaten egg yolks, cream, salt, pepper, sugar, and flour. Fold in
the stiffly beaten whites of eggs. Pour into a well-buttered casserole,
place in a pan of boiling water, and bake in a moderate oven (350° F.)
thirty minutes or until set.

Finger Rolls (see page 18)

Whipped Cream Raspberry Ice

1 quart raspberries	$\frac{1}{2}$ cup water
1$\frac{1}{2}$ cups sugar	Juice of $\frac{1}{3}$ lemon
$\frac{1}{2}$ pint whipping cream	

Crush the berries, press through a sieve, extracting all the juice. Cook
the sugar, water, and lemon juice for ten minutes or until a heavy syrup
is formed. Add this to the fruit juice, cool, and freeze in freezer. When
frozen, fold in the beaten cream, repack, and let stand until ready
to serve.

Pecan Balls

$\frac{1}{2}$ pound sweet butter	2 cups ground pecans
$\frac{1}{2}$ cup sugar	(measure before grinding)
2 teaspoons vanilla	2 cups pastry flour
Confectioner's sugar	

Cream butter and sugar; add vanilla, nuts, and flour. Shape into balls
the size of a marble. Bake in a slow oven (300° F.) twenty-five to
thirty minutes. While hot, roll in confectioner's sugar. When cool,
dust with vanilla sugar (see page 6).

Jellied Consommé Russe
Charcoal-Broiled Chicken
French Fried Potatoes
Green Beans, Hollandaise
Red Cabbage Filled with Cole Slaw
Chocolate Marshmallow Ice Cream
Sandwich Cookies
Iced Coffee

Jellied Consommé Russe

Add caviar and lemon juice to jellied consommé. Top with sour cream and chopped chives.

Charcoal-Broiled Chicken

Season broilers or small frying chickens and cover generously with butter. Place in a low oven (325° F.) uncovered, and allow to pre-cook for about forty-five minutes. Finish broiling over a charcoal grill. Paint with melted butter several times while chickens are over the coals.

For barbecued chickens, spread with barbecue sauce (see page 132) while grilling.

French Fried Potatoes (see page 198)

Green Beans, Hollandaise

Cut beans lengthwise and tie in bunches; cook in boiling salted water. Serve as you would asparagus, covered with Hollandaise Sauce (see page 58).

Red Cabbage Filled with Cole Slaw

Select a large solid head of cabbage, scoop out the center so as to leave the outside leaves intact for refilling. Cut the scooped-out part into shreds and add to shredded white cabbage. Soak one hour in ice water. Just before serving, drain and dry. Mix with French Dressing and refill the cabbage.

Chocolate Marshmallow Ice Cream

6 sticks of Maillard's Chocolate
   (double vanilla)
3 tablespoons strong coffee
½ cup milk

3 egg yolks
½ cup sugar
1 pint whipping cream
½ pound marshmallows, quartered

Melt chocolate in double boiler and add coffee. Scald milk and pour over beaten yolks and sugar. Add to chocolate and cook until thick. Cool, add whipped cream, and freeze. When partially frozen, fold in marshmallows.

Sandwich Cookies

1 cup shortening
½ cup sugar
2 cups flour
$\frac{1}{16}$ teaspoon salt

Juice and grated rind of ½ lemon
⅓ pound nuts, grated
Raspberry jam
Chocolate Icing

Cream the shortening and sugar, add flour, salt, lemon, and nuts. Cover and chill for an hour. Roll wafer-thin on a lightly floured board. Cut with a small round cutter; bake on a greased cooky sheet in a moderate oven (375° F.) until delicately browned. Sandwich two together with jam, top with Chocolate Icing.

Frappéed Yellow Tomato Juice
Stuffed Celery
Pot Roast in Aspic
Cold Mustard Sauce   Corn on Cob
Raspberries with Brown Sugar and Sour Cream
Chocolate Spice Cake
Iced Coffee

Frappéed Yellow Tomato Juice

Season tomato juice; pour into a freezing-tray of refrigerator. Stir several times during the freezing process. When ready to serve, beat until it is a semi-liquid. Serve with a dash of celery salt.

Stuffed Celery (see page 77)

Pot Roast in Aspic

4- or 5-pound rump	Salt, pepper, paprika
1 large chopped onion	1½ pints boiling water
1 clove garlic, grated	2 bay leaves
2 tablespoons butter	½ cup tomato pulp
1 tablespoon flour	

Brown the onion and garlic in the butter; add the well-seasoned meat and sear quickly on all sides. Add the boiling water and bay leaves. Cover and simmer for two and one-half hours. Add the tomato, and more water if necessary; continue cooking until the meat is tender. Thicken the gravy with flour mixed with a tablespoon of cold water.

Aspic

2 tablespoons gelatin	2 beef cubes
¼ cup cold water	1 cup boiling water
3 cups strained pot roast gravy	

Soak gelatin in cold water; dissolve with the beef cubes in the boiling water, and add to the pot roast gravy. Fill a mold with a layer of the aspic; place in the refrigerator to congeal. Put the cooked meat in the center and place small cooked carrots or onions around it. Cover with the remaining gelatin mixture. Again place in the refrigerator to congeal.

Cold Mustard Sauce

1 hard-cooked egg	Vinegar
1 large onion	Salt
1 bunch parsley	Pepper
3 teaspoons prepared mustard	Paprika
1 tablespoon olive oil	Sugar

Chop egg, onion, and parsley very fine. Add mustard, oil, and enough vinegar to make the consistency of chili sauce. Add seasonings.

Corn on Cob (see page 244)

Raspberries

Serve berries with sour cream and brown sugar.

Chocolate Spice Cake

$\frac{1}{3}$ cup butter	$2\frac{1}{4}$ cups flour
$1\frac{1}{2}$ cups sugar	3 teaspoons baking powder
3 eggs, separated	$\frac{1}{8}$ teaspoon salt
1 cake German sweet chocolate, melted	$\frac{1}{2}$ teaspoon allspice
	1 teaspoon cinnamon
1 cup strong coffee	$\frac{1}{2}$ teaspoon cloves

Cream butter and sugar; add well-beaten egg yolks and chocolate. Add coffee alternately with two cups of the flour sifted with the baking powder, salt, and spices. Fold in stiffly beaten whites and the remainder of the flour mixed with the raisins. Bake in a buttered and floured loaf pan in a moderate oven (350° F.) from forty to fifty minutes. Ice with Lemon Frosting.

Lemon Frosting

2 tablespoons butter	1 tablespoon lemon juice
1 cup confectioner's sugar	Little grated rind
Cream	

Cream butter and sugar; add flavoring and cream enough to make it the right consistency for spreading.

Egg Romanoff   *Toasted crackers*
Southern Fried Chicken
Corn Fritters   *Peas Epicurean*
Plum and Peach Compote
Ladyfinger Torte
Coffee

Egg Romanoff

Cut a small section from the pointed end of a hard-cooked egg. Remove yolk, fill with caviar, and replace the cap. Place on a slice of tomato on shredded lettuce and surround with pieces of cold boiled lobster. Serve with Russian Dressing.

Southern Fried Chicken

Disjoint frying chickens, season with salt, pepper, and paprika, and dredge with flour. Heat shortening, one inch deep, in an iron skillet. Place one layer of uniform-sized pieces of chicken in the pan over a low flame; cover and raise flame. Turn frequently until fat no longer bubbles and chicken is brown. Complete frying of each batch before adding fresh pieces of chicken. To keep chicken warm while next batch is frying, place on unglazed paper in oven and dot with butter.

Cream Gravy

Remove all but three tablespoons of fat from the pan in which the chickens were fried. Add two tablespoons flour and brown. Gradually add one and one-half cups cream (or half milk). Season with salt and white pepper. Cook five minutes and then strain.

Corn Fritters

1 can cream style corn	4 egg yolks
1 can niblets	2 cups flour
1 teaspoon salt	2 teaspoons baking powder
¼ teaspoon pepper	4 egg whites

Mix all ingredients, folding in the well-beaten whites last. Drop from spoon into deep fat. Drain on unglazed paper.

Peas Epicurean

2 cups peas	1 teaspoon sugar
3 tablespoons olive oil	½ teaspoon salt
2 tablespoons minced onion	Pepper, water
1 heart lettuce, shredded	1 tablespoon minced parsley

Slowly cook peas, oil, onion, lettuce, sugar, salt, and pepper in enough water to cover, until the peas are tender and most of the liquid has boiled away. Add parsley.

Plum and Peach Compote

Boil one cup sugar, one cup water, rind of one-half lemon, juice of one orange, a few cloves with heads removed, and a stick of cinnamon, to a syrup. Add peeled peaches, cover and boil slowly until tender; then remove. Pierce plums with a fork and boil in same syrup until tender; remove plums and simmer until the syrup thickens; strain over the fruits and add juice of one lemon.

Ladyfinger Torte

22 ladyfingers	1 cup grated almonds
6 eggs, separated	⅛ teaspoon salt
½ cup sugar	3 teaspoons wine or whiskey
Sweetened whipped cream	

Put eleven ladyfingers in a slow oven to dry, then roll into crumbs. Beat egg yolks and sugar until thick and lemon-colored. Add crumbs, three-fourths of the nuts, and salt. Fold in the stiffly beaten egg whites. Place the remaining ladyfingers on the bottom of a buttered spring form and sprinkle with liquor. Pour in the almond mixture and bake in a moderate oven (350° F.) for forty to fifty minutes. When cool, cut through the center, spread with whipping cream, and replace top. Cover with cream and sprinkle with remaining almonds.

Dinner Parties

```
┌─────────────────────────────────────────────┐
│                                               │
│         Tomato Soup Française                  │
│              Croutons                          │
│    Brook Trout      Horseradish Sandwich       │
│    Potato Balls         Chicken Cerise         │
│      Fresh Asparagus Polonaise                 │
│              Dinner Rolls                      │
│  Burnt Almond Mousse         Coconut Cake      │
│                Coffee                          │
│                                               │
└─────────────────────────────────────────────┘
```

Tomato Soup Française

1 large can tomatoes	8 peppercorns
1 large onion, sliced	1 cup water
2 carrots, diced	6 cups soup stock
1 stalk celery, diced	2 tablespoons butter
2 bay leaves	2 tablespoons flour
6 cloves	2 lumps sugar
Parsley	Salt, pepper

Simmer the first nine ingredients for thirty minutes. Press through a strainer. Add five and one-half cups soup stock and simmer one hour. Melt butter and add flour blended with remaining soup stock. Gradually add to the boiling soup with the sugar and seasonings. Boil five minutes. Serve with croutons and a dash of whipped cream, if desired.

Croutons

Remove crusts from stale bread; cut into one-third-inch cubes. Sauté in butter in an iron skillet.

Brook Trout

Clean fish, bring heads and tails together and hold in place with small skewers. Cook in boiling salted, vinegar water until tender — ten to fifteen minutes. Carefully place on serving platter and remove skewers.

Pour melted butter seasoned with lemon juice over them. Sprinkle with minced parsley.

Horseradish Sandwich

Rice one-fourth cup cream cheese. Add one-fourth cup horseradish, one teaspoon lemon juice, salt, and a few grains of sugar. Spread on thin rounds of rye bread. Cover with another round of bread which has been cut with a doughnut-cutter. Place a slice of pimiento olive in the center of each.

Chicken Cerise

Cut chickens into halves or quarters. Dredge with flour, salt, pepper, paprika, and a few grains of ginger. Sauté in butter until brown, and then place in a roasting-pan. Add one-fourth pound butter, one-half cup boiling water, and two tablespoons grated onion. Cover and bake one-half hour, basting frequently. Remove cover and brown the chicken again.

While chicken is browning, add one grated onion to four tablespoons of the butter used in sautéing chicken, and brown. Blend two tablespoons cornstarch with the juice from one can pitted black Bing cherries and two cups soup stock. Add to browned onion and boil three minutes, stirring constantly. Strain. Add cherries, one-half cup sherry wine, salt and pepper to taste. Pour part of the sauce over the chicken on the platter and serve the rest separately.

Fresh Asparagus Polonaise (see page 226)

Burnt Almond Mousse

5 egg yolks, beaten	1 cup sugar
1 cup maple syrup	1 cup chopped roasted almonds
⅛ teaspoon salt	1 teaspoon vanilla
1 quart whipping cream	

Cook syrup, egg yolks, and salt until thick; cool. Caramelize sugar and turn into a slightly buttered pan. When cold, pound to a fine mass. Combine custard, nuts, caramelized sugar, vanilla, and whipped cream. Mold and freeze (four to six hours).

Coconut Cake

1½ cups granulated sugar	1 cup milk
½ cup butter	2½ cups pastry flour
½ teaspoon orange peel	2 teaspoons baking powder
1 teaspoon vanilla	⅛ teaspoon salt
6 egg whites	

Cream sugar and butter together; add orange peel, vanilla, milk, and two cups of flour. Beat well, add the remaining flour into which the baking powder and salt have been sifted. Fold in the whites of eggs, beaten stiff. Bake in three layers (nine-inch pans) in a moderate oven (350° F.) until the cake has risen, then increase the heat.

Boiled Icing

3 cups sugar	3 egg whites, stiffly beaten
¾ cup water	Juice of ½ lemon
¼ teaspoon cream of tartar	1 teaspoon vanilla

Boil sugar, water, and cream of tartar until they spin a thread. Pour slowly over egg whites, beating constantly. Add the flavoring. Remove the brown crust from the layers. Spread frosting and sprinkle fresh grated coconut between the layers and on the sides of the cake. (Cake may be cut into small rounds, iced on all sides, and then rolled in coconut, if preferred.)

Bouillon Royal
Fillet of Sole, Anna
Rolled Watercress Sandwich
Stuffed Squab
Cucumbers Poulette   Baked Orange
Poppyseed Twists
Black Cherry Flambeau
Date and Nut Chews
Cinnamon Stars
Coffee

Custard for Bouillon Royal

2 egg yolks	$\frac{1}{8}$ teaspoon salt
Parsley, chopped	Dash of grated nutmeg
2 tablespoons milk	Dash of cayenne

Mix all ingredients. Pour into baking-pan one-half inch thick. Place in a pan of boiling water. Bake in moderate oven (350° F.) until set. Cool. Remove from pan and cut into fancy shapes. Add to boiling bouillon (see page 77). Serve at once.

Fillet of Sole, Anna

8 fillets of sole	3 tablespoons flour
Salt, paprika	$\frac{1}{2}$ pint cream
$\frac{1}{4}$ cup melted butter	1 large-size can mushrooms, drained
$\frac{3}{4}$ cup white wine	1 teaspoon Worcestershire Sauce
1 tablespoon lemon juice	1 teaspoon mushroom catsup
$\frac{1}{2}$ sliced onion	1 pound shrimps
3 tablespoons butter	1 pint oysters

Place fish in buttered baking-pan, sprinkle with salt and pepper. Add melted butter, wine, lemon juice, and onion. Bake in a hot oven twenty minutes, basting frequently. Remove onion. Make a sauce of the butter, flour, cream, and liquid drained from the mushrooms. Season, and add cooked shrimps, oysters, and mushrooms. Pour the sauce on the fish. Bake for five minutes.

Note: Fillets may be rolled with a shrimp in the center and held together with a toothpick.

Rolled Watercress Sandwich

Chop watercress fine. Add enough mayonnaise to form a paste. Season with salt and paprika. Cut fresh bread into very thin slices and remove crusts. Spread with watercress paste, and roll.

Stuffed Squab

Season squabs inside and out, with salt, a little ginger, paprika, and pepper, and stuff. Place close together in a pan with butter over them; bake in a hot oven for five minutes, then reduce the heat and bake forty to forty-five minutes longer, or until tender, basting frequently. When squabs are half done, add one-half cup currant jelly to the gravy with which the squabs are being basted.

Nut Stuffing

$\frac{1}{2}$ cup chopped pecans	$\frac{1}{2}$ onion, grated
1 cup dried bread crumbs	$\frac{1}{2}$ cup scalded milk
2 tablespoons minced celery	Melted butter
Salt, pepper	

Mix pecans, crumbs, celery, onion, seasoning, and milk with sufficient butter to moisten well.

Cucumbers Poulette

6 large cucumbers	4 egg yolks, beaten
2 tablespoons butter	Salt, pepper
2 tablespoons flour	Juice of 1 lemon

Pare cucumbers, cut into halves and scrape out the seeds. Simmer in boiling salted, acidulated water until tender. Carefully remove from water.

Melt butter, add flour, and gradually pour on two cups cucumber liquid. Boil three minutes and add yolks mixed with two tablespoons water. Heat thoroughly but do not boil. Season with salt, pepper, and lemon juice. Serve cucumbers in shallow vegetable dish; pour the strained sauce over them and sprinkle lightly with finely minced parsley or chopped fresh mint.

Baked Orange

Cut large oranges into halves and remove fruit. Scallop shells. Add fruit to one large-size can crushed pineapple, with the juice of one lemon and sugar to taste. Cook until the consistency of thin marmalade. Flavor with sherry wine, refill orange shells, and sprinkle with pistachio nuts. Bake twenty minutes in a moderate oven (350° F.). Cool, but do not place in refrigerator.

Poppyseed Twists (see page 24)

Black Cherry Flambeau

Canned Bing cherries	1 or 2 empty egg shells
French vanilla ice cream	Brandy

Drain juice from cherries and soak in curaçao or cointreau for several hours. Heat the cherries in the liqueur and one-half cup of the cherry juice. Form ice cream into a pyramid. Dry egg shells and press into top of ice cream. Fill them with brandy. Cover ice cream with cherries, ignite brandy in shells, and send to the table flaming.

French Vanilla Ice Cream

8 egg yolks	Pinch of salt
1 cup sugar	$\frac{1}{8}$ vanilla bean
1 quart whipping cream	

Mix eggs, sugar, and salt. Cook in a double boiler with a vanilla bean until thick, stirring constantly. Cool and remove bean. Scrape out the seeds and soft part and add to the custard. Fold into the whipped cream and freeze in freezer.

Date and Almond Chews

$\frac{1}{2}$ pound almonds	2 egg whites, unbeaten
1 pound dates, cut fine	1 teaspoon vanilla
$\frac{1}{2}$ pound granulated sugar	Candied cherries

Blanch almonds and cut into shreds lengthwise. Mix dates, almonds, sugar, egg whites, and vanilla. Place in refrigerator for one hour.

Form into small cones and top each with half a cherry. Place on a buttered sheet and bake in a slow oven fifteen to twenty minutes.

Cinnamon Stars

6 egg whites	$\frac{1}{8}$ tablespoon salt
1 pound confectioner's sugar	2 tablespoons cinnamon
1 pound grated almonds	

Beat eggs, sugar, salt, and cinnamon twenty minutes or until stiff. Take out four tablespoons of this mixture to be used for the icing. Add almonds to the remainder of the mixture. Cover board well with powdered sugar and roll or pat thin. Cut with a star cutter. Put a little of the icing mixture on each star. Bake in moderate oven (350° F.) until slightly brown on the bottom. Keep in a covered tin.

Shrimps Glacé
Celery Fingers
Consommé with Noodles   *Rolled Toast*
Squab Chicken   *Foie Gras Stuffing*
Peas and Mushrooms
Cherry and Apricot Compote
Chocolate Mousse — Orange Ice
London Bars
Coffee

Shrimps Glacé

3 tablespoons gelatin
¼ cup cold water
1 cup boiling water
1 pint mayonnaise
½ pint whipped cream

½ jar German prepared mustard
Salt, pepper
½ package lemon Jello
2 pounds shrimps, cooked
2 ounces caviar

Prepare the Jello and put a thin layer in an oiled mold. When nearly firm, arrange a ring of shrimps in it, cover with remaining Jello and chill until firm. Soak gelatin in cold water, dissolve in the boiling water and cool. Add to the mayonnaise, whipped cream, mustard, and seasoning. Place in the refrigerator until slightly thickened, add the remaining shrimps and the caviar. Mix well and put on top of the Jello ring. Chill until firm. Serve on a bed of watercress and lettuce leaves with Russian Dressing.

Russian Dressing

1 cup mayonnaise
½ cup catsup
½ cup chili sauce
½ pimiento, minced
2 tablespoons chopped chives
1 tablespoon minced parsley

1 chopped egg
1 tablespoon lemon juice
2 tablespoons caviar
Salt
Dash of cayenne
Paprika

Mix all ingredients together.

Celery Fingers

1 cup minced celery   1 tablespoon minced olives
1 tablespoon chopped walnuts   2 tablespoons mayonnaise
                        Paprika

Mix all together, spread between slices of thin buttered bread. Remove crusts and cut into one-inch strips.

Consommé with Noodles

To rapidly boiling soup add a dash of maggi and fine-cut noodles. Boil for five minutes.

Noodles

Beat one egg slightly. Add enough flour to make a stiff dough. Knead well. Roll out very thin and set aside until sheet is no longer sticky. Fold into a roll. Cut crosswise in fine threads. Toss lightly with the fingers to separate. Spread on a board until thoroughly dry.

Squab Chicken

Season chickens inside and out with salt, pepper, and paprika. Fill with dressing. Place close together in a pan with butter over them, and bake in a hot oven for five minutes. Then reduce the heat and bake forty to fifty minutes longer, basting frequently.

Foie Gras Stuffing

Chicken livers (6 or 7) $\frac{1}{4}$ cup crisp bacon, chopped
1 small can purée of foie gras $\frac{1}{2}$ teaspoon lemon juice
$\frac{1}{2}$ cup chopped mushrooms, sautéed   Salt, paprika
1 teaspoon chopped chives   1 cup stale bread crumbs, or
1 tablespoon chopped parsley   1 cup wild rice, cooked

Sauté livers and purée. Combine with remaining ingredients and moisten with soup stock.

Peas and Mushrooms

Cook peas in a small quantity of salted water, uncovered, until tender. There should be almost no water to drain from the peas when done. Sauté halved mushrooms and add to the peas with butter. Flavor with sherry.

Cherry and Apricot Compote

1 pound pitted sweet cherries	$\frac{1}{2}$ cup water
$\frac{7}{8}$ cup sugar	1 can peeled apricots
1 teaspoon lemon juice	

Boil sugar and water to a heavy syrup. Add cherries, and cook until tender, stirring frequently. Remove from the fire. Add lemon juice and apricots with half their juice. Chill.

Chocolate Mousse

$\frac{1}{2}$ pound Maillard's sweet chocolate	4 tablespoons milk
4 tablespoons sugar	1 teaspoon vanilla
4 eggs, separated	$\frac{1}{16}$ teaspoon salt
1 pint whipping cream	

Melt chocolate in double boiler. Add sugar, egg yolks, and milk beaten together. Cook until thick. When cool, add vanilla and salt; fold in beaten egg whites and whipped cream.

Orange Ice

4 oranges	1 cup sugar
1 lemon	Orange coloring

Combine ingredients and let stand several hours, stirring from time to time, until all the sugar is dissolved. Pour the orange syrup into a mold, fill with the chocolate mixture, and freeze in salt and ice.

London Bars

4 ounces sweet butter	$1\frac{1}{4}$ cups flour
4 tablespoons confectioner's sugar	Apricot jam or raspberry
2 egg yolks	Nut meringue
$\frac{1}{16}$ teaspoon salt	Blanched and shredded almonds

Cream butter and sugar; add egg yolks, salt, and flour. Press dough, one-eighth inch thick, into a buttered and floured pan. Bake in a hot oven until light brown. Remove cake from oven, spread with apricot jam, cover with the nut meringue, sprinkle with blanched, shredded almonds, return to the oven and bake until almonds brown. When cold, cut into strips three inches long and one inch wide.

Nut Meringue

2 egg whites	6 tablespoons confectioner's sugar
$\frac{1}{16}$ teaspoon salt	2 ounces walnut meats, grated
	$\frac{1}{2}$ teaspoon vanilla

Beat egg whites and salt until stiff. Fold in sugar, nuts, and vanilla.

Mushroom Soup   *Breadsticks*
Breast of Wild Duck
Chestnut Purée
Green Beans Polonaise
Frosted Apples
Rolls
Maple Mousse
Madeleines
Coffee

Mushroom Soup

2 tablespoons butter	Salt, cayenne
2 tablespoons flour	1 egg yolk
½ pound chopped mushrooms	½ cup cream
5 cups soup stock	Minced parsley

Melt butter, blend in flour, add mushrooms, and sauté. Mix well with the soup stock. Simmer for thirty minutes, then add salt and cayenne. Just before serving, add egg yolk mixed with cream; do not boil. Put a sprinkling of parsley in each plate.

Breadsticks

Cut off small pieces of Refrigerator Dough (see page 18), roll and shape the size of a lead pencil; place far apart in a buttered pan; brush the top with the beaten yolk of an egg. Let rise and bake in a hot oven (400° F.) until brown and crisp.

Breast of Wild Duck

Pick and draw the ducks. Wash thoroughly just before using. Rub inside and out with salt and pepper, sprinkle generously with celery seed, and put half an onion inside each duck. Place in a roasting-pan, not close together, and bake uncovered in a hot oven (450° F.) forty-five minutes, basting frequently. Some people prefer them slightly rare, so by diminishing the time, they can be cooked according to taste. Serve the breasts only, around a mound of Chestnut Purée.

Chestnut Purée

Cook one pound shelled and skinned chestnuts in two cups salted milk until tender, adding more milk if necessary. Drain, rice, and mound. Place a butter rose on top.

Beans Polonaise

Cut beans lengthwise and cook in salted water; drain. Cover with bread crumbs browned in butter.

Frosted Apples

Pare and core apples, uniform in size. Add one quart water and one cup sugar to parings. Simmer twenty minutes. Strain, color light red, and add apples. Cook slowly until apples are tender. Remove apples and cool. Spread lightly with meringue made of one tablespoon sugar folded into one stiffly beaten egg white. Stick shreds of blanched almonds in the apples. Place in a cool oven (250° F.) to dry the meringue. Serve warm with the duck.

Rolls (see page 18)

Maple Mousse

2 cups maple syrup	1 cup nutmeats
6 egg yolks	½ pound chopped glacéed fruit
⅛ teaspoon salt	1 quart whipping cream

Beat egg yolks until light; add syrup and salt. Cook in double boiler until thick, stirring constantly. Cool. Add nuts and fruit; fold in whipped cream, pour into wet mold, and pack in ice and salt.

Madeleines

½ lemon rind	1 teaspoon vanilla
2 lumps sugar	⅛ teaspoon salt
½ pound sweet butter	6 eggs, separated
½ pound powdered sugar	7½ ounces sifted cornstarch

Rub yellow rind of the lemon over lumps of sugar. Pound fine and sift. Stir butter with the powdered sugar, the lemon sugar, vanilla, and salt until creamy. Add yolks, one at a time, and cornstarch. Stir until the batter becomes light and foamy. Fold in the stiffly beaten whites. Put batter in small buttered and floured shell forms and bake in a medium hot oven (350° F.). Remove and dust with confectioner's sugar.

Soup Julienne   Cheese Straws
Trout with Wine Sauce
Radish Sandwich
Broiled Turkey   Chestnut Gravy
Corn and Bean Pudding
Cranberry Relish
Dinner Rolls
Trilby Ice-Cream Balls
Banbury Tarts
Coffee

Soup Julienne

Add cooked, slivered carrots, turnips, string beans, and peas to soup stock (see page 77).

Cheese Straws

1 tablespoon butter	$\frac{1}{4}$ teaspoon salt
$\frac{2}{3}$ cup flour	$\frac{1}{8}$ teaspoon paprika
1 cup fresh bread crumbs	Dash of cayenne
1 cup grated cheese	1 tablespoon cream

Cream butter, add flour, crumbs, cheese, and seasonings. Mix thoroughly and add cream. Roll one-fourth inch thick, cut one-fourth inch wide and six inches long. Bake until brown, in a moderate oven (375° F.)

Trout with Wine Sauce

5- to 6-pound trout	1 large onion, sliced
2 quarts water	1 stalk celery, diced
$\frac{1}{4}$ cup vinegar	1 carrot, sliced
$\frac{1}{4}$ teaspoon whole pepper	1 bay leaf
Salt	3 whole cloves

Add vegetables and seasoning to the water and boil until it is well flavored. Cook the fish in this water slowly until the meat is firm and leaves the bones. Carefully remove to a serving platter, and skin.

Wine Sauce

1 cup white wine	4 egg yolks, well beaten
$\frac{1}{3}$ cup sugar	$\frac{1}{2}$ cup butter
1 tablespoon cornstarch	Salt
Juice of 2 lemons	Cayenne
Grated rind of 1 lemon	1 cup seeded and skinned grapes
$\frac{1}{2}$ pound blanched and slivered almonds	

Mix sugar, cornstarch, lemon juice, and rind with yolks. Heat wine and butter in a double boiler; gradually add the egg mixture. Cook over boiling water until thick, stirring constantly. Add seasonings and grapes. Pour wine sauce over fish, and sprinkle with blanched and slivered almonds.

Radish Sandwich

Cut small rounds of rye bread; toast on one side; spread the other side with mayonnaise. Chop red radishes very fine; sprinkle with salt and a little vinegar; let stand fifteen minutes, then press dry. Form a circle in the center of the toast with an anchovy. Fill and surround it with the chopped radish.

Broiled Turkey

Select a six- to seven-pound turkey. Split down the back, and partially disjoint the leg from the second joint; season with salt and pepper. Place in a dripping-pan, skin side down. Pour one cup of melted butter over and bake fifteen minutes in a hot oven. Then broil slowly in the broiler for an hour or until tender, basting frequently.

Chestnut Gravy

To two cups turkey gravy, add three tablespoons Madeira wine and three-fourths cup cooked and skinned chestnuts. Chestnuts may be either whole or puréed.

Corn and Bean Pudding

½ cup butter
2 eggs, separated
2 tablespoons flour
½ teaspoon sugar
½ teaspoon salt
¼ teaspoon white pepper
Paprika

1 cup soup stock
1 cup cream
1 quart cooked and shredded beans
2 cups corn
1 chopped green pepper
1 chopped pimiento
1 teaspoon chopped parsley

Melt butter; blend flour, add cream, soup stock, seasonings, and beaten yolks. Fold in the beaten egg whites and the vegetables. Pour into a greased baking-dish and bake in a moderate oven (350° F.) thirty minutes.

Cranberry Relish

1 pound cranberries
2 navel oranges
2 cups sugar

1 package lime Jello
½ cup boiling water
1 cup diced celery

1 cup chopped nut meats

Put cranberries and oranges through food-chopper. Add sugar and let stand two hours, stirring frequently. Dissolve Jello in water. When cool, add to the fruit mixture with the celery and nuts. Pour into a mold and chill until firm.

Trilby Ice-Cream Balls

French vanilla ice cream
  (see page 264)
Diced marshmallows

Blanched, shredded, and roasted
  almonds
Grated fresh coconut (if desired)

When ice cream is partially frozen, add almonds and marshmallows. Complete freezing. Make balls with a scoop; roll in coconut.

Banbury Tarts

1 cup butter
½ cup sugar
2 eggs, separated

2 cups sifted flour
½ cup chopped nuts
Apple or currant jelly

Cream butter, add sugar, and beat until light. Add beaten egg yolks and flour and blend. Form into balls the size of a walnut. Dip balls in slightly beaten whites, then in chopped nuts. Place on a buttered baking-sheet three inches apart. Bake in 350° oven ten minutes. Take pan out of oven and with the tip of a teaspoon make a slight depression on top of each cooky. Return to oven and bake about five minutes longer.

When cookies have cooled slightly, place a small amount of jelly in center of each. The jelly will not melt but form a thin crust if cookies are not too hot.

Claret Consommé
Rolled Toast
Sweetbread Suprême
Duck à L'Orange   *Wild Rice Mold*
Mushrooms and Artichokes
Dinner Rolls
Strawberry Ice
Pecan Lace Cookies
Coffee

Claret Consommé

Cook one and one-half cups claret with a small piece of cinnamon bark and one tablespoon sugar for ten minutes. Add to one quart of consommé. Add a small amount of red fruit coloring. Garnish with a thin slice of lemon.

Rolled Toast

Slice sandwich bread into wafer-thin slices. Remove crusts and brush lightly with creamed butter. Roll on the diagonal. Toast slowly, turning until crisp and brown.

Sweetbread Suprême

2 pounds sweetbreads	1 cup cream
1½ cups ground breast of raw chicken	2 egg whites
3 slices white bread	Salt, pepper

Minced parsley

Parboil sweetbreads. (See page 78.) Mix one cup finely ground sweetbreads with chicken and bread which has been cooked in the cream until all the cream has been absorbed. Gradually add egg whites and mix until smooth. Season with salt, pepper, and finely minced parsley.

Line individual oiled and floured timbale molds, or a ring mold, with part of the mixture, fill center with Filling (see below), cover with the remainder of the chicken and sweetbread mixture and place in a pan of hot water. Cover the mold with buttered paper and bake until firm in 350° oven.

Filling

Melt two tablespoons butter; add two tablespoons cornstarch, and gradually pour on one cup chicken stock. Cook until thick. Add remaining sweetbreads broken into small pieces. Season with sherry wine, salt, and pepper.

Sauce

3 tablespoons butter	5 large mushrooms, sliced and
2 tablespoons flour	sautéed
1 cup chicken stock	1 chopped truffle
½ cup heavy cream	Sal , paprika
Sherry wine	

Melt butter, add flour, chicken stock, and cream gradually. Cook until smooth and thick. Add mushrooms and truffle, seasonings and wine. Serve with Sweetbread Suprême.

Duck à L'Orange

½ cup currant jelly	1½ cup brown gravy
1 bay leaf	Juice of two oranges
Whole black pepper	Rind of 1 orange (grated)
Rind of ½ lemon (grated)	

Roast ducks (see page 227) and make a brown gravy. Melt currant jelly in a saucepan; add bay leaf, a whole black pepper, one-half cup brown gravy, orange juice and rind, and lemon rind. Let boil for ten minutes on a low flame. Add one cup more of brown sauce and boil. Strain and pour over ducks. Garnish with parboiled orange rind strips, and preserved kumquats or skinned orange sections.

Wild Rice Mold

1 cup wild rice	1 quart boiling water
2 teaspoons salt	4 tablespoons butter

Pick over and wash the rice. Cook in double boiler until tender (about forty-five minutes). Melt butter. Add salt and mix with rice. Put into a buttered ring mold, place in a pan half-filled with boiling water, and bake in a moderate oven (350° F.) twenty-five to thirty minutes.

Mushrooms and Artichokes

1 can French artichokes	$\frac{1}{2}$ grated onion
1 pound mushrooms	6 tablespoons butter

Salt, pepper

Drain artichokes; cut into halves. Sauté mushrooms and onions in butter for three minutes. Add artichokes and seasonings. Cover and simmer ten minutes. Fill center of rice ring.

Strawberry Ice

1 quart strawberries	$\frac{1}{2}$ cup water
2 cups sugar	Juice of $\frac{1}{4}$ lemon

Small piece of vanilla bean

Crush the berries, press through a sieve, extracting all the juice. Cook sugar, water, and lemon juice to a syrup. Add vanilla bean for a few minutes and then remove it. Combine syrup and strawberry juice, cool, and freeze in ice-cream freezer.

Pecan Lace Cookies

2 tablespoons butter	$\frac{1}{2}$ cup pastry flour
2 cups brown sugar	1 teaspoon baking powder
2 eggs, well beaten	$\frac{1}{16}$ teaspoon salt
1 teaspoon vanilla	2 cups coarsely chopped pecans

Cream butter and sugar; add eggs and vanilla. Mix thoroughly and add flour, baking powder, salt, and pecans. Drop half-teaspoonfuls far apart on a buttered and floured tin. Bake in a hot oven (400° F.). Cool slightly before removing from pan.

Note: Do not attempt to make these in hot weather.

Caviar aux Blinis
Bouillon with Egg Balls
Cheese Wafers
Breast of Guinea Hen
Mushrooms Vernon
Hearts of Palm Salad, Lorenzo Dressing
Rolls
Strawberries Romanoff
Small Cakes
Coffee

Caviar

Serve in original can surrounded with ice or in a mold of frozen water.

Blinis

4 cups buckwheat flour	4 teaspoons baking powder
4 eggs, well beaten	$\frac{1}{2}$ teaspoon salt
2 cups warm milk	1 cup heavy cream

Sift flour, add eggs and milk. Mix the baking powder and salt, and add to the batter with the cream. Beat well. Bake small cakes on a griddle, and serve hot with caviar and sour cream.

Bouillon (see page 77)

Egg Balls for Bouillon

Chop hard-cooked eggs, season with salt and pepper. Add enough raw egg to hold chopped eggs together. Form into balls and drop into gently boiling bouillon and cook ten minutes.

Cheese Wafers

1 cup grated American cheese	¼ teaspoon baking powder
½ cup butter	3 tablespoons cold water
1 cup flour	Salt

Add baking powder and salt to flour and cut in the butter. Add cheese and water and work to a smooth mixture. Put dough in a cooky press and form into strips, about three inches long, onto a greased baking-sheet. Or, roll dough as for icebox cookies and, when chilled, slice and bake in a 425° oven for ten minutes.

Breast of Guinea Hen

Leave the lower wing joints attached to the skinned breasts. Sprinkle with salt, paprika, and a few grains of ginger. Dip in cream, roll in flour and sauté in butter until light brown. Place in a dripping-pan and pour butter over them. Bake in a hot oven until tender, basting frequently.

For gravy: To three tablespoons fat taken from the dripping-pan add three tablespoons flour and brown well. Gradually add two cups cream. Season with salt and pepper. Serve guinea hen on sautéed slices of Virginia ham.

Mushrooms Vernon

1 pound large mushrooms	Salt
4 tablespoons cracker crumbs	Paprika
2 tablespoons minced parsley	¼ pound melted butter
3 tablespoons minced shallots	1 teaspoon lemon juice

Chop mushroom stems and mix with remaining ingredients. Fill mushroom caps with mixture and broil five minutes.

Hearts of Palm Salad

Cut chilled hearts of palm into strips lengthwise. Place on romaine. Garnish with rings of stuffed olives and rounds of green peppers, sprinkle lightly with chopped salted nuts and paprika. Serve with French Dressing, a light mayonnaise or Lorenzo Dressing.

Strawberries Romanoff

2 quarts berries, sugared	Juice of 1 lemon
1 pint vanilla ice cream	2 ounces cointreau
½ pint whipping cream	1 ounce Bacardi rum

Whip ice cream slightly and fold in whipped cream. Add lemon juice and liqueur and pour over whole sugared, chilled berries.

Stag Dinners

```
┌─────────────────────────────────────────────────┐
│                                                 │
│              Oysters à la Rockefeller           │
│                    Celery                        │
│       Soup Parmesan          Toasted Crackers    │
│                 Steak Bordelaise                 │
│      Potatoes O'Brien       French Fried Onions  │
│      Hearts of Lettuce — Thousand Island Dressing│
│                     Rolls                        │
│                 Frozen Eggnog                    │
│               Marzipan Crème Slices              │
│                    Coffee                        │
│                                                 │
└─────────────────────────────────────────────────┘
```

Oysters à la Rockefeller

Oysters	1 tablespoon Worcestershire Sauce
1 bunch parsley	Salt, paprika
½ cup cooked spinach	1 clove garlic
1 green pepper	Cocktail sauce
1 teaspoon lemon juice	Buttered cracker crumbs
	Bacon

Open large oysters, leaving them on the half-shell. Chop parsley, spinach, and pepper, season with lemon juice. Worcestershire Sauce, salt, and paprika. Add grated garlic with enough cocktail sauce to form a paste. Cover each oyster with one teaspoon of the mixture, sprinkle with cracker crumbs, and place four small pieces of bacon over each. Place in the broiler until the bacon browns. Serve six oysters to each person, on a pie pan or soup plate covered with heated ice-cream salt.

Soup Parmesan

2 quarts bouillon	2 tablespoons cream
2 egg yolks	3½ ounces grated Parmesan cheese

Blend egg yolks with cream. Just before serving, whip cheese into bouillon, and add eggs. Do not allow to boil.

285

Broiled Steak (see page 218)

Bordelaise Sauce

2 shallots	$\frac{1}{2}$ teaspoon peppercorns
$\frac{1}{4}$ cup claret	3 tablespoons butter
$\frac{1}{2}$ sliced onion	2 tablespoons flour
1 sliced carrot	$1\frac{1}{2}$ cups soup stock
3 sprigs parsley	$\frac{1}{2}$ teaspoon Kitchen Bouquet
1 bay leaf	$\frac{1}{2}$ tablespoon Escoffier Sauce
1 clove	Marrow
	Salt

Cook shallots and wine until claret is reduced to two tablespoonfuls. Strain, and simmer vegetables and spices in butter until brown. Add flour and, when well browned, gradually add soup stock or one bouillon cube dissolved in the same amount of water. Simmer ten minutes and strain. Add claret, Kitchen Bouquet, Escoffier Sauce, and cut up marrow that has been cooked in boiling water. Add salt to taste.

Potatoes O'Brien

Fry three cups of potato cubes or balls in deep fat. Drain on unglazed paper and sprinkle with salt. Simmer one sliced onion in two tablespoons butter for five minutes. Remove onion and add three tablespoons chopped pimiento and potatoes. Heat thoroughly.

French Fried Onions

Skin and cut onions crosswise in one-fourth inch slices. Cover with milk and let stand for ten minutes. Drain and dredge heavily with flour. Fry a few at a time in deep hot fat until golden brown. Drain on unglazed paper and sprinkle with salt.

Hearts of Lettuce — Thousand Island Dressing

1 quart mayonnaise	Dash of tabasco sauce
$\frac{1}{2}$ bottle chile sauce	3 gherkins
1 bottle catsup	3 green peppers
2 teaspoons Worcestershire Sauce	2 small onions

Grind gherkins, green peppers and onions; combine with the other ingredients and mix thoroughly. Chill and serve over quartered heads of crisp lettuce.

Frozen Eggnog

1 cup sugar	1 teaspoon vanilla
$\frac{1}{16}$ teaspoon salt	1 pint whipping cream
4 egg yolks, well beaten	6 tablespoons brandy
1 pint milk, scalded	Nutmeg

Add sugar and salt to egg yolks. Gradually add milk. Cook in a double boiler until creamy. Cool, add vanilla and partially freeze in freezer. When half-frozen, add whipped cream and brandy. Continue freezing, being careful that mixture does not get too hard. Serve in glasses with a grating of nutmeg.

Marzipan Slices

7 ounces butter	7 ounces, half pastry flour, half cornstarch
7 ounces sugar	$\frac{1}{8}$ teaspoon salt
5 eggs, separated	1 teaspoon vanilla
	2 teaspoons lemon juice

Cream butter and sugar, add egg yolks, and beat until thick and lemon-colored. Sift dry ingredients. Add alternately with stiffly beaten egg whites and flavoring. Spread on wax paper in two pans twelve by fifteen inches. Bake in a moderate oven (350° F.) until firm but not brown (twelve to fifteen minutes). Remove from paper and cut each sheet into five strips lengthwise. Put two strips together with strained apricot marmalade. Cover all sides with Marzipan Crème. Roll in confectioner's sugar and place in the refrigerator for an hour or until firm. Cut into one-fourth-inch slices.

Marzipan Crème

1 pound marzipan	8 ounces confectioner's sugar
4 ounces sweet butter	$\frac{1}{2}$ egg yolk
	Vanilla

Blend to a smooth paste.

Caesar Salad
Baked Muskelunge
Cucumber Sandwiches
New Potatoes, Parsley Butter   Lima Beans
Stuffed Beets
Chocolate Macaroon Icebox Cake

Caesar Salad *or* Western Green Salad

Lettuce	$\frac{1}{4}$ cup Worcestershire Sauce
Romaine	$\frac{1}{2}$ cup wine vinegar
Salt	$\frac{1}{4}$ cup lemon juice
Freshly ground black pepper	2 tablespoons anchovies cut and
2 cups French fried bread	drained
croutons	6 tablespoons grated Parmesan cheese
1$\frac{1}{2}$ cups olive oil, garlic flavored	2 coddled eggs

Place greens in a salad bowl; sprinkle with salt and pepper. Add croutons, which have been sprinkled with finely chopped garlic, and toss. Pour on oil, Worcestershire Sauce, vinegar, lemon juice and toss. Add anchovies and cheese and toss. Drop in the eggs, which have been coddled for one and a half minutes. Toss and blend thoroughly: serve immediately.

Note: Fry croutons several hours before using.

Baked Muskelunge

Clean fish thoroughly and remove gall carefully. Soak in water with lemon juice in it. Dry, and season with salt and pepper. Line a roasting-pan with heavy white paper and place fish on it. Bake uncovered in 300° oven, basting frequently with butter.

Serve with lemon sauce:

3 egg yolks	½ cup water
1 whole egg	1 tablespoon sugar
Juice of 2 lemons	¼ cup almonds, blanched and sliced

Cook until thick in double boiler, stirring constantly. Add almonds and pour over fish.

Cucumber Sandwich

Cut thin small rounds of bread. Spread one side with mayonnaise. Force mashed and seasoned cream cheese through a pastry tube around the edges. Fill centers with finely diced and seasoned cucumber.

Stuffed Beets

Scoop out the centers of boiled beets and fill with prepared horseradish. Serve around buttered lima beans.

Chocolate Macaroon Icebox Cake

½ pound semi-sweet chocolate	1 cup confectioner's sugar
4 tablespoons water	1 teaspoon vanilla
4 eggs (separated)	Pinch of salt

Macaroons (½ to ¾ pound)

Melt chocolate with water in double boiler. Add well-beaten egg yolks and sugar and cook slowly until smooth, stirring constantly. Cool, add vanilla, and fold in lightly the stiffly beaten whites.

Line a spring form with macaroons; fill with chocolate mixture and cover top with macaroons. Let stand several hours in refrigerator. Serve, garnished with whipped cream.

Note: If a large spring form is used, double recipe for chocolate filling.

Consommé Bellevue
Braised Pheasants — Wild Rice
Celery Root Timbales *Paradise Jelly*
Russian Bonnet
Almond Crescents

Consommé Bellevue

Combine equal quantities of chicken broth and clam broth; season to taste with salt and pepper. Serve with a small amount of whipped cream on each portion.

Puffed Crackers (see page 43)

Braised Pheasants

Quarter pheasants and dip in flour. In an iron skillet, heat about one-half inch of fat. Put in pheasant breasts and brown over brisk fire on meat side only.

In Dutch oven, melt a little bacon fat; add a small onion, sliced. Put in pheasant breasts brown side up, and cover with bacon strips. Fry the legs in the same fat the breasts were browned in. Place legs, meat side down, on the pieces of bacon which cover the breasts. Dot each leg with butter. Cook covered in 350° oven for about forty-five minutes.

Remove pheasants and bacon to skillet, with meat side up and bacon slices under the pieces of pheasant; salt each piece. To onion and fat remaining in Dutch oven, add juice of one-half lemon and a slice of lemon. Add a generous one-half cup of cream and a little water. Let cook up and stir well. Pour this over pheasants and put skillet in 450° oven for fifteen to twenty minutes.

When ready to serve, remove birds from the pan. Stir up juices from the bottom, add boiling water, boil up and strain for gravy.

Celery Root Timbales

Boil eight celery roots (for ten to twelve people). Mash through a colander; add yolks of five eggs, salt and pepper, and fold in the beaten whites of the eggs. Bake in buttered individual molds, placed in a pan of hot water in a 325° oven until firm.

Serve around pheasants or bake in a ring mold and fill center with peas.

Paradise Jelly

12 large quinces	24 red apples
	1 quart cranberries

Cut and peel quinces (do not core). Peel and core apples. Cover each fruit with water and cook separately until tender. Strain and combine juices. To each cup of juice add three quarters of a cup of sugar. Boil until proper consistency. Pour into sterilized jars and seal.

Russian Bonnet

2 cups water	5 egg yolks
⅔ cup sugar	Maillard's chocolate
	1 pint whipped cream

Cook sugar and water to a syrup (not too thick) and pour slowly on the egg yolks. Cook this mixture to consistency of custard, but *do not let boil*. Soften five bars or sections of the chocolate and pour on it the syrup and egg mixture, stirring until smooth. Let cool and fold in the whipped cream. Pour in a mold (one that is high, if possible) and place in refrigerator for four hours or more.

Just before serving, take a tablespoon and make a hole in the bottom of the mold by taking out a scoop of the pudding. Fill this hole with two bars of the chocolate, grated. Put back the piece of pudding that has been removed, thus forming a plug so that the grated chocolate does not fall out. Unmold and sprinkle a bit more grated chocolate on top to garnish.

Almond Crescents

½ cup sweet butter	¼ pound grated and
½ cup sugar	blanched almonds
	1 cup flour

Cream butter and sugar, add nuts and flour; mix until well blended. Chill until firm, and shape into crescents. Bake in a slow oven (325° F.) until dry. Do not brown. Dip while hot in vanilla sugar (see page 6).

Guests for Sunday Night Supper

```
Shirred Eggs and Cheese
Cold Meats
Salad Portuguese
Orange Cake
Coffee
```

Shirred Eggs and Cheese

1 pound American cheese	$\frac{1}{2}$ cup heavy cream
$\frac{1}{2}$ teaspoon mustard	1 teaspoon salt
$\frac{1}{2}$ teaspoon paprika	10 eggs

Cover the bottom of a shallow baking-dish with American cheese sliced one-fourth inch thick. Cover with one-half the cream mixed with seasonings. Break eggs over this, and pour the remainder of the cream mixture on top. Bake in a slow oven for twenty minutes or until cheese is melted and eggs are lightly set.

Platter of Cold Meats

Roll ham into cornucopias; place a border of them around a platter with slices of corned beef, turkey, chicken and tongue in the center. Garnish with parsley.

Salad Portuguese

Rub a salad bowl (preferably wooden) lightly with garlic. Mix slivered carrots, canned artichoke hearts (quartered), lettuce and endive, broken into pieces, with highly seasoned French Dressing and toss well in bowl. Cut Italian salami into thin narrow strips and put over salad.

Orange Cake

4 tablespoons butter	1½ cups pastry flour
1 cup sugar	2 teaspoons baking powder
2 eggs, separated	⅛ teaspoon salt

½ cup orange juice

Cream butter and sugar; add yolks. Beat until thick and lemon-colored. Sift dry ingredients together and add alternately with the orange juice. Fold in stiffly beaten egg whites. Bake in two layers in a moderate oven (350° F.) for twenty minutes. When cold, spread orange filling between the layers and frost with orange icing.

Orange Filling

6 tablespoons sugar	½ teaspoon grated orange rind
1½ tablespoons cornstarch	½ cup orange juice
⅛ teaspoon salt	1 egg yolk, slightly beaten
½ cup water	1 tablespoon butter

½ cup crushed pineapple

Mix sugar, cornstarch, and salt. Gradually add water, rind, juice, and egg yolk. Cook in double boiler until smooth and thick. Fold in the butter and pineapple. Cool before spreading between layers.

Orange Icing

Juice of 1 orange	1½ cups confectioner's sugar
1 orange, lightly grated	1 teaspoon rum

Bring orange juice and rind to a boil; strain and pour as much hot juice over sugar as needed to make the proper consistency for spreading. Add rum, sherry, or whiskey.

Herring L' Aiglon
Boiled Potatoes in Jackets
Pumpernickel Bread
Sliced Roast Beef
Horseradish Ring   *Cole Slaw*
Jelly
Butterscotch Icebox Cake
Coffee

Herring L'Aiglon

1 pint jar herring fillets   Lemon slices
1 pint sour cream   Mustard seed
½ pint whipped cream   Bay leaf
Shaved onion   Apple slices

In layers place a little of the sour and whipped cream, mixed; onions, a few mustard seeds, a bay leaf, a slice of lemon, a slice of apple, and three or four herring fillets. Repeat until all the herring is used. Let stand several hours before serving.

Boiled Potatoes in Jackets

Scrub potatoes and soak in cold water thirty minutes. Cook until tender in enough boiling salted water to cover (one tablespoon salt to one quart water). Drain and shake until dry, uncovered, over the fire.

Horseradish Ring

2 boxes lime Jello   1 bottle horseradish
4 cups boiling water

Dissolve Jello in boiling water. Add the horseradish. Pour into an oiled ring mold and chill until firm. Serve on a bed of shredded lettuce. Fill the center with Cole Slaw.

Cole Slaw

½ head cabbage	2 tablespoons onion juice
Salt	½ cup sugar
2 tablespoons vinegar	Bunch of parsley, chopped
2 tablespoons oil	½ pint sour cream

Shred cabbage; salt, press with a weight, and let stand several hours. Drain off water and add vinegar, oil, onion juice, sugar, and chopped parsley. Before serving, fold in sour cream.

Butterscotch Icebox Cake

Ladyfingers or sponge cake	Vanilla and coffee flavoring
¼ pound sweet butter	1 pint whipping cream
2 cups confectioner's sugar	Grated nuts
4 egg yolks	Ground butterscotch candy

Line bottom and sides of spring form with sponge cake or ladyfingers. Cream butter and sugar and add yolks, flavoring, and whipped cream. Cover the cake layer with one-third of this mixture, sprinkle with nuts and butterscotch, and alternate cake, mixture, butterscotch, and nuts, until all are used. Place in the refrigerator for several hours.

Baked Beans and Frankfurters
Boston Brown Bread
Lettuce and Roquefort Cheese Salad
Rum Cake
Coffee

Baked Beans and Frankfurters

Put a layer of canned baked beans in a deep casserole. Cover with sliced frankfurters and a few teaspoons of catsup. Repeat until the dish is full. Sprinkle the top with brown sugar. Cover with strips of bacon and bake one hour.

Lettuce and Roquefort Cheese Salad

Cut a head of lettuce into chunks. Add one-fourth pound Roquefort cheese broken into small pieces, and French Dressing. Toss lightly until well mixed.

Rum Cake

¼ pound butter	4 eggs, separated
1 cup brown sugar	1 cup sugar
1 large can mixed fruit, drained	1 cup flour
1 teaspoon baking powder	

Melt butter and brown sugar in an iron skillet. Cover with fruit. Beat yolks and sugar together. Add sifted flour and baking powder alternately with beaten whites. Pour batter over fruits and bake twenty-five to thirty minutes in a moderate oven (350° F.). Invert, cool slightly, and pour rum on to taste. Serve with Saint Cecilia Sauce.

Saint Cecilia Sauce

2 egg yolks
⅛ teaspoon salt

1 cup powdered sugar
½ pint whipping cream

1 teaspoon vanilla

Beat yolks, salt, and sugar together. Combine with whipped cream Add vanilla. Put into refrigerator one hour before serving.

Woodchuck
Cold Boiled Ham with Chutney Sauce
Farmer's Chop Suey
Caramel Cake
Coffee

Woodchuck

½ pound butter
6 tablespoons flour
1 pint milk
½ pound diced American cheese

1 pound sautéed mushrooms
1 can tomato soup
1 tablespoon Worcestershire Sauce
Salt, pepper, paprika

8 hard-cooked eggs

Melt butter; add flour and milk. Cook until smooth and thick, stirring constantly. Place in a double boiler and add cheese. Cook until melted, add mushrooms, soup, seasonings, and sliced eggs. Heat thoroughly; serve on toast.

Chutney Sauce

1 cup Major Grey chutney
1 glass currant jelly

1 wineglass sherry
1 teaspoon Worcestershire Sauce

Blend ingredients and serve with boiled ham.

Farmer's Chop Suey

1 onion, chopped
1 cup cucumbers, diced
1 cup radishes, sliced

4 fresh tomatoes, quartered
1 cup green peppers, chopped
1 cup cabbage, shredded

Salt and pepper

Sour-Cream Dressing

2 tablespoons vinegar   1 teaspoon mustard
1 teaspoon salt   Paprika
2 tablespoons sugar   1 cup thick sour cream

Add vinegar and seasonings to sour cream and pour over greens and vegetables.

Caramel Cake

$\frac{3}{4}$ cup butter $2\frac{2}{3}$ cups flour
2 cups brown sugar   2 teaspoons baking powder
4 eggs, separated $\frac{1}{8}$ teaspoon salt
3 tablespoons caramel syrup $\frac{2}{3}$ cup milk
                1 teaspoon vanilla

Cream butter and sugar, add well-beaten yolks, caramel syrup (made by caramelizing sugar in an iron skillet), and sifted dry ingredients alternately with the milk. Fold in the stiffly beaten egg whites. Bake in three layers in a moderate oven (350° F.) for twenty minutes.

Brown Sugar Frosting

2 cups brown sugar   2 egg whites, beaten
$\frac{1}{2}$ cup water   1 teaspoon vanilla

Cook sugar and water until it forms a soft ball when dropped into ice water. Gradually pour over egg whites. Add vanilla and continue beating until it is the right consistency for spreading.

Ham Jambolia
Artichoke and Cheese Salad
Graham Cracker Torte
Coffee

Ham Jambolia

1 large onion, chopped	Water
3 tablespoons butter	1 tablespoon sugar
1 green pepper, chopped	Salt, pepper, paprika
1 can tomatoes	2 cups cooked diced ham *or*
1 cup washed rice	boiled shrimps

Brown onion in butter, add pepper and tomatoes and bring to a boil. Add rice and cook slowly until tender, adding only enough water to prevent burning. Season, add ham or shrimps, and cook until thoroughly heated.

Artichoke and Cheese Salad

6 artichokes	3 grapefruit
1 pound cottage cheese	French Dressing
2 packages cream cheese	Anchovy paste

Remove outside leaves from cooked artichokes. Scoop out chokes and cut hearts into pieces. Mix cottage cheese with cream cheese and season. Add artichoke hearts and mound in the center of a platter. Cover with sections of grapefruit and surround with the tender leaves of the artichokes. Sprinkle with paprika and serve with a French Dressing, flavored with anchovy paste.

Graham Cracker Torte

$\frac{1}{2}$ cup butter	Grated rind of an orange
1 cup sugar	$\frac{1}{2}$ cup flour
3 eggs, separated	2 teaspoons baking powder
1 teaspoon vanilla	$\frac{1}{2}$ pound graham crackers, rolled
	1 cup milk

Cream butter and sugar. Add well-beaten yolks, vanilla, and orange rind. Add sifted dry ingredients and cracker crumbs alternately with milk. Fold in the stiffly beaten egg whites. Bake in two layers in a moderate oven (375° F.) for twenty minutes. Put Custard Filling between layers, and frost with butter frosting.

Custard Filling

½ cup sugar
1 tablespoon cornstarch
⅛ teaspoon salt

2 egg yolks
1 cup scalded milk
½ teaspoon vanilla

Mix dry ingredients and add slightly beaten egg yolks. Pour the milk in gradually. Cook in a double boiler until smooth and thick, stirring constantly. Cool and flavor.

Butter Icing

2 cups powdered sugar
4 tablespoons butter

4 tablespoons water
1 teaspoon vanilla

3 tablespoons cocoa

Cream sugar and butter, add water, vanilla, and cocoa.

Smoked Sturgeon — Scrambled Eggs
Boiled Potatoes and Cottage Cheese
French Chocolate Cake
Peach and Orange Compote

Scrambled Eggs

Break as many eggs as needed into a bowl. Add one tablespoon cream for each egg; salt and pepper. Beat until very light; pour into a double boiler with one teaspoon butter for each egg. Cook, stirring with a fork, until firm but creamy. Serve with slices of smoked sturgeon or smoked turkey.

New Potatoes and Cottage Cheese

Boil new potatoes in their skins in salted water. Peel and pour over melted butter, salt, and pepper. Serve with cottage cheese, sour cream, and caraway seeds.

French Chocolate Cake

½ cup cocoa	½ teaspoon baking soda
¾ cup boiling water	½ cup sour cream
½ cup butter	2 cups pastry flour
2 cups sugar	⅛ teaspoon salt
1 teaspoon vanilla	3 egg whites

Dissolve cocoa in water and cool. Cream butter and sugar. Add cocoa mixture, vanilla, baking soda mixed with the sour cream. Fold in the flour and salt, which have been sifted four times, alternately with the stiffly beaten egg whites. Bake in two layers in a moderate oven (350° F.) twenty minutes. Cool before removing from pan. Spread chocolate icing between layers and over cake.

Chocolate Icing

½ cup brown sugar	2 squares bitter chocolate
½ cup water	2 cups confectioner's sugar
2 tablespoons butter	1 teaspoon vanilla

Pinch of salt

Boil brown sugar, water, and butter for a few minutes; add chocolate. When melted, remove from fire, add confectioner's sugar, salt, and vanilla and beat until smooth.

Peach and Orange Compote

Boil two cups sugar and one cup water five minutes. Cook twelve peeled peaches in the syrup until tender; remove and chill. Cut thin slices of peel from four oranges and simmer in the syrup until soft. Pour over the peaches. Serve cold.

Italian Meat Balls and Spaghetti
French Bread
Platter of Assorted Sausage
Lettuce and Anchovy Salad
Chilled Fruits with Maraschino
Hazelnut Squares
Coffee

Meat Balls

1 pound ground round steak	1 egg
¼ pound ground veal	¼ cup cold water
1 tablespoon bread crumbs	½ grated onion
Salt and pepper	

Mix all the ingredients and form into balls the size of a walnut. Cook in soup stock until well done. Remove from broth and mix with one-third of the Italian Sauce.

When ready to serve, place spaghetti on a large platter, arrange meat balls on top, and sprinkle with Parmesan cheese. Serve with additional Italian Sauce.

Italian Sauce

4 carrots, grated	4 tablespoons olive oil
4 onions, grated	2 tablespoons butter
1 stalk celery, diced	2 cans Italian tomato paste
1 clove garlic, grated	1 can tomatoes
Parsley	3 cups soup stock
4 slices bacon, slivered	½ pound sautéed mushrooms
Salt, pepper, paprika	

Simmer carrots, onion, celery, garlic, parsley, and bacon in the oil and butter. Add tomato paste, canned tomatoes, and soup stock. Cover and cook slowly for two and one-half to three hours. Strain, add the mushrooms, and season highly.

Lettuce and Anchovy Salad

Head lettuce
Anchovy fillets
4 hard-cooked egg yolks
1 teaspoon salt
½ teaspoon pepper
1 teaspoon sugar

½ teaspoon paprika
1 teaspoon dry mustard
2 tablespoons cream
4 tablespoons olive oil
1 tablespoon Worcestershire Sauce
2 tablespoons tarragon vinegar

1 teaspoon onion juice

Rice egg yolks, mix with dry ingredients. Gradually add liquids with vinegar to taste; rub a salad bowl with a clove of garlic. Cut lettuce into chunks, add a can of cut anchovies, and mix with dressing. Top with shredded egg whites.

Chilled Fruits with Maraschino

Use all the fresh fruits in season: strawberries, raspberries, pears, peaches, seedless grapes, melon balls, and cherries. Put alternate layers of the fruit with sugar in a bowl. Pour cherry brandy mixed with maraschino over all. Serve very cold.

Hazelnut Squares

½ pound butter
1 cup sugar
1 egg yolk, beaten
2½ cups flour

1 teaspoon vanilla
½ teaspoon cinnamon
1 egg white, unbeaten
½ cup chopped hazelnuts

Cream butter and sugar. Add the egg yolk, flour, salt, and cinnamon. Spread one-fourth inch thick on a cooky pan. Brush with egg white and sprinkle with nuts. Bake in hot oven, then medium till brown. While warm, cut into small squares.

Deviled Eggs with Mushrooms
Baked Ham
Potato Salad
Rye Bread Rolls
French Doughnuts
Coffee

Deviled Eggs with Mushrooms

12 hard-cooked eggs	$\frac{1}{4}$ teaspoon pepper
1 pound mushrooms, chopped	$\frac{1}{4}$ teaspoon paprika
and sautéed	2 cups white sauce
$\frac{1}{2}$ teaspoon salt	Buttered bread crumbs

$\frac{1}{4}$ cup grated cheese

Cut eggs in half lengthwise. Remove yolks, rub them through sieve, and add some of the mushrooms and seasoning. Refill whites with this mixture and press two halves together. Place in a casserole and cover with the white sauce, mixed with the remaining mushrooms. Sprinkle with buttered crumbs mixed with the cheese. Bake in a hot oven (400° F.) until brown.

Potato Salad

5 or 6 pounds potatoes	$\frac{1}{2}$ cup water
$\frac{1}{2}$ cup cider vinegar	$\frac{1}{2}$ cup salad oil

1 onion, chopped
$\frac{1}{2}$ cup sour cream or 3 tablespoons mayonnaise
Salt, pepper, minced parsley, riced egg

Boil potatoes in jackets and slice very thin while warm. Bring vinegar, onion, and water to a boil. Put layer of potatoes in a bowl; salt, pepper, a sprinkling of oil, and a few spoons of the vinegar mixture. Continue in layers until all the potatoes are used. Fold in sour cream or mayonnaise last and sprinkle with parsley or riced egg.

Rye Bread Rolls

¼ cup lard	Grated rind of ½ orange
1 tablespoon salt	1 cake yeast
2 cups boiling water and milk	4 cups rye flour
½ cup molasses	2 cups white flour

Caraway seeds

Dissolve lard and salt in one and one-half cups of the liquid. When lukewarm, add molasses, orange rind, and yeast, dissolved in the remaining half-cup of lukewarm liquid. Stir in flour. Knead until smooth and elastic, using as little additional white flour as possible to keep the dough soft. Brush with butter and allow to rise in a warm place until double its bulk. Toss on board, cut and shape into small rolls, one and one-half inches wide and three inches long. Place far apart on a floured pan. Brush the tops with slightly beaten egg white to which a half-tablespoon of cold water has been added. Sprinkle with caraway seeds. Bake in a hot oven (400° F.) for twenty-five minutes, or until brown and crisp.

French Doughnuts

1 cup water	⅛ teaspoon salt
½ cup butter	1 tablespoon sugar
1 cup flour	5 eggs

Grated rind of 1 lemon

Heat water and butter to the boiling point; add flour, salt, and sugar all at once and stir the batter over low flame until it leaves the sides of the pan and forms a ball. Remove from fire. Have eggs at room temperature and add one egg and lemon rind. Stir thoroughly and let stand until cool. (Do not chill or put in a draft.) Add the other four eggs, one at a time, stirring briskly after each addition.

Put batter in a pastry bag and press circles onto heavy waxed paper or on the end of a greased pancake-turner. Drop a few at a time into deep fat (350° to 375° F.) and fry to a golden brown. Drain on unglazed paper and sprinkle with powdered sugar.

Crab Gumbo
Corn Dodgers
Corned Beef   Rye Bread
German Potato Salad
Guava Preserves
Cream Cheese   Assorted Crackers
Pear Compote

Crab Gumbo

2 onions, chopped fine	1 pound shrimps, boiled
2 tablespoons bacon fat or butter	1 pound fresh crabmeat
4 tablespoons flour	Parsley
2 quarts soup stock	Bay leaf
2 small cans tomatoes	Salt
2 pounds fresh okra	Pepper

Brown onions in melted fat. Add flour, soup stock, tomatoes, and okra. Cook about two hours. Then add shrimp, crabmeat, and lobster (if desired). Add seasonings. Heat thoroughly and serve with a small mound of rice in the center of each plate.

Corn Dodgers

2 cups white corn meal	1 teaspoon salt
1 teaspoon sugar	2 tablespoons melted butter

$1\frac{3}{4}$ cups boiling water

Sift dry ingredients; add butter and water to form a stiff dough. Form into thin cakes and brown on both sides on a greased griddle. Bake in a slow oven until well dried out.

Corned Beef

Cover a piece of corned beef with cold water and bring slowly to the boiling point. Boil five minutes and skim. Add a stalk of celery, a few bay leaves, a large onion, and two cloves garlic. Reduce the heat and simmer for several hours. Before it is completely tender, remove and place in the oven; sprinkle with brown sugar, bake slowly until tender and the top is glazed.

German Potato Salad

10 medium size potatoes	1 egg
1 large onion, grated	2 tablespoons hot bacon fat
Salt, pepper	$\frac{1}{2}$ cup hot vinegar
$\frac{1}{2}$ teaspoon celery seed	$\frac{1}{4}$ cup water

Boil potatoes in their skins; peel while hot, and slice. Mix lightly with onion, salt, pepper, and celery seed. Beat egg until light; add melted fat and hot vinegar with hot water. Pour this over seasoned potatoes; if necessary, add more vinegar, salt, and pepper. Add two chopped hard-cooked eggs and garnish with minced parsley.

Pear Compote

Select firm pears, peel. Place in a saucepan with a little water, an equal amount of red wine, a stick cinnamon, one-half lemon, sliced, and sugar to taste. Cook slowly until tender. Serve cold.

Bologna Cups   Corn Scramble
Rye Toast
Cold Tongue and Chicken
Pickled Beets   Dill Pickles
Camembert and Swiss Cheese
Fresh-Fruit Coffee Cake
Coffee

Bologna Cups

Sauté unskinned, thinly sliced bologna sausage in butter until the edges curl up. Fill with corn scramble.

Corn Scramble

4 tablespoons butter	1 can tomato soup
1 tablespoon grated onion	4 eggs, slightly beaten
1 tablespoon minced green pepper	½ teaspoon salt
2 cups corn kernels	Pepper, paprika

Grated cheese

Melt butter, add vegetables and soup. Heat to boiling point. Reduce heat and add eggs and seasonings. Cook, stirring constantly until set but not firm. Serve at once in bologna cups or on toast. Sprinkle with grated cheese and a few grains of paprika.

Coffee-Cake Dough

⅔ cup butter	4 egg yolks
½ cup sugar	3 eggs
1 teaspoon salt	½ lemon (juice)
1 cup scalded milk	½ orange (rind)
2 yeast cakes	4⅔ cups flour

Melt butter, sugar, and salt in milk. Cool until lukewarm. Add yeast and, when thoroughly dissolved, add remaining ingredients. Beat until

dough is blistered.   Allow to rise for six hours, then place in the refrigerator overnight.   Before using let dough rise again.

Fresh-Fruit Coffee Cake

Line a buttered spring form with coffee-cake dough, rolled one-fourth
inch thick.   Sprinkle with cracker crumbs or grated bread crumbs.   Fill
with two quarts sour, pitted cherries mixed with one and one-half cups
sugar, two tablespoons flour, and one teaspoon cinnamon.   Dot with
pieces of butter (about one quarter cup) and spread thick sour cream
over the fruit.   Bake thirty to forty minutes in a hot oven (400° F.).

Note: If blueberries or peaches are substituted for cherries, use only
one cup of sugar.

Individual Plates of Hors D'Oeuvres
Chicken Pie
Waldorf Salad
Coconut Torte
Coffee

ASSORTED HORS D'OEUVRES

Ham and Cheese Canapé

⅓ pound American cheese	2 eggs, separated
½ teaspoon baking powder	Salt
1 tablespoon Worcestershire Sauce	Paprika

Grate cheese, add baking powder, Worcestershire Sauce, and yolks beaten light. Fold in stiffly beaten whites and seasoning. Toast small rounds of bread on one side. Spread untoasted side with deviled Virginia ham. Cover with cheese mixture and place in broiler until puffed and light brown.

Egg Stuffed with Caviar

Cut hard-cooked eggs in halves. Remove yolk and fill with caviar, seasoned with lemon and onion juice. Rice yolks and arrange as a border around caviar.

Ripe Olives

Stuff large pitted ripe olives with blanched almonds.

Rolled Cervelat

Rice cream cheese; add prepared horseradish to taste. Spread on thinly sliced cervelat and roll.

Mock Pâté de Foie Gras

Boil a one-pound piece of calf liver in salted water with a clove of garlic and a bay leaf, and cook until well done. When cold, skin and grind. Add one-half cup chicken fat or creamed butter, and season with salt, pepper, ginger, grated onion, lemon juice, and Worcestershire Sauce. Beat until smooth. Mound on rounds of rye bread toasted on one side. Garnish with riced egg yolks and slices of ripe or pimiento olives.

Chicken Pie

4- to 5-pound hen	2 tablespoons flour
1 stalk celery	2 egg yolks
2 cloves	½ cup cream
12 small white onions	Pepper
1 teaspoon salt	1 tablespoon lemon juice
2 tablespoons butter	2 tablespoons parsley
½ pound mushrooms, sautéed	

Cut hen into pieces. Cover with boiling water and add the celery and cloves. Simmer for two hours or until tender. Twenty minutes before it is done, add the onions and salt. Remove the chicken and onions from the broth, and boil down to two cups; strain. Melt butter, add the flour, broth, and yolks, slightly beaten and mixed with the cream, reserving two tablespoons of egg mixture. Cook two minutes, stirring constantly. Season. Add mushrooms, onions, and chicken, which has been cut from the bones and left in large pieces. Put in a casserole and cover with a crust. Slit the top of the dough before baking, to allow steam to escape. Brush lightly with the reserved egg-cream mixture. Bake in a hot oven (450° F.) for fifteen minutes, then reduce heat to moderate (350° F.) and bake fifteen minutes longer.

Crust for Chicken Pie

1 cup flour	½ teaspoon celery salt
1 teaspoon baking powder	3 tablespoons shortening
⅓ teaspoon salt	6 tablespoons milk

Sift dry ingredients together, cut in the shortening, and gradually add milk, mixing to a soft dough. Roll one-fourth inch thick.

Waldorf Salad

Mix equal parts of apple and diced celery. Marinate in the juice of a lemon one hour before using. Add cubed pineapple and fold in mayonnaise mixed with whipped cream. Sprinkle with chopped salted nuts.

Coconut Torte

2 cups coconut	1 cup Zwieback crumbs
4 eggs, separated	1 teaspoon baking powder
$\frac{1}{2}$ cup sugar	$\frac{1}{8}$ teaspoon salt

1 teaspoon vanilla

Toast coconut on a large baking-sheet in a moderate oven (350° F.) ten minutes. Beat egg yolks and sugar until thick and lemon-colored. Add crumbs mixed with baking powder, salt, and one and one-half cups coconut. Fold in vanilla and stiffly beaten egg whites. Bake in two greased and floured cake pans in a moderate oven (375° F.). Place sweetened whipped cream between layers and over cake; sprinkle with remaining coconut.

Lobster Newburg
Cold Half Spring Chicken
Cherry and Pecan Salad
Cheese Platter
Gâteau Robert
Coffee

Lobster Newburg

2 boiled lobsters	5 egg yolks
¾ cup sherry wine	1 cup top milk
¼ cup butter	1 cup cream
Salt, pepper, paprika	1 teaspoon confectioner's sugar

Put live lobsters, head first, into a kettle with enough boiling salted water to cover. Allow two tablespoons salt to one quart water. Boil twenty minutes, drain, and cool quickly. Take out the intestinal vein and remove the meat in large pieces from the lobsters. Marinate in the wine for one hour. Melt butter in a double boiler, add lobster, wine, and seasonings. Cover and cook ten minutes. Add the eggs mixed with the milk, cream, and sugar. Cook until thick, stirring constantly. Serve on toast.

Cherry and Pecan Salad

Pit fresh Bing cherries. Mix them with broken pecans, seedless grapes, and fruit-salad dressing. Serve in a bowl lined with lettuce; garnish with cheese balls.

Gâteau Robert

1 cup butter	4 teaspoons baking powder
2 cups sugar	1 cup milk
3½ cups pastry flour	2 teaspoons vanilla
⅛ teaspoon salt	7 egg whites, stiffly beaten
1 dozen preserved marrons	

Cream butter and sugar thoroughly; add the sifted dry ingredients alternately with the milk and vanilla; fold in egg whites. Pour batter into three buttered and floured layer-cake pans. Bake in a moderate oven (375° F.) twenty minutes. Cool, spread cream filling and sliced marrons between layers. Cover the top layer with Caramel Frosting, and spread sides with Cream Filling.

Cream Filling

¾ tablespoon gelatin   1 pint whipping cream
2 tablespoons water   ½ cup confectioner's sugar
1 teaspoon vanilla

Soak gelatin in water and dissolve over hot water. Cool and add to the whipped cream with the sugar and vanilla.

Caramel Frosting

¾ cup brown sugar   ¼ cup water
½ cup white sugar   2 tablespoons cream
2 tablespoons butter

Boil sugar and water until it spins a thread. Add cream and cook five minutes. Remove from fire, add butter, let cool, and beat until proper consistency for spreading.

Diable Sardines
Chicken Tetrazzini
Vegetable Salad
Boston Cream Cake
Coffee

Diable Sardines

12 skinned boneless sardines	6 tablespoons catsup
3 teaspoons butter	3 teaspoons Escoffier Sauce
1½ teaspoons anchovy paste	Dash of Tabasco
6 teaspoons lemon juice	¾ teaspoon dry mustard

Broil sardines until thoroughly heated; place on toast. Melt butter, mix with anchovy paste and remaining ingredients. Heat and pour over hot sardines.

Chicken Tetrazzini

box spaghetti	3 cups boiled chicken, cut into
1 can tomato juice	one-inch cubes
1 pound mushrooms, sautéed	Grated American cheese

Cook spaghetti in boiling salted water for ten minutes. Drain and rinse in cold water. Add tomato juice and cook slowly until spaghetti has absorbed the juice. Combine mushrooms, chicken, one-half cup cheese, and a sauce made of the following:

4 tablespoons butter	2 cups chicken stock
3 tablespoons flour	1 cup heavy cream
Salt, pepper, paprika	

Arrange a border of the spaghetti on a platter, fill with the creamed chicken and serve with cheese.

Vegetable Salad

Combine cooked peas, beans, carrots, and cauliflower. Add a cup of sliced water chestnuts. Serve with boiled salad dressing to which whipped cream has been added.

Boston Cream Cake

4 eggs, separated	1 full cup flour
1 cup sugar	1 teaspoon baking powder
4 tablespoons hot water	$\frac{1}{8}$ teaspoon salt

1 teaspoon vanilla

Beat egg yolks and sugar until thick and lemon-colored. Add water, and sifted dry ingredients. Fold in stiffly beaten egg whites and flavoring. Bake in two layers in a moderate oven (350° F.) for twenty minutes. Put Custard Filling between the layers and spread the top of the cake with chocolate frosting or sprinkle with confectioner's sugar. (One-half of frosting recipe on page 306 will cover the top.)

Custard Filling

3 egg yolks	$\frac{1}{2}$ cup powdered sugar
2 tablespoons flour	2 cups rich milk
1 tablespoon cornstarch	2 tablespoons butter

1 cup whipped cream with vanilla to taste

Cook ingredients in double boiler until thick. When cold, add whipped cream. Cut each layer in half, through center and spread with filling. Sprinkle top with powdered sugar or frosting.

Herring Ring
Thousand Island Dressing
Chicken Mexicaine
Cucumber Salad
Cornbread Sticks
Peach Suzanne
Pound Cake
Coffee

Herring Ring

1 large jar Bismarck herring	¼ pound sweet butter
1 large can tuna fish	1 tablespoon grated onion
1 jar pimiento olives	1 tablespoon lemon juice

Place a border of olives in the bottom of an oiled ring mold. Grind herring with the tuna and remaining olives. Add to the creamed butter with the seasonings. Mix, pack in ring mold, and place in the refrigerator until firm. Invert on lettuce and surround with quartered tomatoes, artichoke bottoms, or garnish with riced egg and caviar. Serve with Thousand Island Dressing (see page 55).

Chicken Mexicaine

5 pounds boiled chicken	1 large onion, grated
Flour	1 clove garlic, grated
Salt, paprika	1 green pepper, chopped
½ cup butter	1 cup tomatoes, strained
1 pound sautéed mushrooms	

Remove meat from the bones in large pieces. Dredge with flour mixed with salt and paprika. Brown in hot butter and remove to a casserole. Simmer onion, garlic, and green pepper in the same butter until tender. Mix with tomatoes and mushrooms. Season and pour over the chicken. Cover and bake in a slow oven (350° F.) thirty to forty minutes. When ready to serve, sprinkle with minced parsley and minced chives.

Cucumber Salad

3 cucumbers, peeled and sliced thin   1 tablespoon minced chives
6 spring onions, finely diced   2 tablespoons minced parsley
½ cup vinegar   1 green pepper, minced
1 tablespoon sugar   1 teaspoon salt
¼ teaspoon pepper

Mix the cucumbers and spring onions. Combine remaining ingredients, pour over the vegetables and chill.

Peach Suzanne

6 stewed whole peaches   6 tablespoons maraschino
¾ cup peach syrup   3 tablespoons shredded, blanched
¾ cup raspberry syrup   almonds
3 jiggers Kirsch

Heat the peaches in the fruit juices. Sprinkle with nuts. Pour Kirsch over them; light, and serve.

Pound Cake

1 cup butter   1 cup milk
2 cups sugar   2½ teaspoons baking powder
4 eggs   1 teaspoon vanilla
3 cups flour   Grated rind of one orange
Grated rind of one lemon

Cream butter and sugar, add yolks, and beat. Add gradually two and one-half cups flour alternately with milk. Add remaining flour with baking powder and stir only until smooth. Add flavoring and rinds. Fold in stiffly beaten whites. Bake in buttered loaf pan in moderate oven (350° F.) one hour.

Note: A nut crunch top may be put on this as follows: Combine two tablespoons of butter with one-quarter cup of honey and bring to a boil. Remove from fire and add one cup of chopped nuts. Pour on warm cake and spread evenly. Place cake low under slow broiler and broil until nuts are toasted.

Shad Roe Ring   *Ripe Olive Roll*
Cold Turkey   *Assorted Cold Cuts*
Cranberry Jelly
Celery Root Salad
Cheese Mixture
Crackers   *Bread*
Fruit Thais
Chocolate Coconut Cookies
Lebkuchen
Coffee

Shad Roe Ring

1½ to 2 shad roe	1½ pints cream, whipped
6 eggs, separated	Salt, pepper

Parboil roe and put through ricer. Add yolks and seasonings; fold in stiffly beaten whites and cream. Put in buttered and floured ring, cover and set in a pan of hot water. Bake in a moderate oven (350° F.) for one-half hour.

Sauce

4 hard-cooked eggs	Pint of mustard chow-chow
Large bunch parsley	1 stalk celery
½ cup butter, melted	

Grind eggs, parsley, chow-chow and celery; add butter and a bit of sugar. Serve in center of ring.

Ripe Olive Roll

Mix chopped ripe olives with mayonnaise highly seasoned with horse-radish, salt, and a little lemon juice. Cut wafer-thin slices of bread, remove crusts, spread with the olive-paste, and roll.

Cranberry Jelly

1 pound cranberries	½ green apple
1 cup water	Sugar

Cook cranberries, water, and apple over low fire, in a covered saucepan until very tender. Press through a sieve. Measure pulp (there should be two cups). Heat to the boiling point. Add one cup sugar for each cup cranberries, and heat only until the sugar is melted. Pour into individual molds, rinsed in cold water. Serve each mold on a slice of orange.

Celery Root Salad

3 celery roots	½ teaspoon salt
4 tablespoons salad oil	1 teaspoon onion juice
1 tablespoon vinegar	2 tablespoons cream
¼ teaspoon pepper	2 hard-cooked eggs
Parsley, minced	

Scrub celery root well; cook several hours until tender in salted water. Peel and slice. Marinate in the oil, vinegar, seasoning, and cream. If celery absorbs the dressing, add more in same proportion. Garnish with riced egg and minced parsley.

Cheese Mixture

3 parts Pabstette cheese	1 part cream cheese
1 part butter	

Mix thoroughly and season with paprika and Worcestershire Sauce.

Fruit Thais

Use assorted fruits, such as peaches, apricots, pears, pineapple, bananas, and pitted Bing cherries, or use drained canned fruit. Arrange fruits in layers in a baking-dish. Sprinkle each layer with brown sugar, dabs of butter, and shredded blanched almonds. Pour one-half cup sherry wine over all and cover the top with crushed macaroon crumbs. Bake twenty minutes and serve hot.

Chocolate Coconut Cookies

2 squares bitter chocolate	1 can Sweetened Eagle
1 can moist coconut	Condensed Milk
1 cup chopped nut meats	1 teaspoon vanilla

Melt chocolate and stir in other ingredients. Chill for a short time. Drop from a spoon on a greased and floured cooky sheet and bake in moderate oven (350° F.) about ten minutes.

Note: These cookies scorch rather easily; watch closely during baking.

Lebkuchen

4 eggs	$1\frac{1}{2}$ teaspoons baking powder
1 pound brown sugar	$1\frac{1}{2}$ cups flour
1 teaspoon cinnamon	Pinch of salt
1 teaspoon cloves	$\frac{1}{2}$ cup nuts, coarsely chopped
1 teaspoon allspice	$\frac{1}{2}$ cup citron, coarsely chopped

Beat eggs until light; add sugar, sifted dry ingredients, nuts, and citron. Bake in a pan, approximately twelve by sixteen inches, for eighteen to twenty minutes in 375° F. oven. Frost with a thin white icing made of confectioner's sugar and water, while warm. Cut in strips.

Smoked Salmon   *Quiche Lorraine*
Lettuce and Hard-Boiled Egg Salad
North Shore Dressing
Chocolate Angel Food Cake

Smoked Salmon

Arrange thin slices of smoked salmon on a platter. Garnish with lemon quarters and parsley.

Quiche Lorraine

12 strips lean bacon, fried	¾ teaspoon salt
½ cup Swiss cheese, grated	Pinch of sugar
½ cup American cheese, grated	Pinch of nutmeg
4 eggs	Cayenne
2 cups cream	Black pepper, freshly ground

Large unbaked pie shell

Beat eggs, cream, and seasoning just long enough to mix thoroughly. Rub a little soft butter over the surface of the pie shell and sprinkle the bacon, broken into small pieces, over the bottom; cover with the cheese and pour the egg mixture over all.

Preheat oven to 450° and bake at this temperature ten to fifteen minutes; reduce heat to 300° and continue baking until custard has set (twenty-five to thirty minutes). If not golden brown on top, place under a hot broiler for a minute before serving.

Note: Thinly sliced ham or chipped beef sizzled in butter can be used instead of bacon.

Lettuce and Hard-Boiled Egg Salad — North Shore Dressing

1 cup mayonnaise	½ cup catsup
½ cup French Dressing	1 tablespoon chives

Mix ingredients well together; add salt and pepper to taste. Pour over and mix with broken chunks of lettuce and sliced hard-boiled eggs.

Chocolate Angel Food Cake

12 large egg whites   1 cup flour (sift before measuring)
1 teaspoon cream of tartar   2 cups sugar (fine-grained)
$\frac{1}{2}$ cup Van Heusen Cocoa

Pre-heat oven to 400°. Beat whites until frothy. Add cream of tartar and beat with wire whisk until stiff but not dry. Sift flour, sugar, and cocoa together; fold in very gradually to the egg whites. Bake about forty minutes. (This new method of baking angel cake in a hot oven requires less time.)

Filling

$\frac{2}{3}$ cup confectioner's sugar   1 pint whipping cream
3 tablespoons cocoa   1 teaspoon vanilla

Add sugar, chocolate, and vanilla to whipped cream. Place in refrigerator for several hours before using.

Split cake in half and spread filling between and over cake.

Buffets

```
Shrimps de Jonghe
Baked Canadian Bacon — Fried Chicken
Spaghetti          Cucumbers in Sour Cream
Bing Cherry Ring    Fruit Mayonnaise
Assorted Pickles      Cheese Platter
Almond Chocolate Torte    Cinnamon Slices
              Coffee
```

Shrimps de Jonghe

3 pounds boiled shrimps	1 cup bread crumbs
1 teaspoon salt	Dash of cayenne, paprika
1 clove garlic, grated	4 tablespoons minced parsley
¾ cup butter	½ cup sherry wine

Mix salt and garlic. Cream butter, add garlic and salt, bread crumbs, seasonings, parsley, and sherry. Place alternate layers of shrimps and bread-crumb mixture in a buttered baking-dish. Bake in a hot oven twenty to twenty-five minutes.

Baked Canadian Bacon

Place bacon, fat side up, in an uncovered roasting-pan. Bake in 350° oven for one and one-half hours. During last half-hour of baking, cover the top with brown sugar and baste with fruit juice or ginger ale.

Fried Chicken (see page 254)

Spaghetti

1 large onion, chopped fine	1 can tomatoes
1 cup olive oil	½ pound fresh mushrooms
1 pound ground round steak	Salt, dash of cayenne
1 can thick tomato paste	2 boxes spaghetti
1 cup water	1 cup Italian cheese, grated

Simmer onion in oil until light brown. Add meat and cook until well seared; add tomato paste, water, tomatoes, and mushrooms. Cook slowly for two hours. Season. Boil two packages spaghetti in boiling salted water for fifteen minutes. Drain and rinse in cold water. Mix with one-half the sauce. Heat thoroughly and place on a platter. Sprinkle with cheese, and pour the remaining sauce over all.

Cucumbers in Sour Cream (see page 41)

Bing Cherry Ring

1 can Bing cherries	1 cup sugar
2 cups orange juice	3 tablespoons gelatin
1½ cups sherry wine	Nut meats

Combine the juice from the cherries with one and one-half cups of orange juice, the wine, and sugar; bring to a boil. Soak gelatin in remaining orange juice. Dissolve in the hot fruit syrup. When the mixture begins to set, put into a mold or individual molds, placing cherries, which have been stuffed with pecans or other nut meats, in the jelly.

Fruit Mayonnaise

1 tablespoon butter	Juice of one lemon
2 tablespoons flour	Juice of one orange
1½ cups fruit juice	Two eggs (separated)
(pineapple or grapefruit)	½ cup whipping cream
Sugar	

Melt butter and flour. Add fruit juices and sweeten to taste. Cook until thick. Add egg yolks. Remove from fire. Cool, and add beaten whites and whipped cream.

Almond Chocolate Torte

10 eggs, separated	1 teaspoon cloves
2 cups sugar	1 lemon (juice and rind)
¼ pound bitter chocolate, grated	2 cups ground almonds
1 tablespoon cinnamon	1 wineglass brandy
1 cup sifted cracker meal	

Beat egg yolks and sugar until thick and lemon-colored; add the chocolate, spices, lemon rind and juice, almonds and brandy. Alternately fold in the stiffly beaten egg whites and cracker meal. Bake in a buttered spring form in a moderate oven (350° F.) fifty to sixty minutes.

When cold, frost with icing made by creaming one tablespoon butter with one cup confectioner's sugar, flavor with rum and add enough cream to make consistency for spreading.

Cinnamon Slices

Coffee-cake dough	Granulated sugar
Melted butter	Sliced almonds
Ground cinnamon	Lemon juice

Roll a small piece of yeast dough (see page 313) as thin as possible on a well-floured board.   Cut in slices four inches by two and one-half inches and place on a well-buttered cooky pan.   Brush slices with melted butter and sprinkle thickly with a mixture of cinnamon and sugar. Cover entire top with sliced almonds, and pour a little melted butter over each slice.   Let rise for an hour.   Bake in moderate oven (350° F.) ten to fifteen minutes until light brown.   Remove from pan while hot.

Chicken Mousse
Tongue in Madrilène Jelly
Sea Food Tetrazzini
Salad Bowl
Avocado Pears Filled with Strawberries
Garnierter Liptauer   *Relishes*
Schiller Locken   *Orange Gâteau*
Nut Bars
Coffee

Chicken Mousse

3 egg yolks	2 cups minced chicken
1½ cups milk	Onion and lemon juice
2 tablespoons gelatin	Salt, pepper, paprika
¼ cup cold water	1 tablespoon minced parsley
½ cup hot chicken stock	1 cup whipping cream

Beat egg yolks, add milk, and cook in double boiler until consistency of a thin custard. Soak gelatin in cold water, dissolve in soup stock, and add to the custard with the chicken and seasonings. When cold, fold in the whipped cream. Pour into an oiled mold and chill until firm. Serve with a light mayonnaise.

Tongue in Madrilène

Remove skin and roots from a hot boiled tongue. Run a skewer through the tip and fleshy part to keep the tongue in shape. Leave until cold in the water in which it was boiled, then remove skewer. Cover the bottom of a round pan with Madrilène and, when firm, decorate with asparagus tips and hard-cooked egg. Cover with Madrilène, adding it by spoonfuls so as not to disarrange the garnishings. When this layer is firm, put in a tongue and again cover with Madrilène.

Note: Canned Madrilène may be used, or refer to page 110.

Sea Food Tetrazzini

2 packages spaghetti	1 quart cream
2 cups tomato juice	3 large lobsters
¼ pound butter	2 pounds crabmeat
5 tablespoons flour	Salt, pepper

Sherry wine

Cook spaghetti until tender; drain; add tomato juice. Simmer about one-half hour. Make cream sauce of butter, flour, and cream. Add sea food and heat; add sherry wine to taste. Combine with spaghetti.

Avocado Pears Filled with Strawberries

2 tablespoons gelatin	Juice of 2 oranges
¼ cup cold water	Juice of 2 lemons
1½ cups water	¼ cup sugar
1 glass currant jelly	Avocado halves

Strawberries

Soak gelatin in cold water. Boil water, jelly, juices, and sugar five minutes. Dissolve gelatin in hot liquid and let it cool. Fill avocados with whole strawberries. Pour cooled aspic over berries and let it jell.

Garnierter Liptauer (mixed cheese)

2 cakes cream cheese	Paprika
¼ pound Roquefort cheese	½ teaspoon lemon juice
¼ pound sweet butter	1 to 2 tablespoons sour cream
1 teaspoon minced parsley	(to blend mixture to
1 teaspoon sardellen paste	a paste)

Rice the cheese and add to the creamed butter with the remaining ingredients. Place in the refrigerator. When ready to serve, shape into a mound on a plate. Dust with paprika and garnish with parsley.

Puff Paste for Schiller Locken

½ pound flour	¼ to ½ cup ice water
1 teaspoon salt	½ pound sweet butter

Sift flour and salt in a bowl. Add enough water to form a dough and knead for one minute. Chill between pans of ice. Roll dough into a square, chip butter down the center, fold each side over, and roll. This is called a turn. The dough must have six turns and be thoroughly chilled after each turn and before making into Schiller Locken.

Schiller Locken

Roll Puff Paste into a thin sheet; cut into strips one-half inch wide. Wind these around cone-shaped sticks, having edges overlap. Roll in sugar and place on a baking sheet. Bake until brown in a moderate oven. Remove from sticks and when ready to serve, fill centers with sweetened whipped cream, flavored with mocha or vanilla.

Orange Gâteau

$\frac{1}{4}$ cup butter
1 cup sugar
2 eggs, well beaten

$1\frac{2}{3}$ cups flour
$2\frac{1}{2}$ teaspoons baking powder
$\frac{1}{8}$ teaspoon salt

$\frac{1}{2}$ cup milk

Cream butter and sugar. Add eggs, then the sifted dry ingredients alternately with the milk. Bake in a Mary Ann pan, or a round cake pan, in a moderate oven, twenty-five to thirty minutes. If baked in the latter, when it is cold remove the center, leaving an inch border and enough thickness in the bottom to hold filling. Spread the bottom with apricot jam and cover with peeled orange sections. Pour over Orange Filling, and decorate with sweetened whipped cream.

Orange Filling

2 tablespoons butter
2 tablespoons flour
1 cup orange juice

Juice of 1 lemon
Grated rind of 2 oranges
$\frac{1}{2}$ cup sugar

2 egg yolks

Melt butter in double boiler; add flour and blend. Add juices, rind, and sugar; then egg yolks (which have been diluted with a little water so that eggs will not curdle). Stir constantly until thick. Cool before spreading on cake.

Nut Bars

4 egg whites	$\frac{1}{4}$ pound almonds, grated
$\frac{1}{16}$ teaspoon salt	$\frac{1}{4}$ pound hazelnuts, grated
$\frac{3}{4}$ pound sugar	1 teaspoon vanilla

$\frac{1}{2}$ teaspoon lemon juice

Beat egg whites and salt until stiff; fold in the sugar. Put aside four tablespoons of this meringue. To the rest add the nuts and flavoring. Place in refrigerator for two hours. Spread in shape of narrow bars on buttered tins. Cover with reserved meringue and bake six to eight minutes in a hot oven.

Crabmeat and Oysters au Gratin
Spaghetti en Casserole
Pâté de Foie Gras and Mushroom Patties
Steak Tartare   Liver Timbale
Chicken Curry
Choice of
Bismarcks or Schnecken   Dobos Torte
Othellos   Linzer Drops
Toffee Squares   Walnut Layer Torte

Crabmeat and Oysters au Gratin

1 pound crabmeat	1 tablespoon green pepper, chopped
1 quart oysters	2 tablespoons flour
2 tablespoons butter	Cream
½ onion, grated	Lemon juice, salt

Cook oysters in their liquor until edges curl; strain, reserving liquor. Sauté onion and green pepper lightly in butter. Add flour, oyster liquid, and enough cream to make a thick sauce. Season with salt and lemon juice; add oysters and crabmeat. Place in a baking-dish, sprinkle with buttered crumbs, and bake until heated.

Spaghetti en Casserole

½ cup dried mushrooms	1 can tomatoes
2 cups soup stock	2 boxes spaghetti
1 cup olive oil	1 pound sautéed chicken livers
2 large onions, chopped	½ pound sliced mushrooms, sautéed
2 green peppers, chopped	Parmesan cheese
1 clove garlic, grated	1 teaspoon sugar
1 can Italian Spaghetti Sauce	Salt, dash of cayenne

Soak dried mushrooms for several hours in soup stock. Heat oil in an iron skillet, add onion, pepper, and garlic and simmer for ten minutes. Add Italian Spaghetti Sauce, tomatoes, soup stock, and dried mushrooms. Cook slowly for two hours. Cook the spaghetti fifteen minutes in boiling salted water. Drain and rinse with cold water. Mix with sauce, chicken livers, mushrooms and some Parmesan cheese. Season.

Put in a casserole, cover with cheese, and place in a hot oven until cheese has melted.

Pâté de Foie Gras and Mushroom Patties

2 tablespoons butter	1 cup hot milk
2 tablespoons flour	3 ounces pâté de foie gras
¼ teaspoon salt	1 pound mushrooms, sautéed
Paprika, dash of cayenne	Patty shells

Melt butter, add flour and seasonings; gradually add milk, stirring constantly; cook until smooth and thick. Add the pâté de foie gras and mushrooms; mix thoroughly. Serve in patty shells.

Steak Tartare

Remove fat from two pounds of round steak. Grind three times with twelve anchovies. Season highly with onion juice, lemon juice, Worcestershire Sauce, Escoffier Sauce, salt, and pepper. Mix with three raw egg yolks. Mold and garnish with rolled anchovies, minced Bermuda onions, and riced egg yolks.

Liver Timbale

Sauté one-half pound chicken livers in two tablespoons butter; grind three times, season with salt, pepper, onion juice, lemon juice, and a few grains ginger. Soak three tablespoons gelatin in one cup soup stock. Dissolve over hot water; chill. When it begins to congeal, line an oiled mold with a thin coating of gelatin to form a glaze. Add remaining gelatin to liver paste, and blend with one-half pint whipped cream. Put into mold and chill until firm.

Chicken Curry

4 cups cooked chicken, diced	½ or 1 teaspoon curry powder,
½ cup butter	to taste
½ cup cream	¼ cup chopped chutney
2 cups White Sauce	

Sauté chicken in butter, add cream and curry powder. Bring to a boil, add chutney and White Sauce.

Bismarcks

Roll rich coffee cake dough (see page 313) one-half inch thick; cut with a biscuit-cutter. Moisten edges with beaten egg. (Prepare only a few at a time, so egg does not dry.) Put one-half teaspoon jam or jelly in center. Cover with a piece of dough and press edges together. Spread with melted butter. Cover, and allow to rise one to two hours. Fry in deep hot fat, turning once. Drain on unglazed paper. Sprinkle with sugar.

OR

In place of frying them, they can be baked in a moderate oven (350° F.) fifteen or twenty minutes. Before removing from the oven, brush with confectioner's sugar moistened with water.

Schnecken

Roll rich coffee-cake dough one-half inch thick; brush with melted butter, sprinkle with sugar, cinnamon, chopped pecans, and raisins. Roll and cut into one-inch pieces.

Melt four tablespoons butter, add one-half cup brown sugar and one tablespoon water. Cook until thick. Put one tablespoon of the syrup into each greased muffin tin, sprinkle with pecan halves, and place a roll in each. Brush with melted butter, allow to rise until light, and bake in a moderate oven (350° F.) twenty minutes, until brown. Invert pan, remove schnecken, and serve caramel side up.

Dobos Torte

1 cup flour	$\frac{1}{8}$ teaspoon salt
7 eggs, separated	1 cup confectioner's sugar

Sift flour once, measure and sift four times more. Beat egg yolks, salt, and sugar until thick. Fold in flour and stiffly beaten (but not dry) egg whites. Spread thin layers of dough on buttered and floured layer-cake pans. (Removable bottoms are preferable.) Bake in moderate oven (375° F.) six to eight minutes. Remove at once from pans and repeat until dough is all used. This will make six or seven layers; increase recipe to make a higher cake of more layers.

Put layers together with the following filling:

$\frac{1}{2}$ pound sweet chocolate	$1\frac{1}{2}$ cups confectioner's sugar
3 tablespoons water	$\frac{1}{2}$ pound butter, scant
3 eggs	1 teaspoon vanilla

Melt chocolate with water in double boiler. Mix eggs and sugar, add to chocolate, and cook until thick, stirring constantly. Remove from stove, cool, add vanilla and butter, which has been creamed until light, and beat until blended.

Spread between layers, and cover top and sides. To keep layers from slipping, put toothpicks through top layers until filling sets. Allow the torte to set twenty-four hours before serving.

Instead of putting filling on top layer, it is sometimes covered with a glaze. To glaze torte, melt three tablespoons of sugar in a skillet. Put it over the top and spread with a hot knife.

Othellos

Make a rich icebox cooky dough. Roll it into a roll the diameter of a half-dollar. Slice dough about an eighth of an inch thick and bake. Put two cookies together with a half of a marshmallow, cut crosswise, between them. Place in a warm oven until the marshmallows melt enough to hold the two cookies together.

Frost with Chocolate Frosting (see page 306).

Linzer Drops

½ cup butter	Lemon rind, grated
1 cup sugar	1 cup flour
2 eggs	1 cup almonds, ground

Cream butter and sugar, add beaten eggs, lemon rind, flour and nuts. Form into balls. Bake on buttered sheets. Ten minutes after they are in the oven, make an indentation in the top of each with a thimble. Finish baking and fill with jelly.

Toffee Squares

1 cup butter	1 egg yolk
1 cup brown sugar	1 teaspoon vanilla
2 cups flour	½ pound milk chocolate
1 cup chopped nuts	

Cream butter and sugar until light. Add beaten yolk, vanilla, and sifted flour. Spread thinly on a cooky sheet and bake in a 350° F. oven for fifteen to twenty minutes. Melt chocolate and spread on cooky surface while warm. Sprinkle with nuts and cut into squares.

Walnut Layer Torte

9 eggs, separated	2 teaspoons baking powder
1½ cups confectioner's sugar	⅛ teaspoon salt
1 pound grated walnuts	1 teaspoon cinnamon
½ cup fine bread crumbs	Grated rind of one lemon

Beat egg yolks and sugar until thick and lemon-colored. Add nuts and crumbs mixed with remaining dry ingredients. Fold in the stiffly beaten egg whites and lemon rind. Fill three well-buttered and floured cake tins and bake in a moderate oven (350° F.) twenty to twenty-five minutes. When cold, put Nut Filling (see below) between layers and ice with Rum Icing.

Nut Filling

3 egg yolks, beaten	**¾ cup sugar**
⅛ teaspoon salt	**1 cup grated walnuts**
¾ cup milk	**1 teaspoon vanilla**

Cook egg yolks, salt, milk, and sugar in a double boiler until thick, stirring constantly. Cool, add nuts and vanilla.

Rum Icing

2 tablespoons butter	**Rum**
2 cups confectioner's sugar	**2 tablespoons cream**

Cream butter, add sugar, flavoring, and cream until thin enough to spread.

Evening Snacks

Grilled Hamburger on Rye Toast

Toast large rounds of rye bread on one side. Place on the untoasted side De Luxe Hamburger Patties (see page 175), covering bread completely so edges will not burn. Dot with butter, and broil until well seared.

OR

Moisten ground beef with just enough ice water to hold together. Spread on lightly toasted, split hamburger bun; dot with butter, salt and pepper and broil. Serve with other half of toasted bun on top.

Toasted Cheese and Ham Sandwiches

$\frac{1}{2}$ package Shefford Snappy Cheese	1 tablespoon butter
1 can Pet Milk	$\frac{1}{8}$ teaspoon dry mustard

Paprika

Stir over flame until smooth. Place in refrigerator for several hours. Cut circles of bread, toast on one side, cover with slices of Dewey ham, and spread with cheese mixture. Put under broiler to brown.

Saloon Style Eggs

Cut a slice of white bread, one-half inch thick. With a small cutter, cut out a round circle in center of slice. Fry in butter, turn, and drop an egg in center. Fry until egg is set, and under side is browned.

In the Chafing-Dish:

Welsh Rarebit
Lobster for the Chafing-Dish

Welsh Rarebit

1 pound aged American cheese	$\frac{1}{2}$ teaspoon salt
2 tablespoons butter	$\frac{1}{2}$ cup beer, heated
1 egg	1 tablespoon Worcestershire Sauce
1 teaspoon dry mustard	Paprika
	Toast

Put butter in a chafing-dish or double boiler with cheese which has been cut or chopped into small pieces. Stir until cheese is melted; then add the egg beaten with the mustard and salt. Cook until blended, stirring constantly. Gradually pour in the beer and Worcestershire Sauce, continuing to stir until smooth. Serve at once on toast. Sprinkle with paprika.

Lobster for the Chafing-Dish

1 pound lobster meat	1 cup cream
2 tablespoons butter	Salt, paprika
2 truffles, chopped	Dash of cayenne
3 egg yolks	Sherry wine

Cut lobster into one-inch pieces. Melt butter in chafing-dish; add truffles, egg yolks well mixed with cream, and lobster. Cook until well thickened, stirring constantly. Season and add sherry to taste.

The Cocktail Party

Hors D'Oeuvres
Canapes

Hors d'Oeuvres:

Cheese Puff Mixture   Peanut Butter and Bacon
French Fried Shrimp
Chicken Livers on Apple Rounds
Fried Meat Balls   Sausage Squares
Celery Parisienne
Ham and Chutney Sandwiches
Cocktail Ham Biscuits   Fried Cheese Balls
Sardellen Butter   Chicken Liver Paste
Roquefort and Cream Cheese Mixture
Appetizer Pie   Sandwich Loaf
Russian Towers   Filled Dotlets
Egg Stuffed with Pâté de Foie Gras
Avocado Spread   Marinated Mushrooms
Cold Shrimps, Crabmeat, or Lobster Ravigote
Ravigote Sauce
French Fried Artichokes   Herring Salad
Antipasto   Appetizers
Canapes

Cheese Puff Mixture

3 ounces cream cheese	1 teaspoon onion juice
½ teaspoon baking powder	1 egg yolk

Salt, paprika

Mix all the ingredients together. Cut rounds or fingers from fresh bread; toast slightly on one side. Spread rounds with deviled ham or chutney, or place a skinned and boneless sardine on fingers. Spread cheese mixture on top, sprinkle with paprika, and, just before serving, toast until puffed and brown.

Peanut Butter and Bacon

Cut bread into small diamonds or squares. Toast one side. Spread untoasted side with peanut butter mixed with chili sauce and sprinkle with minced, sautéed bacon. Place in a hot oven until heated.

French Fried Shrimps

Clean shrimps, leaving tails on. Beat one egg until light. Add one cup milk alternately with one cup flour mixed with one teaspoon baking powder and one teaspoon salt. Hold shrimps by the tail and dip in batter. Fry until brown in hot fat. Drain on unglazed paper.

Chicken Livers on Apple Rounds

Core and slice small apples crosswise. Sauté in butter until tender, place slices on rounds of toast, and top each with a sautéed chicken liver.

Fried Meat Balls

Form well-seasoned ground round steak into balls the size of a marble. Dredge lightly with flour and fry in hot fat until brown. Drain on unglazed paper; serve on toothpicks.

Sausage Squares

Spread wafer-thin slices of bologna sausage with cream cheese, seasoned with horseradish. Place five slices together, chill until firm, cut into inch cubes and serve on toothpicks.

Celery Parisienne

12 celery hearts	12 whole black peppers
Soup stock	French Dressing
Anchovy paste	

Cut celery hearts in half lengthwise. Cook in soup stock with black peppers until tender. Drain and cover with French Dressing, flavored with anchovy paste. Allow to stand several hours before serving.

Ham and Chutney Sandwiches

Toast small rounds of bread on one side. Mix chutney sauce with either deviled or chopped boiled ham. Put a mound of this on untoasted side of bread. Spread with following:

¼ pound American cheese, grated	¼ teaspoon dry mustard
2 tablespoons butter	1 egg
Salt, paprika	

Cream cheese with butter, add mustard, salt, paprika, and beat in egg. Spread on toast and bake in quick oven. Sprinkle with paprika.

Cocktail Ham Biscuits

⅔ cup flour
6 tablespoons grated cheese
½ teaspoon salt

2 tablespoons butter
2 to 3 tablespoons milk
Deviled ham

Mix flour, cheese, and salt, chop in the butter, and add enough milk to form a stiff dough. Roll very thin and cut with a small round cutter. Moisten edges with slightly beaten egg. Spread one-half of the rounds with ham or cooked pork sausage meat. Cover with remaining rounds and press edges together. Brush with melted butter and bake twelve to fifteen minutes in hot oven (400° F.).

Fried Cheese Balls

1½ cups grated American cheese
1 tablespoon flour
¼ teaspoon salt

Dash of cayenne
3 egg whites
Cracker meal

Cream cheese, add flour and seasonings, then the stiffly beaten egg whites. Shape in small balls, roll in cracker meal, and fry in deep hot fat. Drain on unglazed paper.

Sardellen Butter

Blend one tube of sardellen paste with one-half pound creamed sweet butter. Season with onion and lemon juice. Pack in a small mold or jelly glass and chill before serving.

Chicken-Liver Paste

Slowly cook half-pound chicken livers in hot chicken fat for a few minutes. Press through a sieve. Add two tablespoons chicken fat or creamed sweet butter, two tablespoons minced sautéed mushrooms, salt, a dash of cayenne, lemon juice, and onion juice to taste. Blend thoroughly. Shape into a mound, garnish with riced, hard-cooked egg, and serve warm.

Roquefort and Cream Cheese Mixture

½ pound Roquefort cheese
3 ounces cream cheese
4 tablespoons butter, melted

1 teaspoon Worcestershire Sauce
Grated onion or minced chives
Salt, paprika

Cream the cheese, add butter and seasonings, and mix thoroughly.

Appetizer Pie

Cut a slice of bread crosswise from the center of a large round loaf of rye bread. Remove the crust and spread with softened butter. Cover two inches of the center with caviar, seasoned with lemon and onion juice. Around that, in circles, place mixtures of:

red salmon, seasoned with onion juice, lemon, and moistened with mayonnaise;

sardellen paste and cream cheese;

mashed boneless and skinless sardines mixed with cream cheese, seasoned with lemon and Worcestershire Sauce;

minced ham and green pepper with mayonnaise;

riced whites and yolks of hard-cooked eggs;

ground pimiento, olives, and nuts mixed with mayonnaise; or any sandwich spread;

remembering that variety of color makes the pie attractive.

Cut in pie-shaped wedges but serve intact.

Sandwich Loaf

Remove crusts from loaf of white bread, and cut into five slices lengthwise. Spread each slice with creamed butter, the three middle slices on both sides. Spread the buttered side of the bottom slice with ham, chicken, shrimp, or salmon salad; cover with a slice buttered on both sides; spread it with minced cucumber and cream cheese, seasoned with salt and minced chives. Place a third slice over this, spread with egg salad; cover, spread with caviar, or anchovy and cheese, and place last slice of bread over it. Wrap in wax paper, place in refrigerator until firm. Cover sides with cream cheese softened with mayonnaise; sprinkle with chopped nuts.

Russian Towers

Cut very thin circles of rye bread one and one-half to two inches in diameter; spread with creamed butter, then with caviar seasoned with onion juice. Top the caviar with a smaller circle of buttered rye bread and spread with hard-cooked egg yolks mashed and blended with Russian salad dressing. Add a still smaller disk, spread with potted or deviled ham, and on this place a rolled anchovy fillet. Top with pearl onion. Season cream cheese with cream and chili sauce and use in pastry tube to decorate.

Filled Dotlets

Make the same dough as for Profiterolles (see page 226). Drop one-half teaspoon of the batter on a buttered sheet and bake. (One egg makes eighteen.) When cool, cut a slit in each and fill with a fish salad, chicken salad, or anchovy paste mixed with cream cheese.

Egg Stuffed with Pâté de Foie Gras

Cut hard-cooked eggs into halves lengthwise and remove yolks. Stuff egg whites with pâté de foie gras, and pipe with riced egg yolks which have been mixed to a paste with mayonnaise.

Avocado Spread

Mash a large ripe avocado pear. Season highly, with grated onion, lemon juice, chili powder, salt, pepper, and celery salt, and enough mayonnaise to make a soft paste. Spread on large heated potato chips.

Marinated Mushrooms

1 pound mushrooms	1 bay leaf
Juice of 1 lemon	1 pinch of thyme
1 cup vinegar	2 shallots, cut fine
1 clove garlic	$\frac{1}{4}$ cup olive oil
1 teaspoon salt	1 tablespoon catsup
Pinch of freshly ground pepper	Small amount of chevril, chopped

Boil mushrooms five minutes in water that is salted and seasoned with juice of one lemon; drain and dry. Boil together for five minutes the vinegar, garlic, bay leaf, salt, ground pepper, thyme, and shallots. Cool and remove garlic; add olive oil, catsup, and mushrooms. Allow to marinate for three hours in the refrigerator. Before serving, strain dressing, pour back over mushrooms, and sprinkle with the chevril.

Cold Shrimps, Crabmeat, or Lobster Ravigote

Line a bowl with lettuce. Fill with crabmeat, lobster meat or shrimps. Serve with Ravigote Sauce.

Ravigote Sauce

1 cup whipped cream	2 hard-boiled eggs, chopped
1 cup oil mayonnaise	1 teaspoon tarragon vinegar
$\frac{1}{2}$ cup chili sauce	1 teaspoon walnut catsup
1 teaspoon green pepper, chopped	1 teaspoon lemon juice
1 teaspoon pearl onions, chopped	1 teaspoon salt
1 teaspoon pickled beets, chopped	Paprika

Blend all ingredients and chill before serving.

French Fried Artichokes

Dip artichoke hearts in flour, then in a batter made of one cup flour, one-half teaspoon salt, one-half teaspoon sugar, three eggs beaten separately, one-half teaspoon olive oil, one-half cup beer, and two tablespoons water. Fry in deep fat and drain on unglazed paper.

Herring Salad

5 milch herrings	3 to 4 dill pickles, diced
5 hard-cooked eggs, diced	1 small onion, grated
4 boiled potatoes, diced	Heavy sour cream
6 beets, diced	Cooked salad dressing

Soak herrings in cold water overnight, then skin, bone, and dice. Add eggs, potatoes, beets, pickles, and grated onion. Combine with salad dressing which has been mixed with cream to taste.

OR

4 milch herrings	4 tablespoons blanched, chopped
2 sour apples, grated	almonds
2 onions, grated	$\frac{1}{8}$ teaspoon cloves
1 boiled potato, grated	1 large sour pickle, minced
2 tablespoons vinegar	1 teaspoon sugar
Dash of cayenne	

Remove milch from herrings and soak herring in water overnight. Drain and put through a food-chopper; press milch through a sieve. Combine with remaining ingredients. Garnish with riced egg, minced cooked beets, and parsley.

Antipasto

1½ cups shredded carrot	Raw cauliflower buds
Pearl onions	Mushrooms (canned), cut up
Pickled onions	Anchovies
Green olives, cut up	Tuna fish or salmon
Ripe olives, cut up	French Dressing
Celery, cut up	Worcestershire Sauce
Pickles, dill and sweet, cut up	Chili sauce
Mayonnaise	

Marinate carrots in French Dressing for one hour. Add the other ingredients one-half hour before ready to serve, using more French Dressing, Worcestershire Sauce, chili sauce, and a little mayonnaise, to make mixture moist. Two large cans of tuna fish are a good foundation for this, using the other ingredients to taste and in proportion. Fresh salmon may be used and is excellent.

Appetizers

Place an oyster on a thin slice of bacon. Sprinkle lightly with pepper, paprika, lemon juice, and Worcestershire Sauce. Roll, fasten with a toothpick, and broil until bacon is crisp. Serve with Cocktail Sauce.

Season chicken livers with salt and pepper, wrap in a piece of bacon, and fasten with a toothpick. Broil until bacon is crisp.

Place a stuffed olive in a steamed raw prune, roll in a piece of bacon, fasten with a toothpick, and broil until the bacon is crisp.

Marinate shrimps in chili sauce with chopped garlic, roll in a piece of bacon, dip in chili sauce again, fasten with a toothpick. Chill. Broil until bacon is crisp.

Roll thin slices of salami or Westphalian ham into cornucopias and fill with cream cheese which has been softened with cream and seasoned.

Put a toothpick through a hole of a buttered oysterette; place a rolled anchovy on it and top with a small pearl onion.

Arrange slices of chipped beef to form a six-inch square. Spread with cream cheese mixed with chopped almonds and seasoned with horse-radish, salt, and paprika. Roll, chill until firm, and cut into half-inch slices.

Spread paper-thin slices of tongue or bologna sausage with cream cheese which has been seasoned with Worcestershire Sauce, salt, and paprika. Stack five slices together. Chill until firm, cut into small squares.

Place on a toothpick a pickled onion, a cube of Swiss or American cheese, and a cube of salami.

Cut dill pickles into half-inch slices, mound with herring salad, and sprinkle with riced egg.

Pour boiling water over scallops for one minute, drain and dry. Season with salt and pepper, roll in flour, dip in beaten egg, roll in bread crumbs, and fry in deep fat. Serve on toothpicks around a bowl of tartare sauce.

Sprinkle large potato chips with Parmesan cheese and toast.

Cut off ends and hollow out centers of large dill pickles. Stuff with a mixture of one small can deviled tongue, one tablespoon minced celery, one teaspoon mayonnaise, and one-half teaspoon Diablo Sauce. Place in refrigerator for several hours. Cut into thin slices and serve on toasted butter crackers.

Spread halves of Jumbo pecans with Roquefort or cream cheese (mashed). Put two halves together.

Roll smoked salmon into small cornucopias and fill with cream cheese mixed with horseradish, or Roquefort cheese mixed with India relish.

Stuff olives with caviar, mushrooms, or blanched almonds.

Stuff small pieces of celery with Steak Tartare. Garnish with pearl onions.

Soak dates overnight in brandy. Remove pits and stuff with peanut butter mixed with a small amount of grated horseradish.

Cream three parts Roquefort cheese with one part anchovy paste. Add a dash of cayenne and place in refrigerator to harden. Wrap small portion in crisp lettuce. Hold together with a toothpick.

Mix sausage meat with minced chives and form into balls. Roll in bread or cracker crumbs and fry in deep fat. Serve on a toothpick.

Cover large stuffed olives with cream cheese and roll in chopped salted nuts.

One can shrimps, one small cooked cauliflower (separated), one small can sliced okra, mixed with mayonnaise.

Four large tomatoes quartered, one jar artichoke bottoms diced, one teaspoon pearl onions, one teaspoon caviar. Mix with French Dressing.

One pound cottage cheese, one teaspoon minced parsley, chopped chives, one teaspoon fresh grated horseradish, one-fourth cup sour cream, salt, and paprika.

Two cans tuna fish and one small can baby lima beans in tomato sauce.

Peel two large cucumbers; cut off ends and remove centers. Soak one hour in cold salt water. Fill with one can tuna fish which has been mixed with two tablespoons mayonnaise, and seasoned with onion juice, lemon juice, Worcestershire Sauce, salt, and paprika. Chill and cut into slices one-half inch thick.

Cut fresh figs, lengthwise, and fill with seasoned cream cheese.

Mix diced cucumbers, thinly sliced radishes, canned tiny button mushrooms, and marinate in French Dressing.

Remove yolks from halves of hard-cooked eggs; fill whites with French peas or tiny diced vegetables mixed with mayonnaise.

Mix three boiled and diced Idaho potatoes, one pound of sautéed mushrooms, one can of boneless and skinless sardines, and one-half bunch of chopped watercress with three tablespoons of mayonnaise and five tablespoons of French Dressing.

Mix two cans of boneless and skinless sardines with two cakes of cream cheese. Season with lemon juice, onion juice, Worcestershire Sauce, salt, and paprika. Chill and form into a cone-shaped mound. Cover with thin circular slices of pimiento olives. Place in refrigerator until firm. Garnish with several small leaves from a pineapple put into the top.

Mix three ounces of cream cheese, one-half cup of Parmesan cheese, one cup of whipped cream, one clove of grated garlic, with three-fourths tablespoon of gelatin which has been soaked in one tablespoon of cold water and dissolved in one tablespoon of boiling water. Season highly with salt and paprika, put into an oiled mold, and chill until firm.

Marinate eight small beets with a sliced onion for several hours. Drain and chop fine with one hard-cooked egg and a small can of anchovies. Mix with oil mayonnaise.

Dissolve one-half tablespoon gelatin in one-half cup of soup stock. Mix with one small can of salmon, one can of caviar, one chopped hard-cooked egg, and six minced sweet pickles. Season with salt, paprika, onion juice, and lemon juice.

Canapés

Drop Profiterolles batter in tiny balls on a baking-sheet. Bake until centers are well done. Cut a slit in the side of each and fill with potted tongue, chicken or ham mixed with enough Indian chutney to moisten. Brush tops of dotlets with beaten egg to which one tablespoon cream has been added. Place in the oven a few minutes to glaze.

Scoop out the pulp of a ripe avocado, mash, and season with salt, paprika, minced chives, and lemon juice. Spread thickly on small pieces of toast. Arrange small strips of bacon on each, and place in the broiler until the bacon is crisp.

Cut thin circles of bread. Put firmly together sandwich-fashion with a thin layer of potted ham, tongue, or chicken. Dip in a batter made of one tablespoon flour, one-eighth teaspoon salt, one beaten egg, and one-fourth cup milk. Fry in deep fat; drain on unglazed paper.

Cut bread in crescent-shaped pieces and toast on one side. Mix crab-meat or minced lobster meat with enough White Sauce to form a paste and season with salt, cayenne, and lemon juice. Spread this on the untoasted side of the crescent. Cover with Cheese Dream Mixture, and brown in oven.

Mash liver sausage and season with onion juice and minced parsley. Spread on unbaked rich pie dough and roll like a jelly roll. Place in refrigerator for several hours. When ready to use, cut into slices, brush with beaten egg which has been diluted with one tablespoon cream, and bake in a hot oven.

OR

Sauté one-half pound chopped mushrooms in butter. Mix with one beaten egg and enough thick White Sauce to form a paste; season with salt, paprika, onion juice, minced parsley, and Worcestershire Sauce. Cool and use in place of the liver sausage.

Spread rounds of rye bread with anchovy paste mixed with sweet butter. Place anchovy fillet on top and cover with minced raw mushrooms. Sprinkle with paprika, dot with butter, and bake ten minutes.

Sprinkle rounds of buttered bread with Parmesan cheese and place on each an artichoke heart. Fill with thinly sliced lobster meat mixed with thick White Sauce. Season with salt, pepper, mushroom catsup, and a dash of Tabasco Sauce. Cover with buttered crumbs and brown.

Remove stems from large mushrooms. Mince Westphalian ham and mushroom stems, add thick White Sauce to make a paste, and season. Fill caps rounding full, sprinkle with buttered crumbs, and bake until brown.

Remove stems from mushrooms, and sauté caps in butter. Place in each cap an oyster and a bit of butter. Sprinkle with salt, pepper, and minced parsley. Bake in a hot oven until oysters are plump. Serve on rounds of toast.

Cut bread into small rounds or squares; put a layer of deviled ham and a thin slice of American cheese between two pieces of bread. Brush both sides with creamed butter; place four at a time in a waffle iron and toast golden brown.

Sauté one-third cup of finely chopped mushrooms and one-half tablespoon of minced onion in three tablespoons butter. Add two tablespoons flour and two-thirds cup of cream and cook until mixture thickens. Add one cup canned minced clams (drained), two tablespoons grated cheese, and two egg yolks, well beaten. Season with salt, cayenne, and lemon juice. Pile on circular pieces of toast or in oyster or clam shells. Sprinkle with grated cheese, then buttered crumbs, and bake until crumbs are brown.

Sauté chopped mushrooms in butter. Cool, add mayonnaise, onion juice, salt, and paprika. Spread on paper-thin slices of bread, with crusts removed. Roll and toast in broiler.

Sprinkle a skinned and boned sardine with riced egg yolk and minced parsley. Place on a sautéed bread finger. Garnish at either end with a rosette of cream cheese highly seasoned with salt, cayenne, and Worcestershire Sauce.

Mix one cup grated American cheese with one-half cup butter, one cup flour, and one-fourth teaspoon salt. Add enough milk to form a stiff dough. Roll very thin. Cut into strips twice as large as an anchovy fillet, Lay anchovy on strip, fold over like an envelope, pinching edges of dough together. Bake in moderate oven (350° F.) until brown. Serve hot.

Cut bread into rectangles two by three inches. Sauté in butter until crisp and brown. Drain on unglazed paper. Cover each with a paper-thin slice of smoked salmon. In the center make a circle with a pastry tube of unsweetened whipped cream; fill with caviar seasoned with lemon juice and onion juice.

Table of Weights and Measures

3 teaspoons	1 tablespoon
2 tablespoons	1 liquid ounce
4 tablespoons	$\frac{1}{4}$ cup
1 wine glass	$\frac{1}{4}$ cup
2 cups	1 pint
4 cups flour	1 pound
2 cups granulated sugar	1 pound
$2\frac{2}{3}$ cups powdered sugar	1 pound
$2\frac{2}{3}$ cups brown sugar	1 pound
4 tablespoons flour	1 ounce
2 tablespoons butter, sugar or salt	1 ounce
1 square unsweetened chocolate	1 ounce
1 ounce chocolate	$\frac{1}{3}$ cup cocoa
1 pound walnuts or pecans in shell	$\frac{1}{2}$ pound shelled
1 cup shelled walnuts or almonds	$\frac{1}{4}$ pound
1 cup shelled pecans	$\frac{1}{3}$ pound
$\frac{1}{3}$ cup blanched almonds	1 ounce
1 cup milk	8 ounces

Table of Contents for Index

Index

Appetizers

HORS D'OEUVRES AND APPETIZERS

COCKTAIL HORS D'OEUVRES AND CANAPÉS
349–360

FIRST COURSES

Breads

BREADS, MUFFINS, AND BISCUITS

FINGER SANDWICHES

Soups

Soup Garnishes

Egg and Cheese Dishes

Meat and Fish Sauces

Meat Garnishes

Poultry

Stuffings and Gravies

Compotes

Jams, Jellies, Pickles

Potatoes

Dumplings, Noodles, and Spaghetti

Vegetables

Desserts

CAKES AND TORTES

COOKIES AND SMALL CAKES

Page

SWEET SAUCES

FRUIT DESSERTS

Page

FROZEN DESSERTS

Evening Snacks